SUPER POWERS!

ART BALTAZAR & FRANCO
WRITERS

ART BALTAZAR
ARTIST & LETTERER

SUPERMAN created by Jerry Siegel and Joe Shuster
SUPERGIRL based on the characters created by Jerry Siegel and Joe Shuster
By special arrangement with the Jerry Siegel family

KRISTY QUINN Editor - Original Series
JEB WOODARD Group Editor - Collected Editions
LIZ ERICKSON Editor - Collected Edition
STEVE COOK Design Director - Books
AMIE BROCKWAY-METCALF Publication Design
BOB HARRAS Senior VP - Editor-in-Chief, DC Comics

DIANE NELSON President
DAN DiDIO Publisher
JIM LEE Publisher
GEOFF JOHNS President & Chief Creative Officer
AMIT DESAI Executive VP - Business & Marketing Strategy, Direct to Consumer & Global Franchise Management
SAM ADES Senior VP - Direct to Consumer
BOBBIE CHASE VP - Talent Development
MARK CHIARELLO Senior VP - Art, Design & Collected Editions
JOHN CUNNINGHAM Senior VP - Sales & Trade Marketing
ANNE DePIES Senior VP - Business Strategy, Finance & Administration
DON FALLETTI VP - Manufacturing Operations
LAWRENCE GANEM VP - Editorial Administration & Talent Relations
ALISON GILL Senior VP - Manufacturing & Operations
HANK KANALZ Senior VP - Editorial Strategy & Administration
JAY KOGAN VP - Legal Affairs
THOMAS LOFTUS VP - Business Affairs
JACK MAHAN VP - Business Affairs
NICK J. NAPOLITANO VP - Manufacturing Administration
EDDIE SCANNELL VP - Consumer Marketing
COURTNEY SIMMONS Senior VP - Publicity & Communications
JIM (SKI) SOKOLOWSKI VP - Comic Book Specialty Sales & Trade Marketing
NANCY SPEARS VP - Mass, Book, Digital Sales & Trade Marketing

RUFF RUFF!
BARK BARK!

SUPER POWERS

DC Comics
2900 West Alameda Avenue
Burbank, CA 91505
Printed by LSC Communications, Owensville, MO, USA. 7/7/17. First Printing.
ISBN: 978-1-4012-6842-8
Library of Congress Cataloging-in-Publication Data is available.

PEFC Certified
Printed on paper from sustainably managed forests, controlled sources
PEFC/29-31-337
www.pefc.org

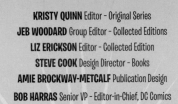

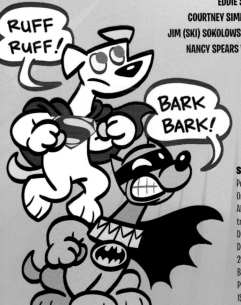

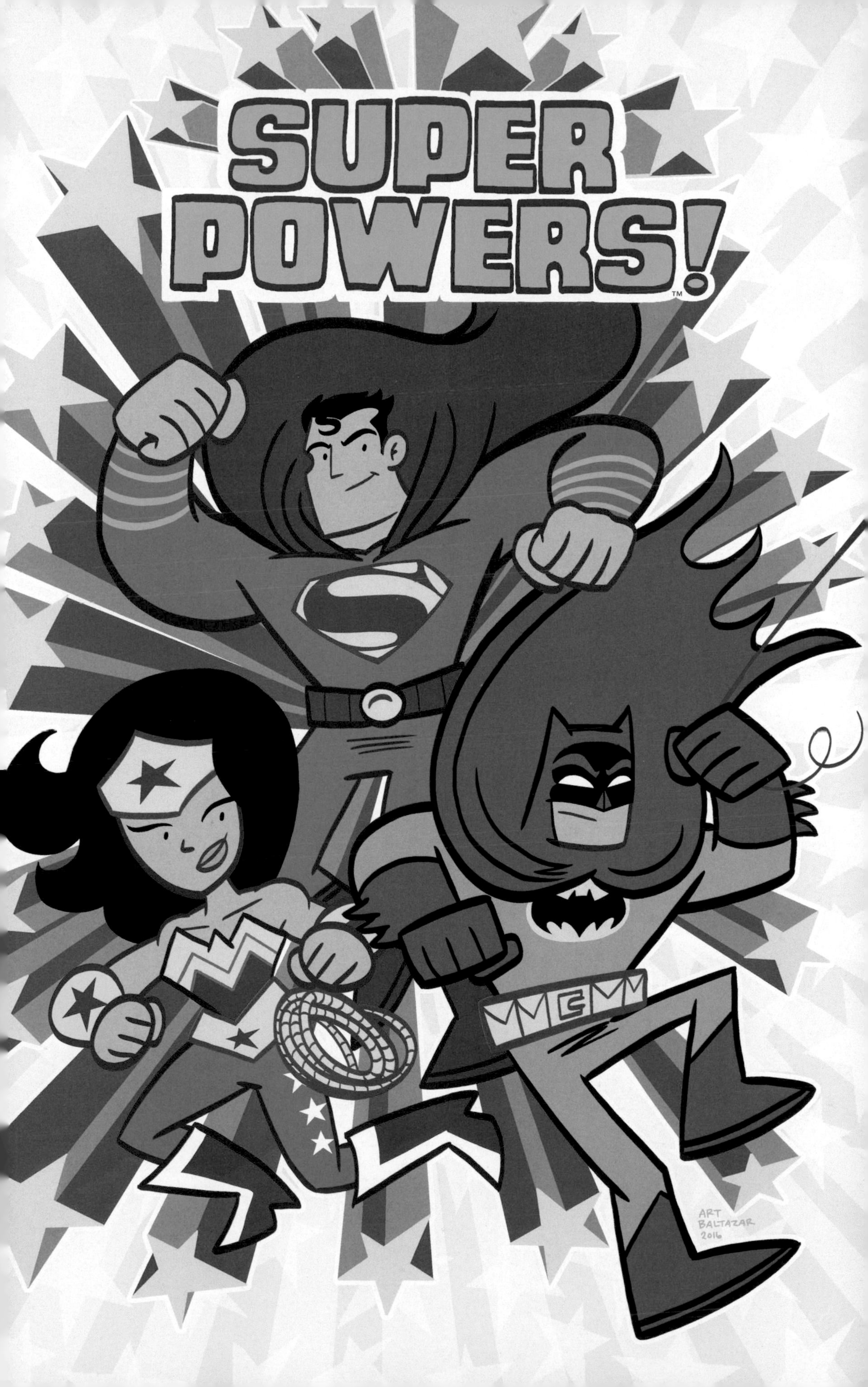
SUPER POWERS!™
ART BALTAZAR 2016

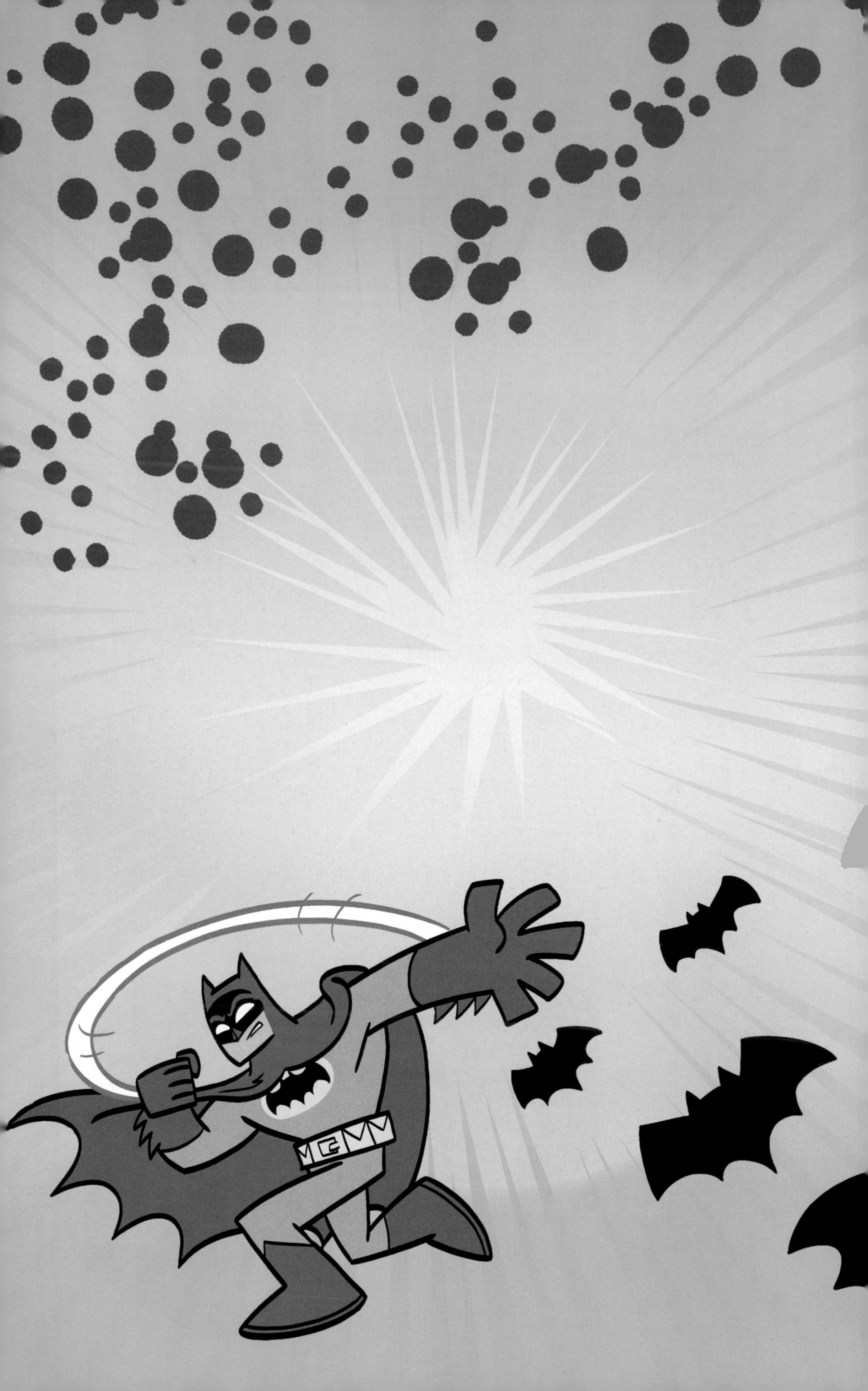

DC COMICS PROUDLY PRESENTS...

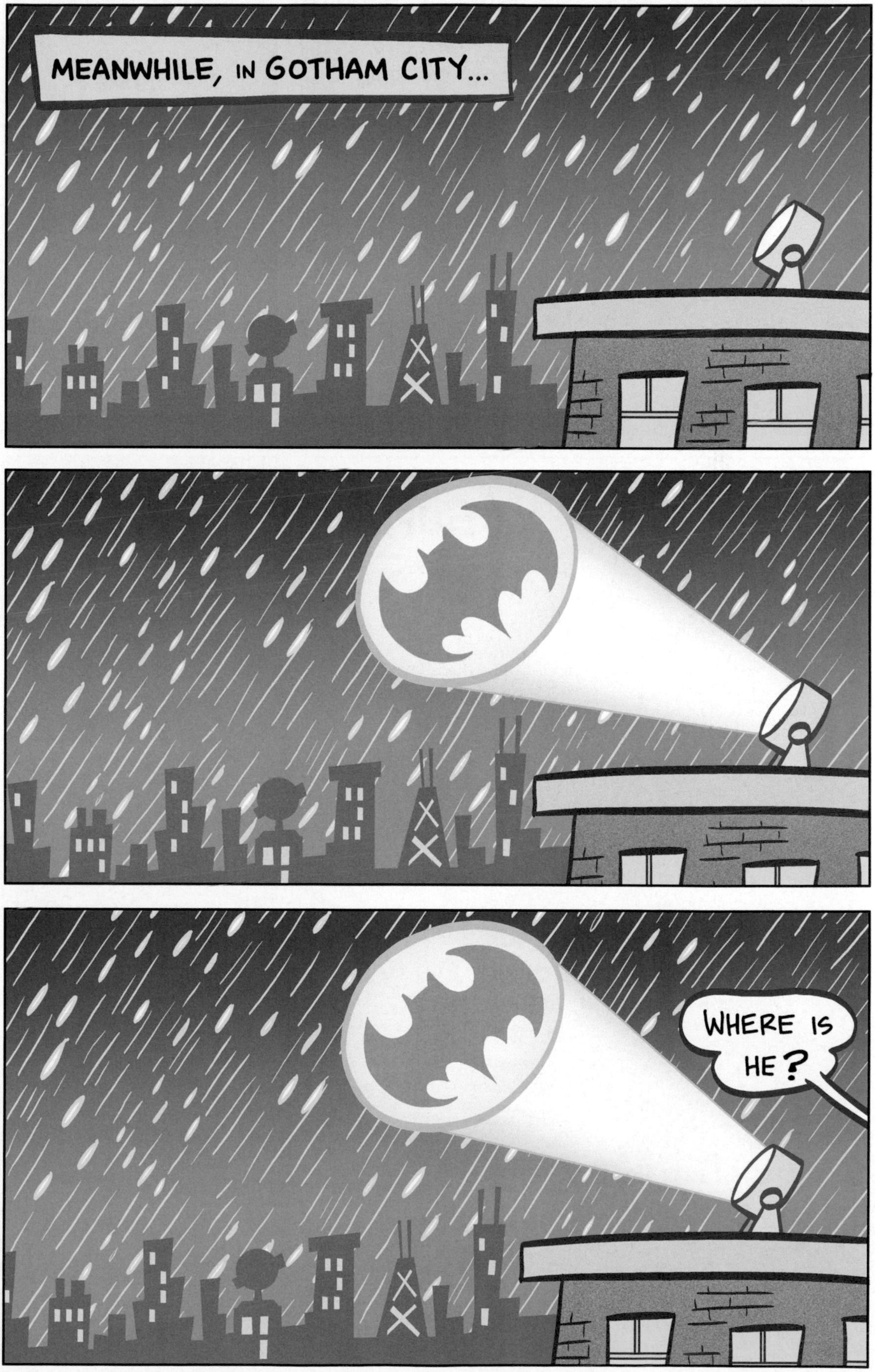
MEANWHILE, IN GOTHAM CITY...
WHERE IS HE?

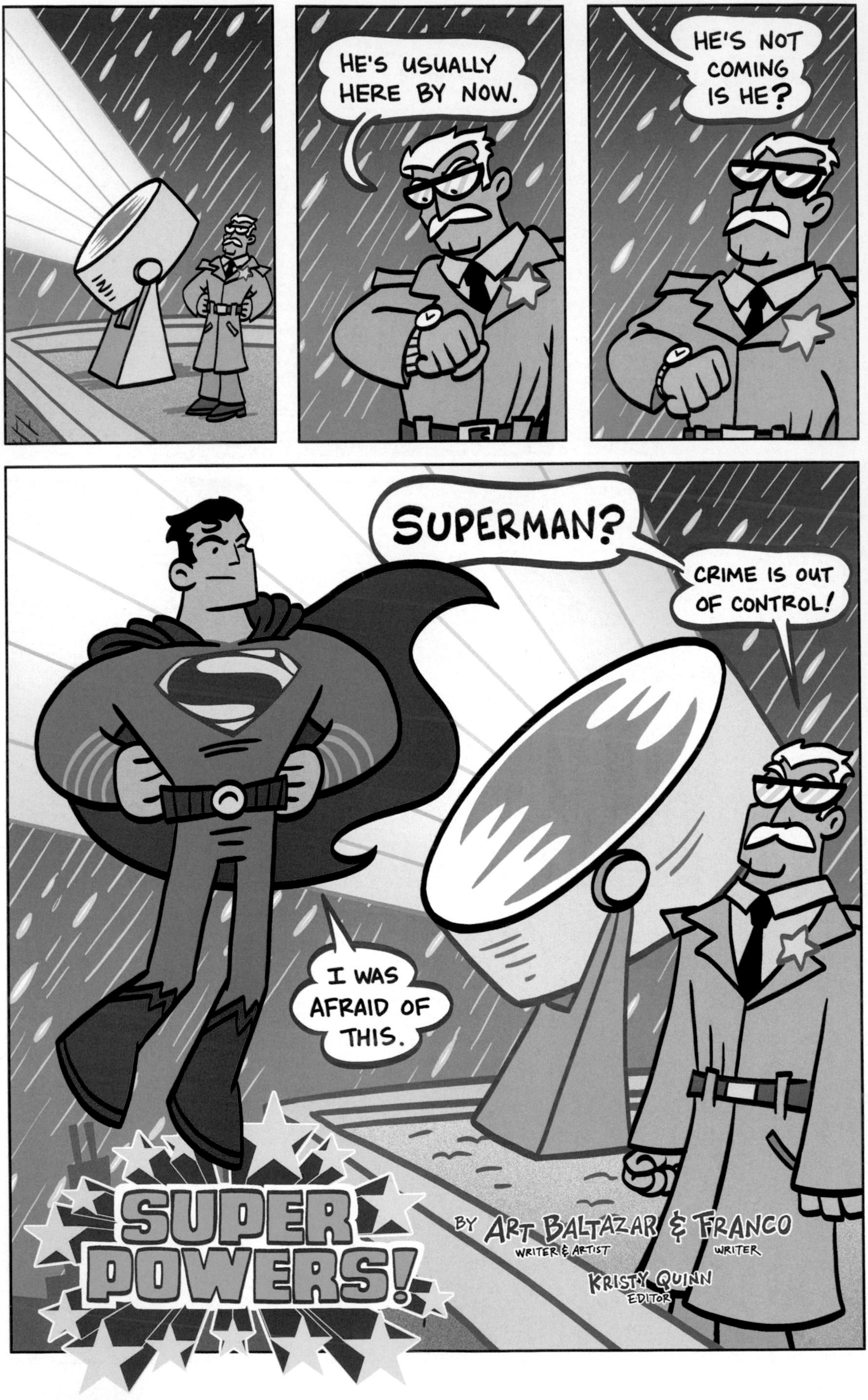
HE'S USUALLY HERE BY NOW.
HE'S NOT COMING IS HE?
SUPERMAN?
CRIME IS OUT OF CONTROL!
I WAS AFRAID OF THIS.
SUPER POWERS!
BY ART BALTAZAR WRITER & ARTIST & FRANCO WRITER
KRISTY QUINN EDITOR

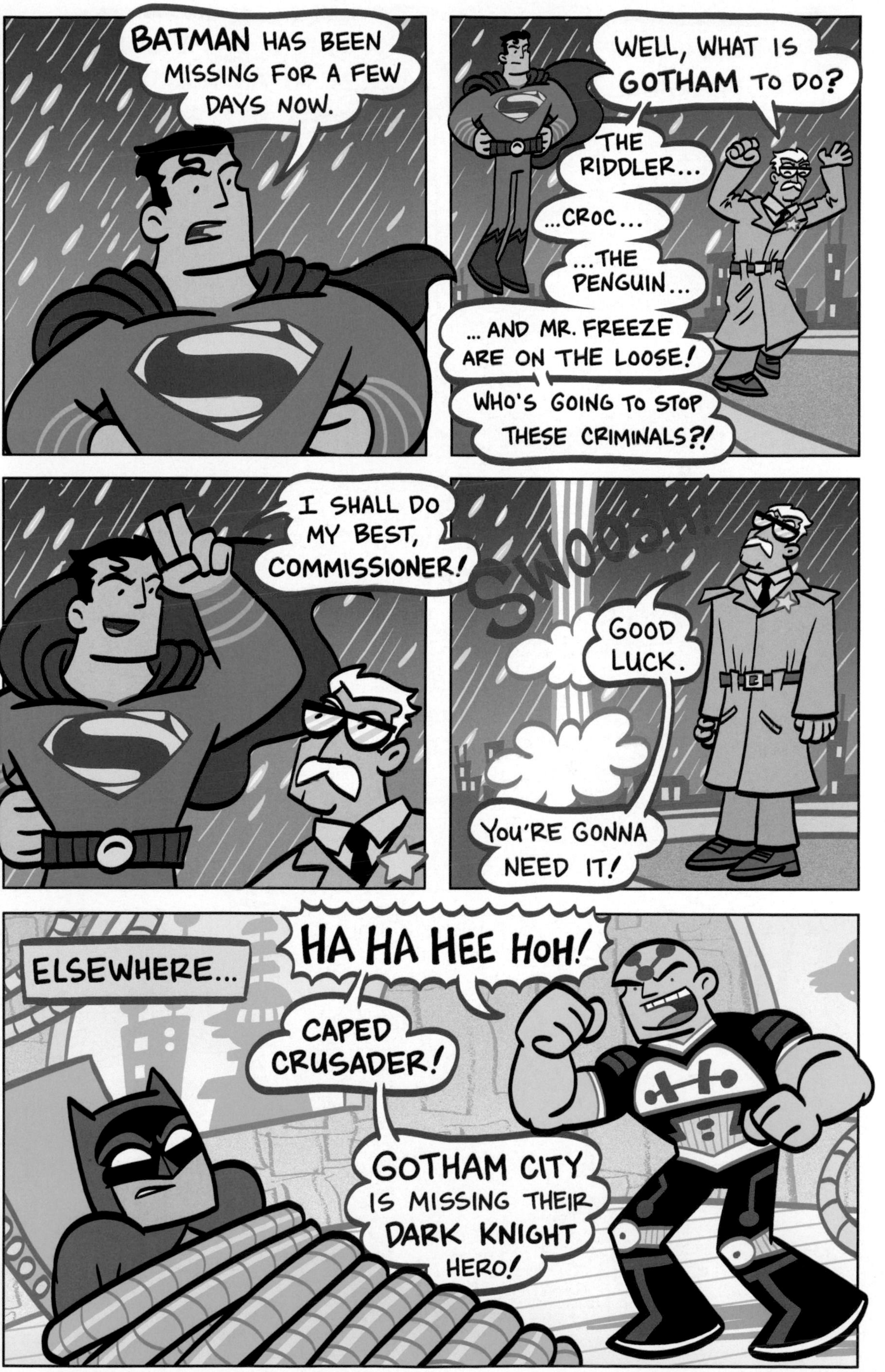
BATMAN HAS BEEN MISSING FOR A FEW DAYS NOW.
WELL, WHAT IS GOTHAM TO DO?
THE RIDDLER...
...CROC...
...THE PENGUIN...
... AND MR. FREEZE ARE ON THE LOOSE!
WHO'S GOING TO STOP THESE CRIMINALS?!
I SHALL DO MY BEST, COMMISSIONER!
SWOOSH!
GOOD LUCK.
YOU'RE GONNA NEED IT!
ELSEWHERE...
HA HA HEE HOH!
CAPED CRUSADER!
GOTHAM CITY IS MISSING THEIR DARK KNIGHT HERO!

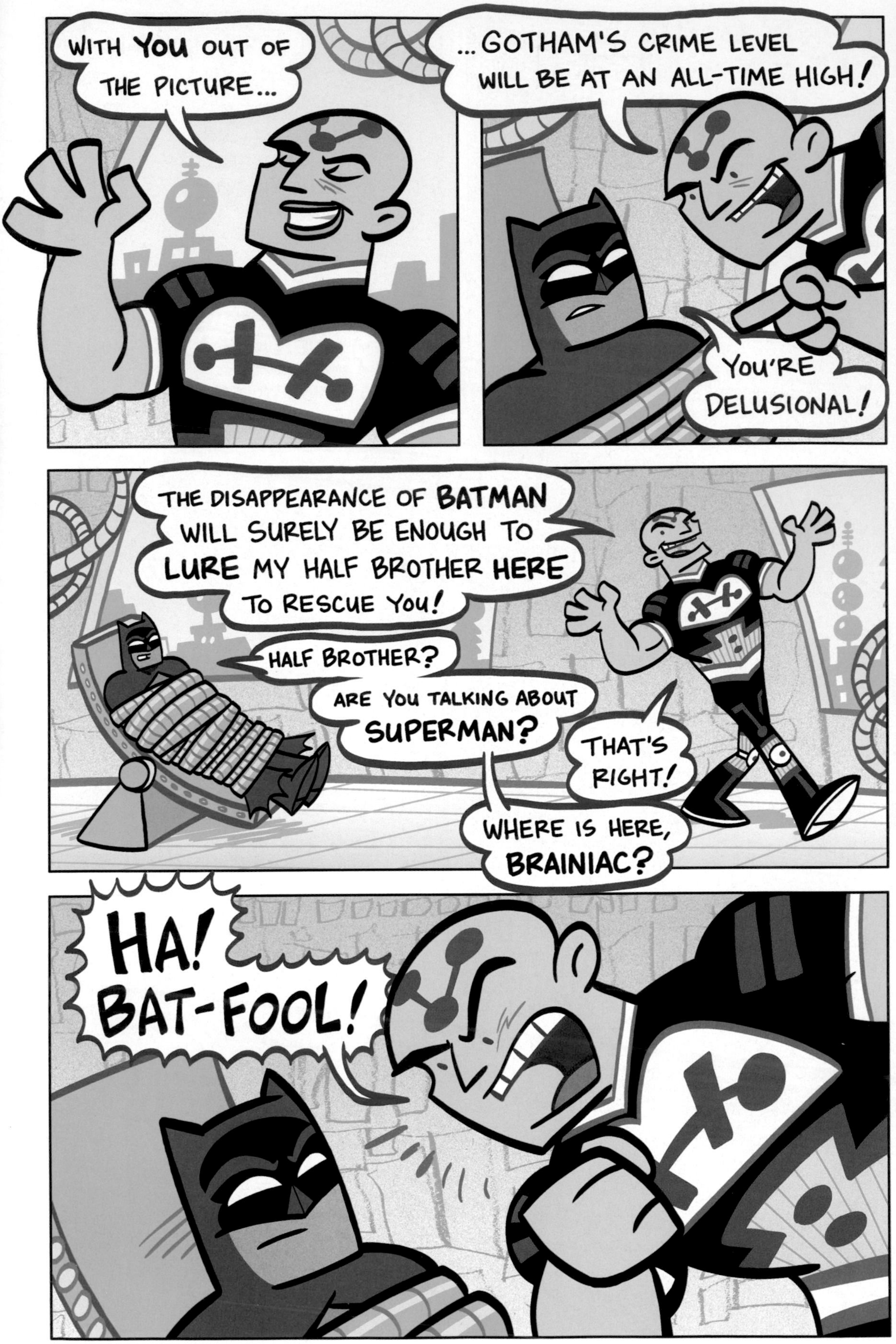
WITH YOU OUT OF THE PICTURE...
...GOTHAM'S CRIME LEVEL WILL BE AT AN ALL-TIME HIGH!
YOU'RE DELUSIONAL!
THE DISAPPEARANCE OF BATMAN WILL SURELY BE ENOUGH TO LURE MY HALF BROTHER HERE TO RESCUE YOU!
HALF BROTHER?
ARE YOU TALKING ABOUT SUPERMAN?
THAT'S RIGHT!
WHERE IS HERE, BRAINIAC?
HA! BAT-FOOL!

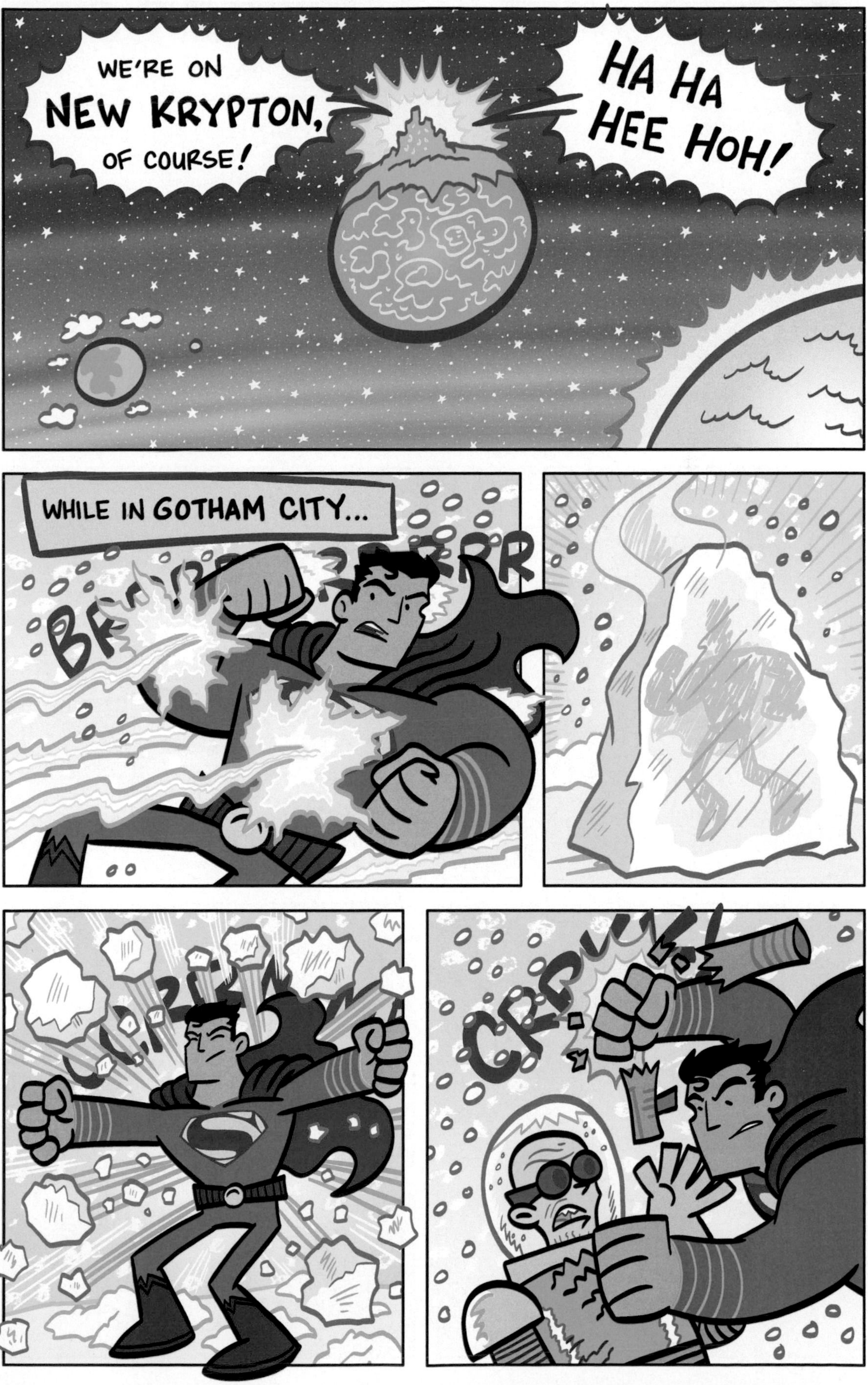
WE'RE ON NEW KRYPTON, OF COURSE!
HA HA HEE HOH!
WHILE IN GOTHAM CITY...

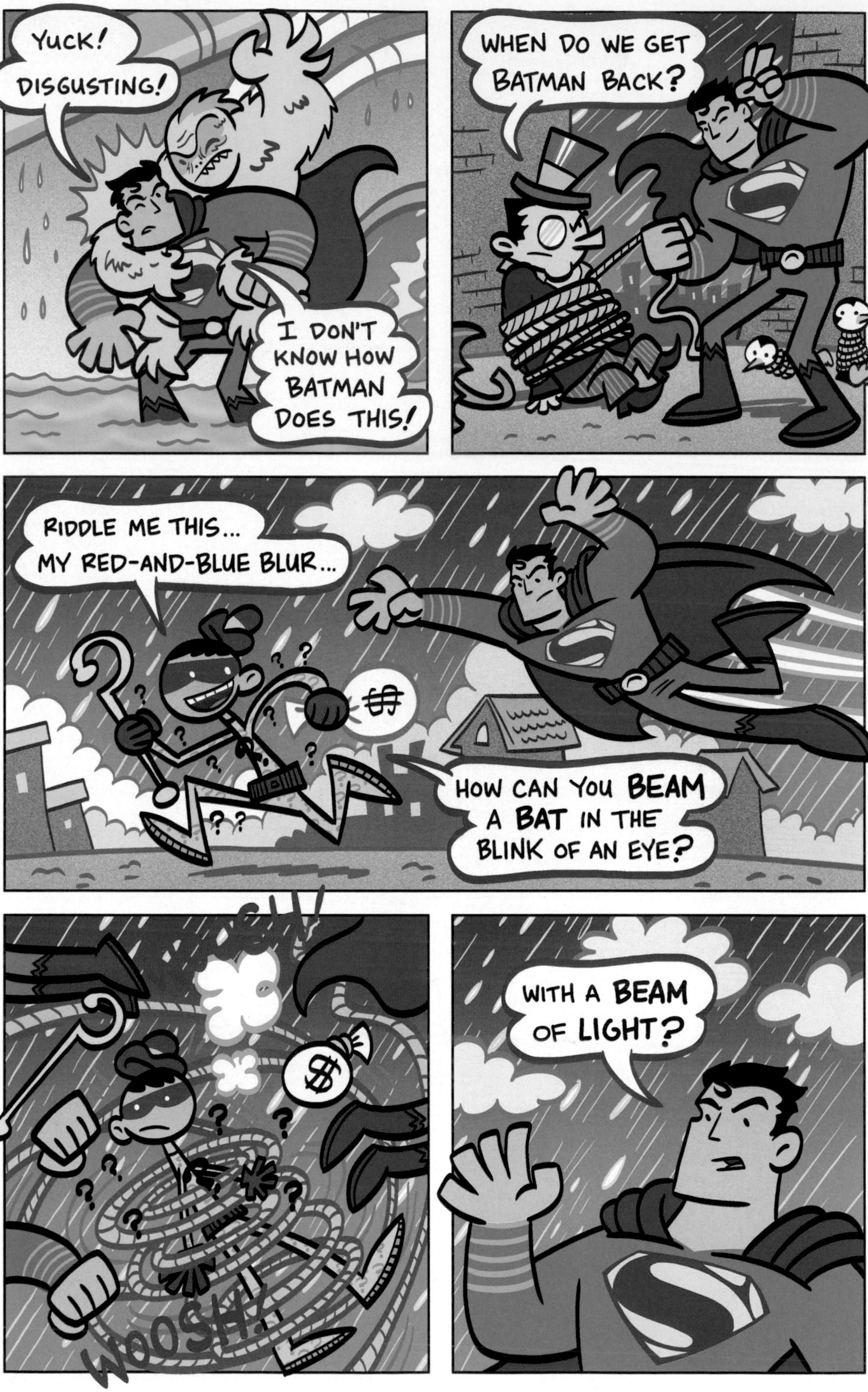
YUCK!
DISGUSTING!
I DON'T KNOW HOW BATMAN DOES THIS!
WHEN DO WE GET BATMAN BACK?
RIDDLE ME THIS... MY RED-AND-BLUE BLUR...
HOW CAN YOU BEAM A BAT IN THE BLINK OF AN EYE?
WOOSH!
WITH A BEAM OF LIGHT?

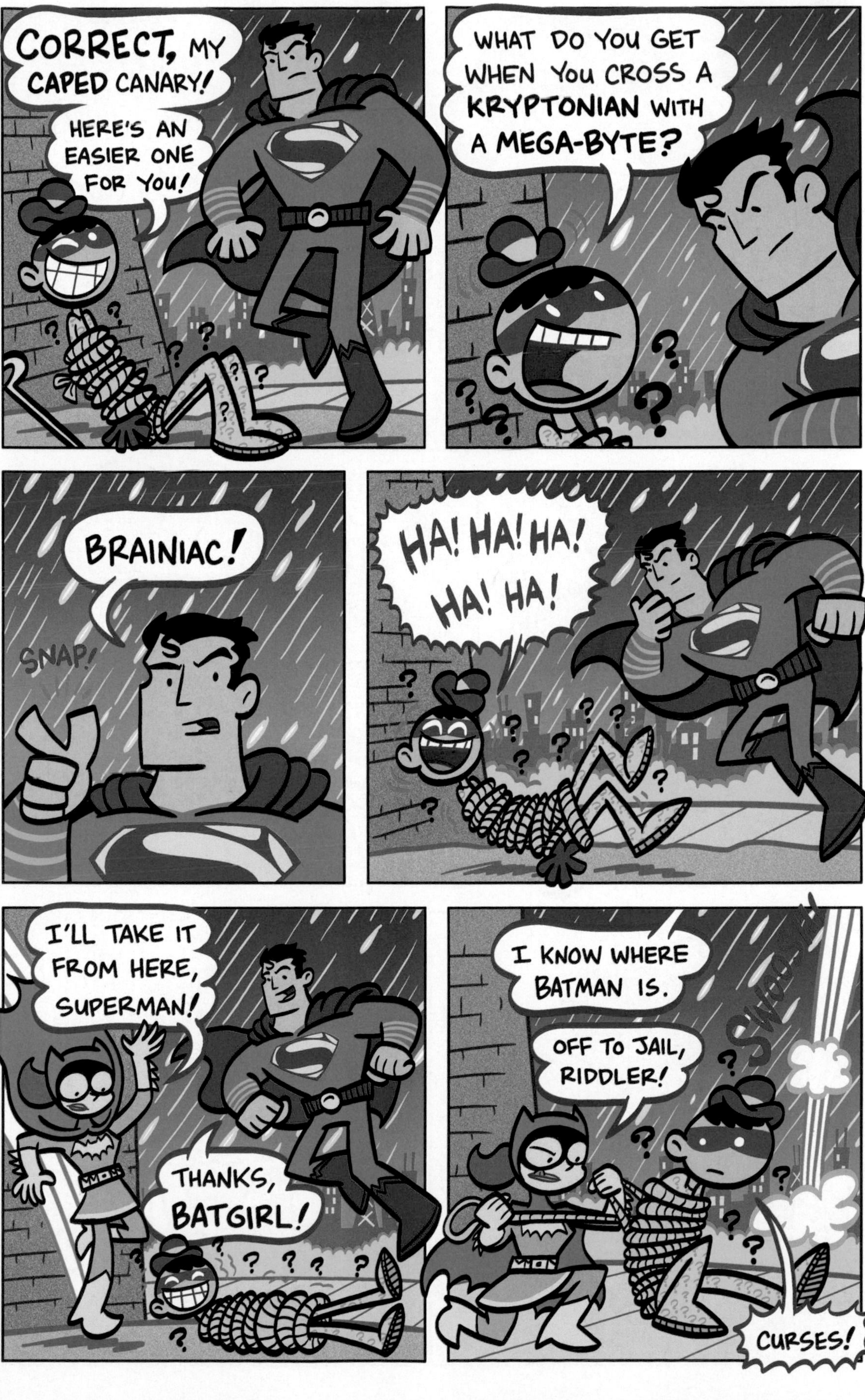
CORRECT, MY CAPED CANARY!
HERE'S AN EASIER ONE FOR YOU!
WHAT DO YOU GET WHEN YOU CROSS A KRYPTONIAN WITH A MEGA-BYTE?
BRAINIAC!
SNAP!
HA! HA! HA! HA! HA!
I'LL TAKE IT FROM HERE, SUPERMAN!
THANKS, BATGIRL!
I KNOW WHERE BATMAN IS.
OFF TO JAIL, RIDDLER!
CURSES!

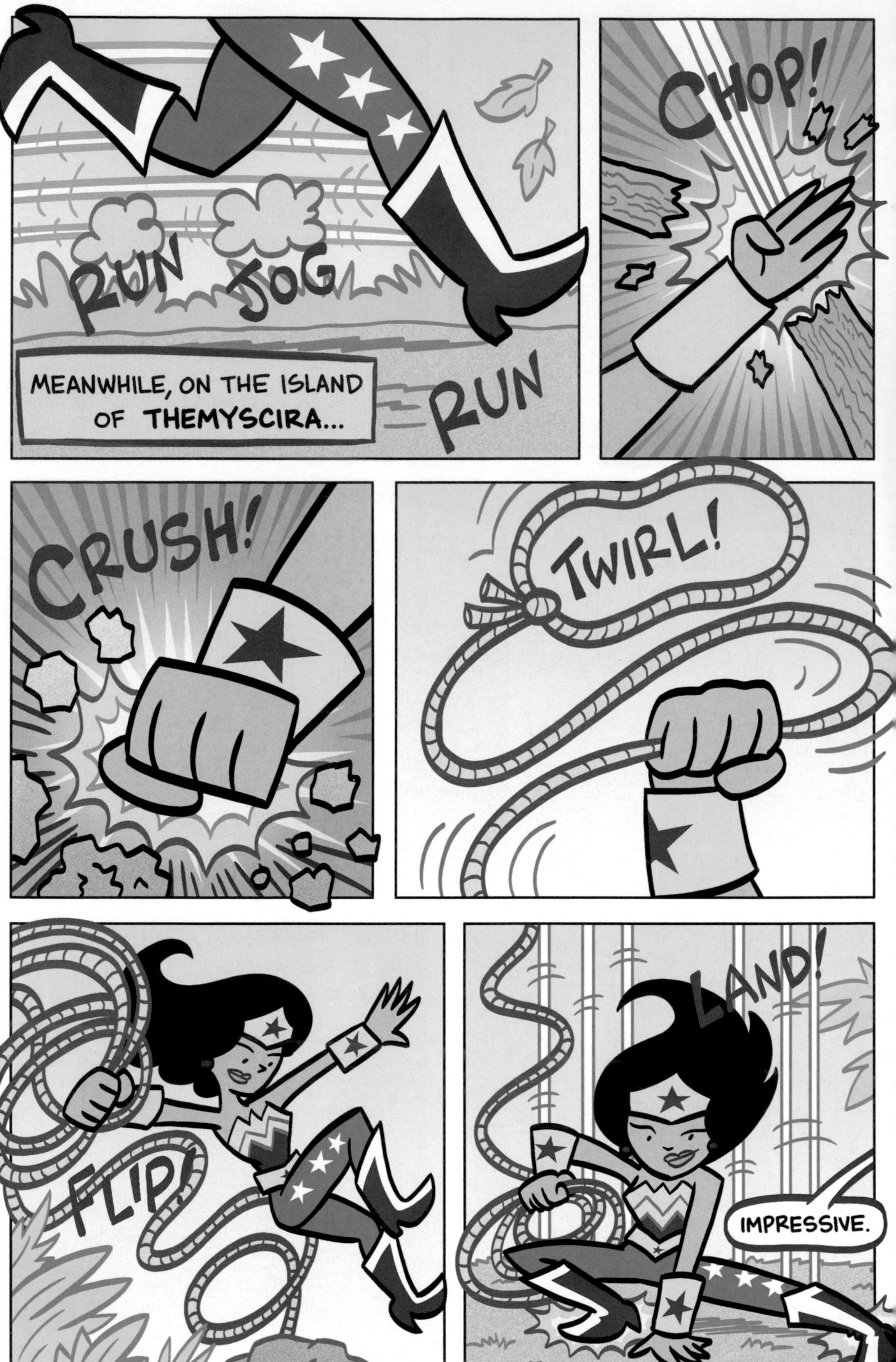
RUN
JOG
MEANWHILE, ON THE ISLAND OF THEMYSCIRA...
RUN
CHOP!
CRUSH!
TWIRL!
FLIP!
LAND!
IMPRESSIVE.

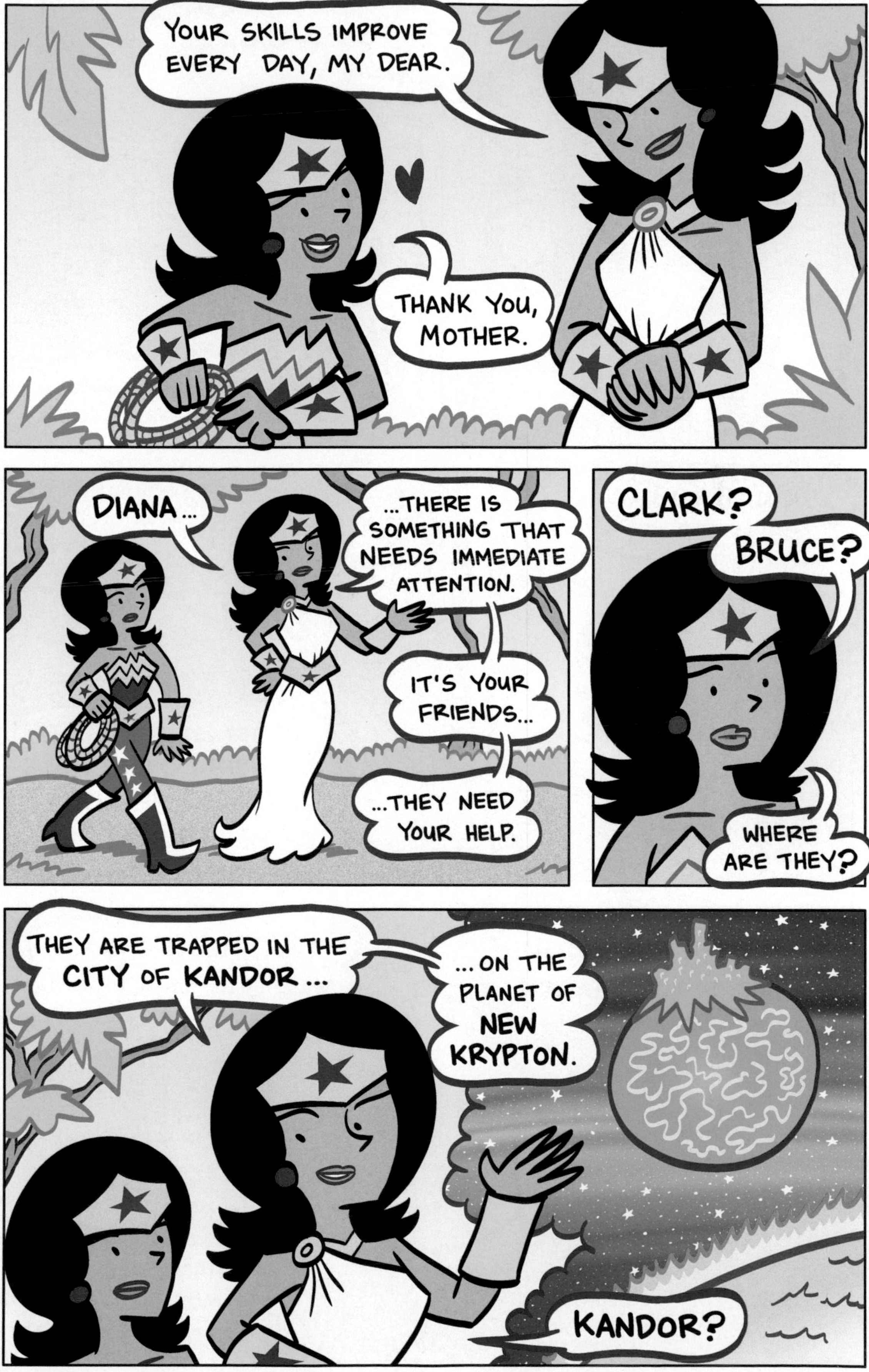
YOUR SKILLS IMPROVE EVERY DAY, MY DEAR.
THANK YOU, MOTHER.
DIANA...
...THERE IS SOMETHING THAT NEEDS IMMEDIATE ATTENTION.
IT'S YOUR FRIENDS...
...THEY NEED YOUR HELP.
CLARK?
BRUCE?
WHERE ARE THEY?
THEY ARE TRAPPED IN THE CITY OF KANDOR...
...ON THE PLANET OF NEW KRYPTON.
KANDOR?

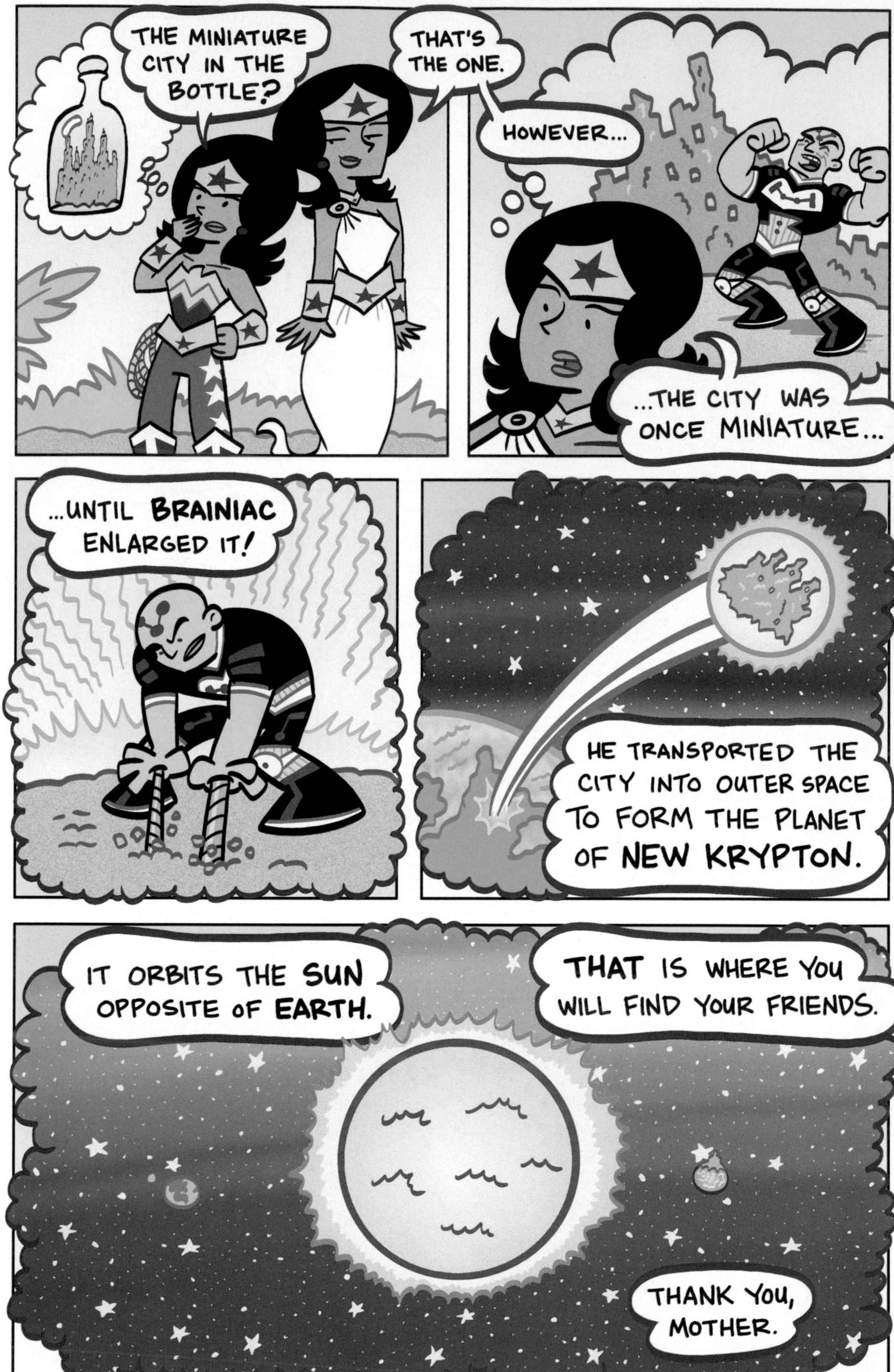
THE MINIATURE CITY IN THE BOTTLE?
THAT'S THE ONE.
HOWEVER...
...THE CITY WAS ONCE MINIATURE...
...UNTIL BRAINIAC ENLARGED IT!
HE TRANSPORTED THE CITY INTO OUTER SPACE TO FORM THE PLANET OF NEW KRYPTON.
IT ORBITS THE SUN OPPOSITE OF EARTH.
THAT IS WHERE YOU WILL FIND YOUR FRIENDS.
THANK YOU, MOTHER.

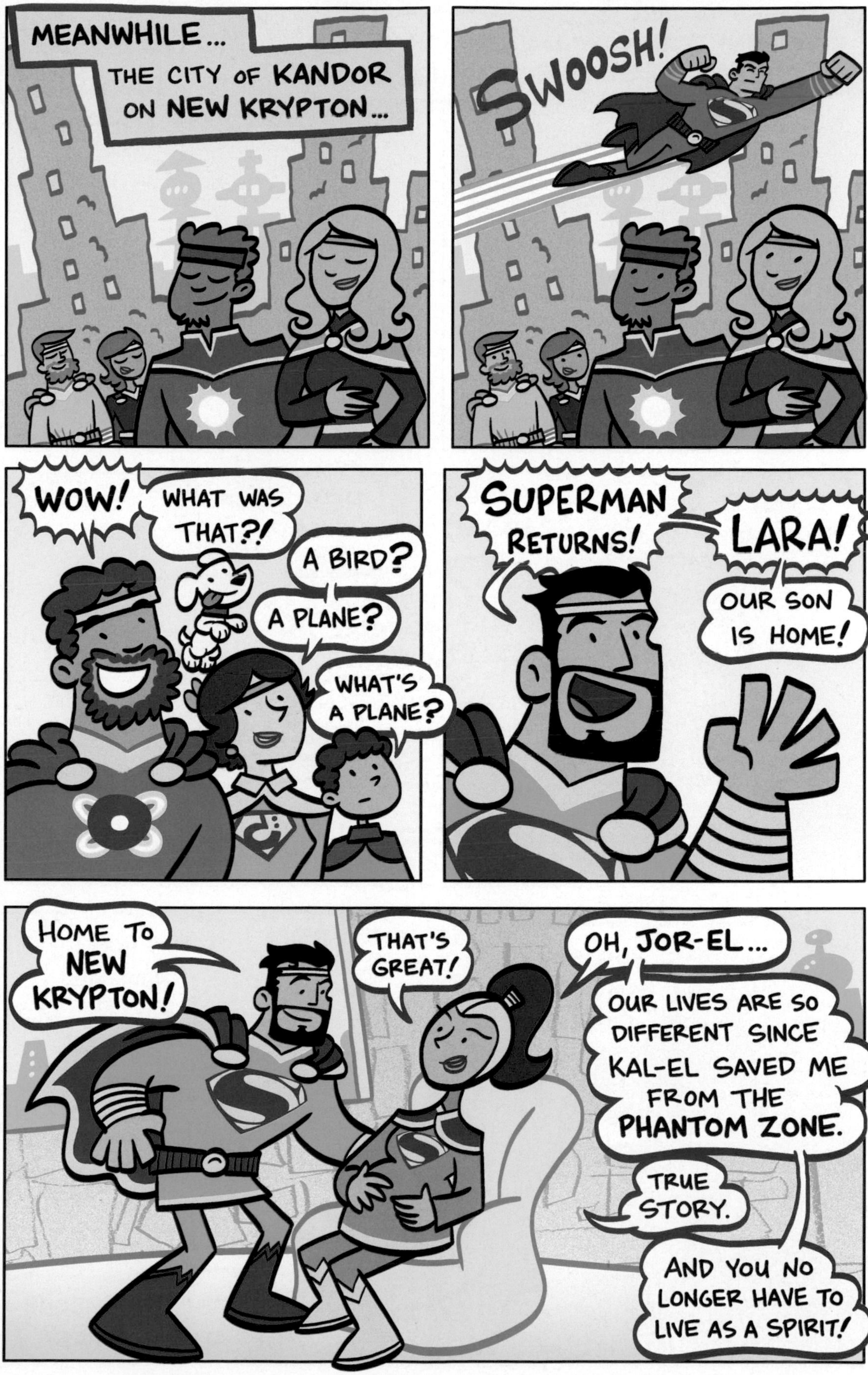
MEANWHILE...
THE CITY OF KANDOR ON NEW KRYPTON...
SWOOSH!
WOW!
WHAT WAS THAT?!
A BIRD?
A PLANE?
WHAT'S A PLANE?
SUPERMAN RETURNS!
LARA!
OUR SON IS HOME!
HOME TO NEW KRYPTON!
THAT'S GREAT!
OH, JOR-EL...
OUR LIVES ARE SO DIFFERENT SINCE KAL-EL SAVED ME FROM THE PHANTOM ZONE.
TRUE STORY.
AND YOU NO LONGER HAVE TO LIVE AS A SPIRIT!

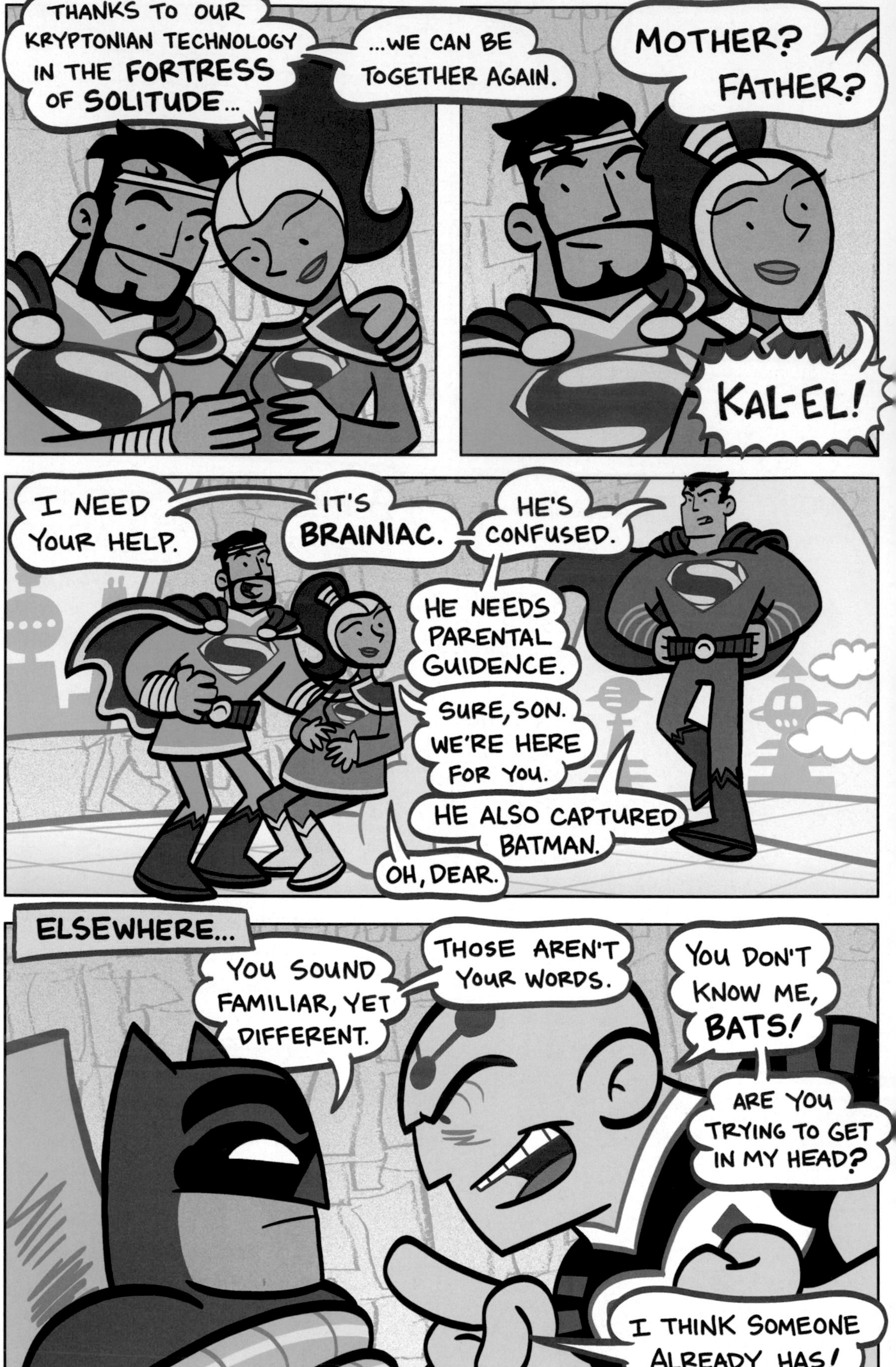
THANKS TO OUR KRYPTONIAN TECHNOLOGY IN THE FORTRESS OF SOLITUDE...
...WE CAN BE TOGETHER AGAIN.
MOTHER? FATHER?
KAL-EL!
I NEED YOUR HELP.
IT'S BRAINIAC.
HE'S CONFUSED.
HE NEEDS PARENTAL GUIDENCE.
SURE, SON. WE'RE HERE FOR YOU.
HE ALSO CAPTURED BATMAN.
OH, DEAR.
ELSEWHERE...
YOU SOUND FAMILIAR, YET DIFFERENT.
THOSE AREN'T YOUR WORDS.
YOU DON'T KNOW ME, BATS!
ARE YOU TRYING TO GET IN MY HEAD?
I THINK SOMEONE ALREADY HAS!

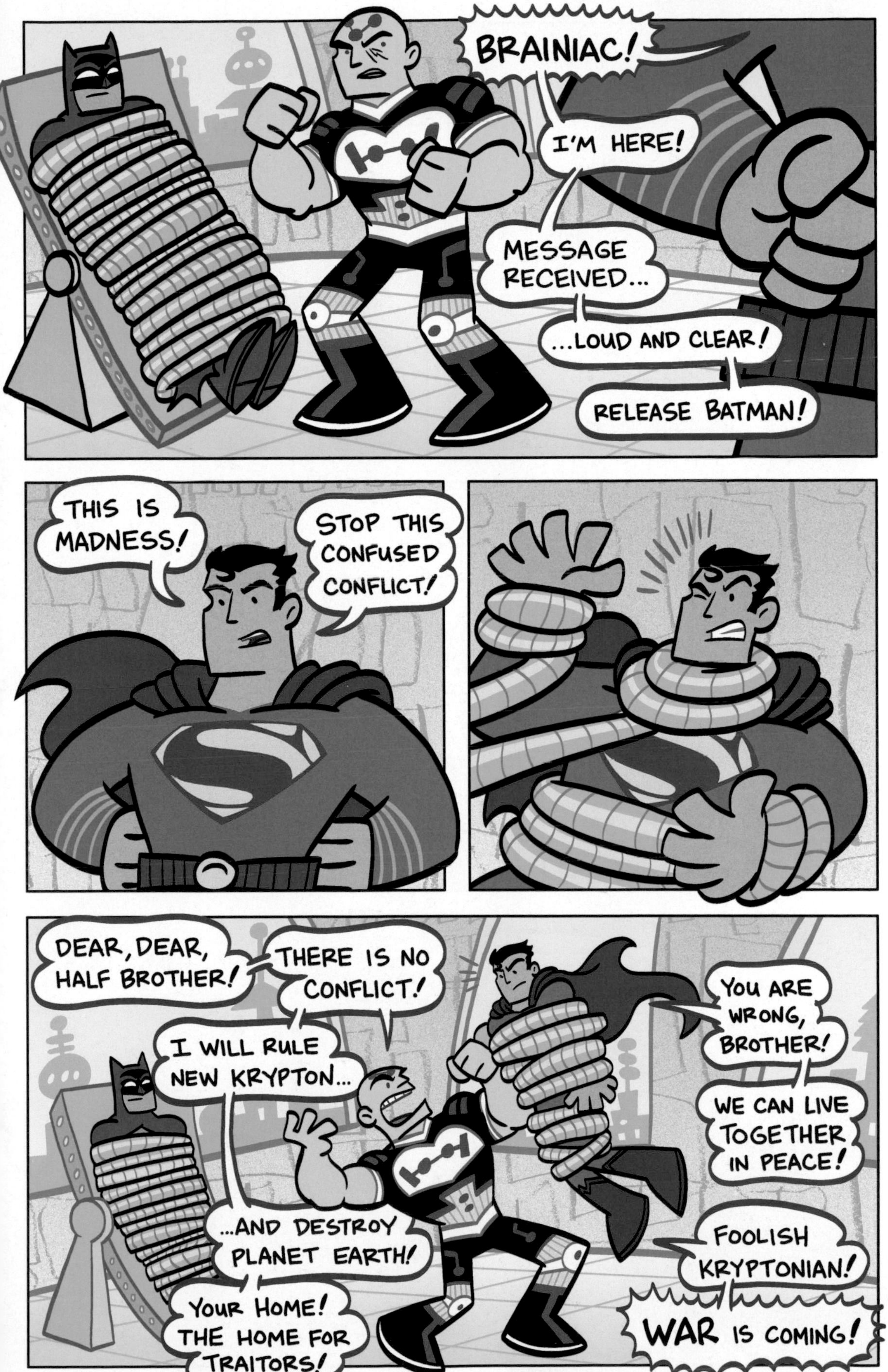
BRAINIAC!
I'M HERE!
MESSAGE RECEIVED...
...LOUD AND CLEAR!
RELEASE BATMAN!
THIS IS MADNESS!
STOP THIS CONFUSED CONFLICT!
DEAR, DEAR, HALF BROTHER!
THERE IS NO CONFLICT!
I WILL RULE NEW KRYPTON...
...AND DESTROY PLANET EARTH!
YOUR HOME! THE HOME FOR TRAITORS!
YOU ARE WRONG, BROTHER!
WE CAN LIVE TOGETHER IN PEACE!
FOOLISH KRYPTONIAN!
WAR IS COMING!

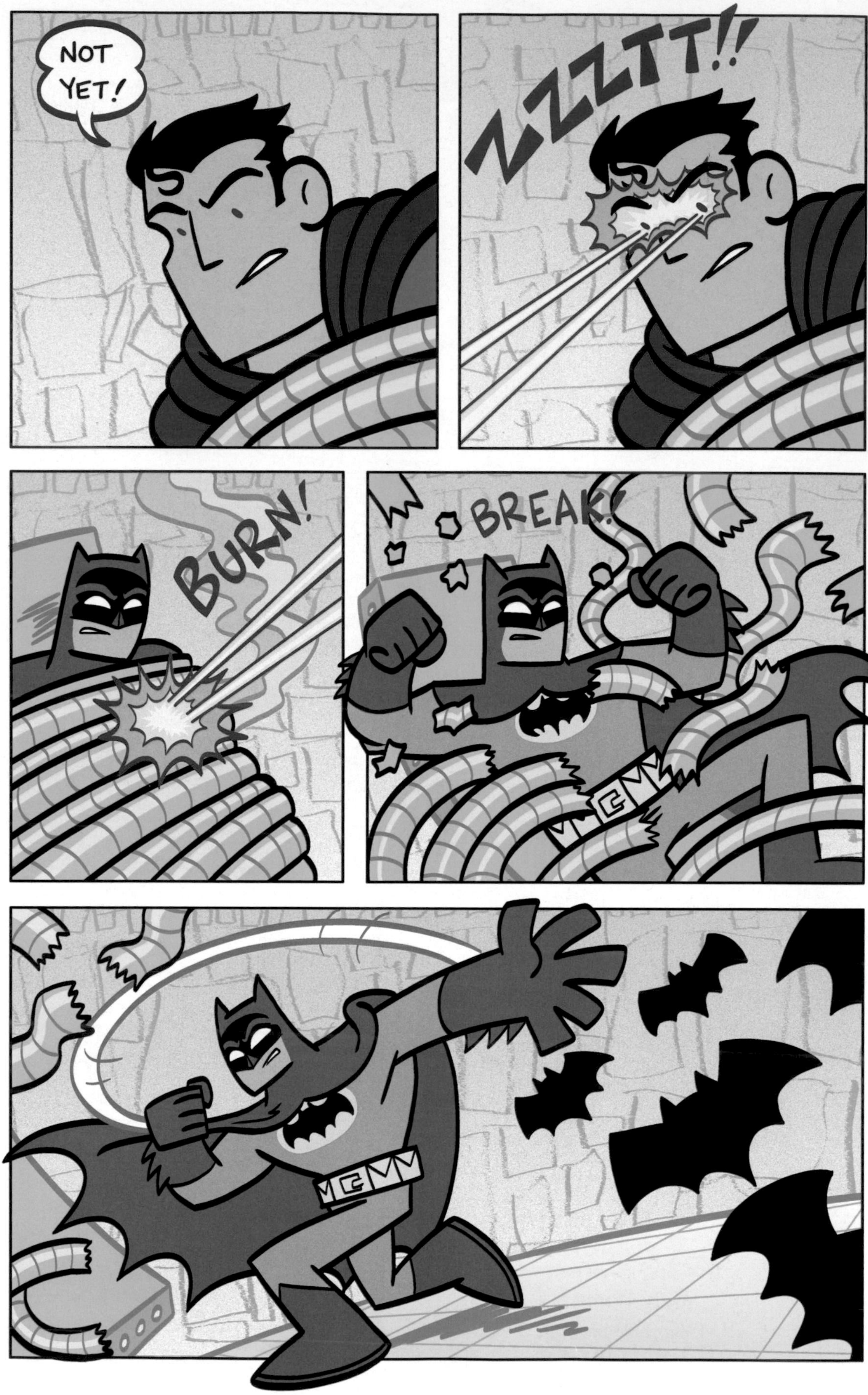
NOT YET!
ZZZZTT!!
BURN!
BREAK!

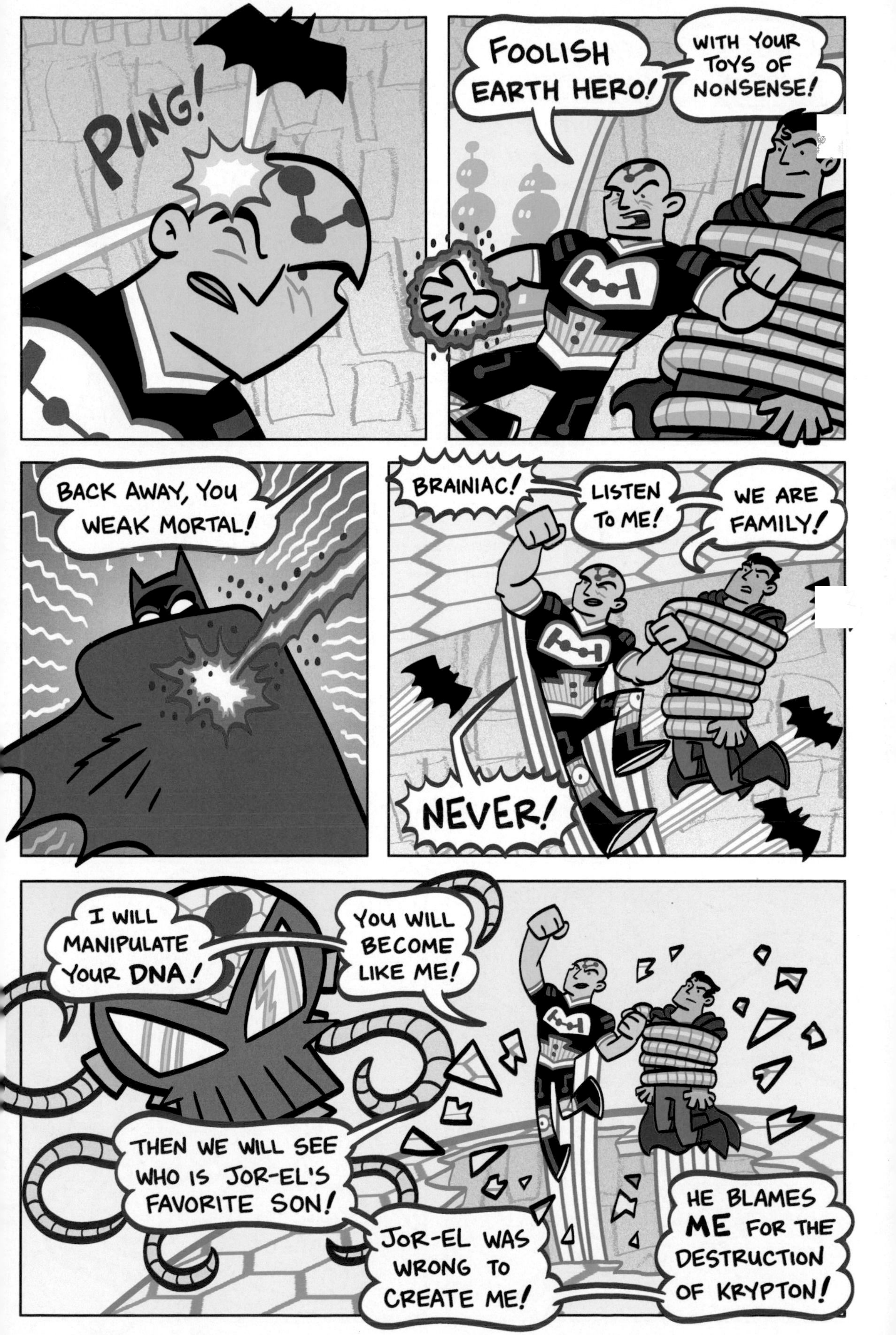
PING!
FOOLISH EARTH HERO!
WITH YOUR TOYS OF NONSENSE!
BACK AWAY, YOU WEAK MORTAL!
BRAINIAC!
LISTEN TO ME!
WE ARE FAMILY!
NEVER!
I WILL MANIPULATE YOUR DNA!
YOU WILL BECOME LIKE ME!
THEN WE WILL SEE WHO IS JOR-EL'S FAVORITE SON!
JOR-EL WAS WRONG TO CREATE ME!
HE BLAMES ME FOR THE DESTRUCTION OF KRYPTON!

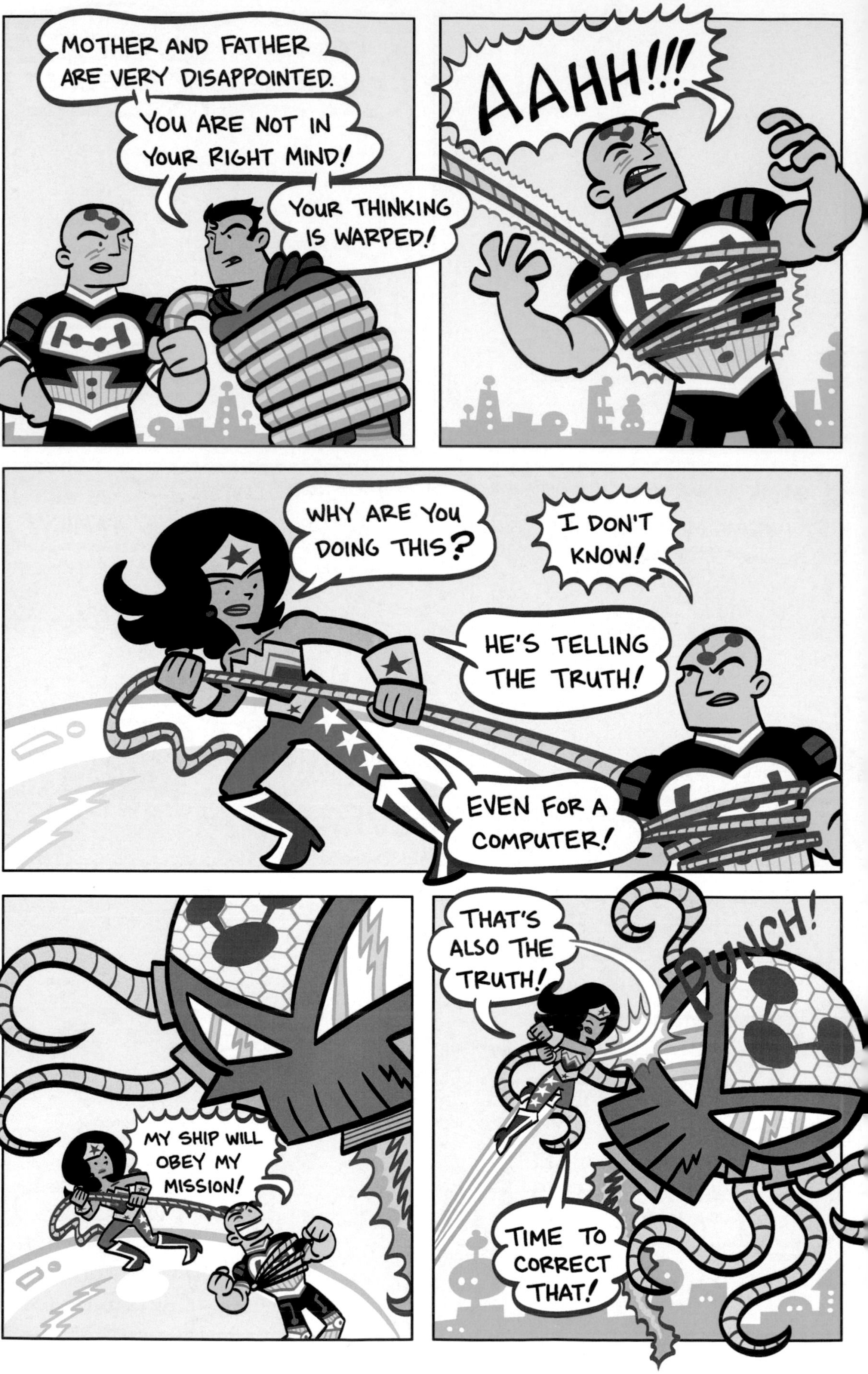
MOTHER AND FATHER ARE VERY DISAPPOINTED.
YOU ARE NOT IN YOUR RIGHT MIND!
YOUR THINKING IS WARPED!
AAHH!!!
WHY ARE YOU DOING THIS?
I DON'T KNOW!
HE'S TELLING THE TRUTH!
EVEN FOR A COMPUTER!
MY SHIP WILL OBEY MY MISSION!
THAT'S ALSO THE TRUTH!
PUNCH!
TIME TO CORRECT THAT!

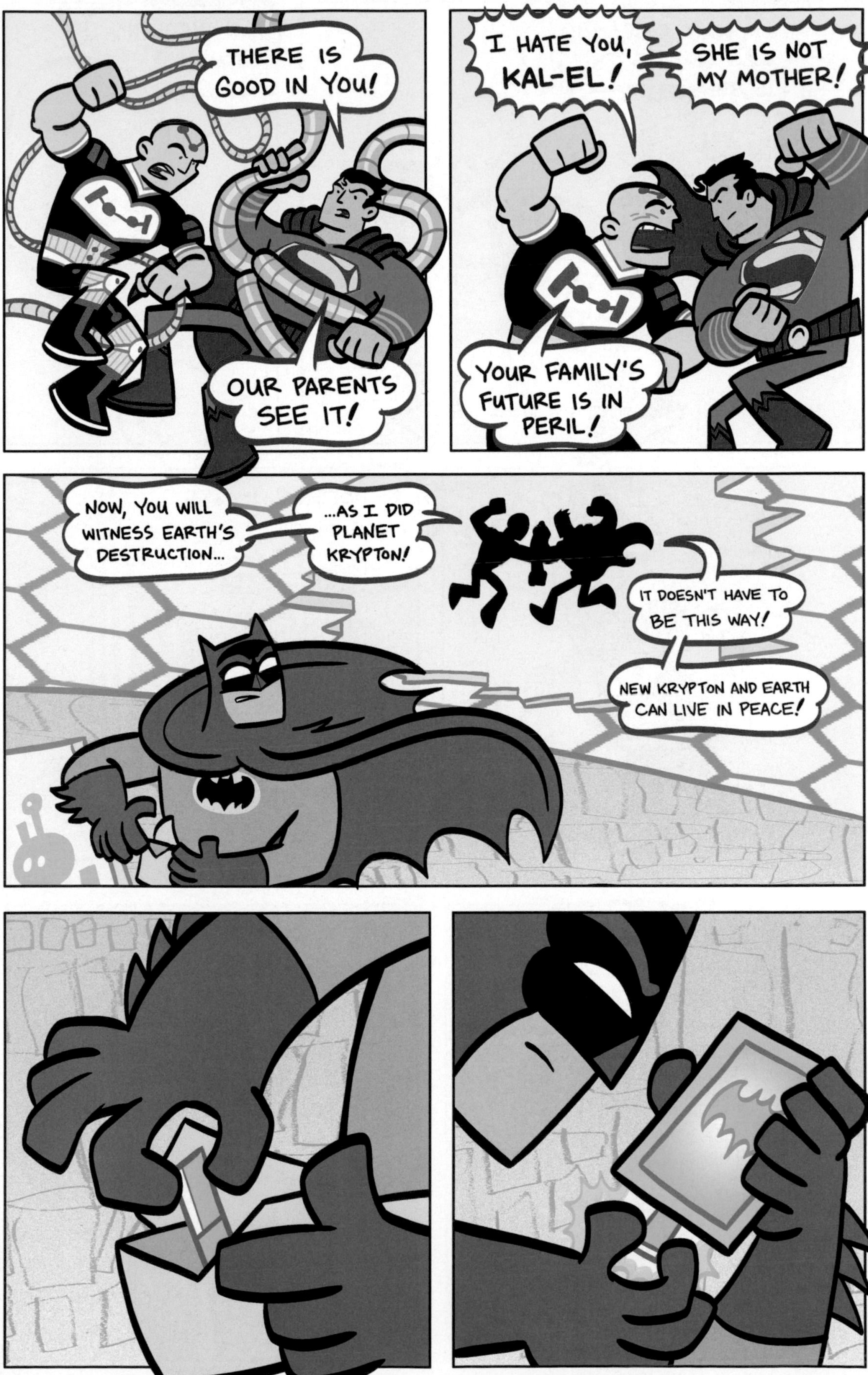
THERE IS GOOD IN YOU!
OUR PARENTS SEE IT!
I HATE YOU, KAL-EL!
SHE IS NOT MY MOTHER!
YOUR FAMILY'S FUTURE IS IN PERIL!
NOW, YOU WILL WITNESS EARTH'S DESTRUCTION...
...AS I DID PLANET KRYPTON!
IT DOESN'T HAVE TO BE THIS WAY!
NEW KRYPTON AND EARTH CAN LIVE IN PEACE!

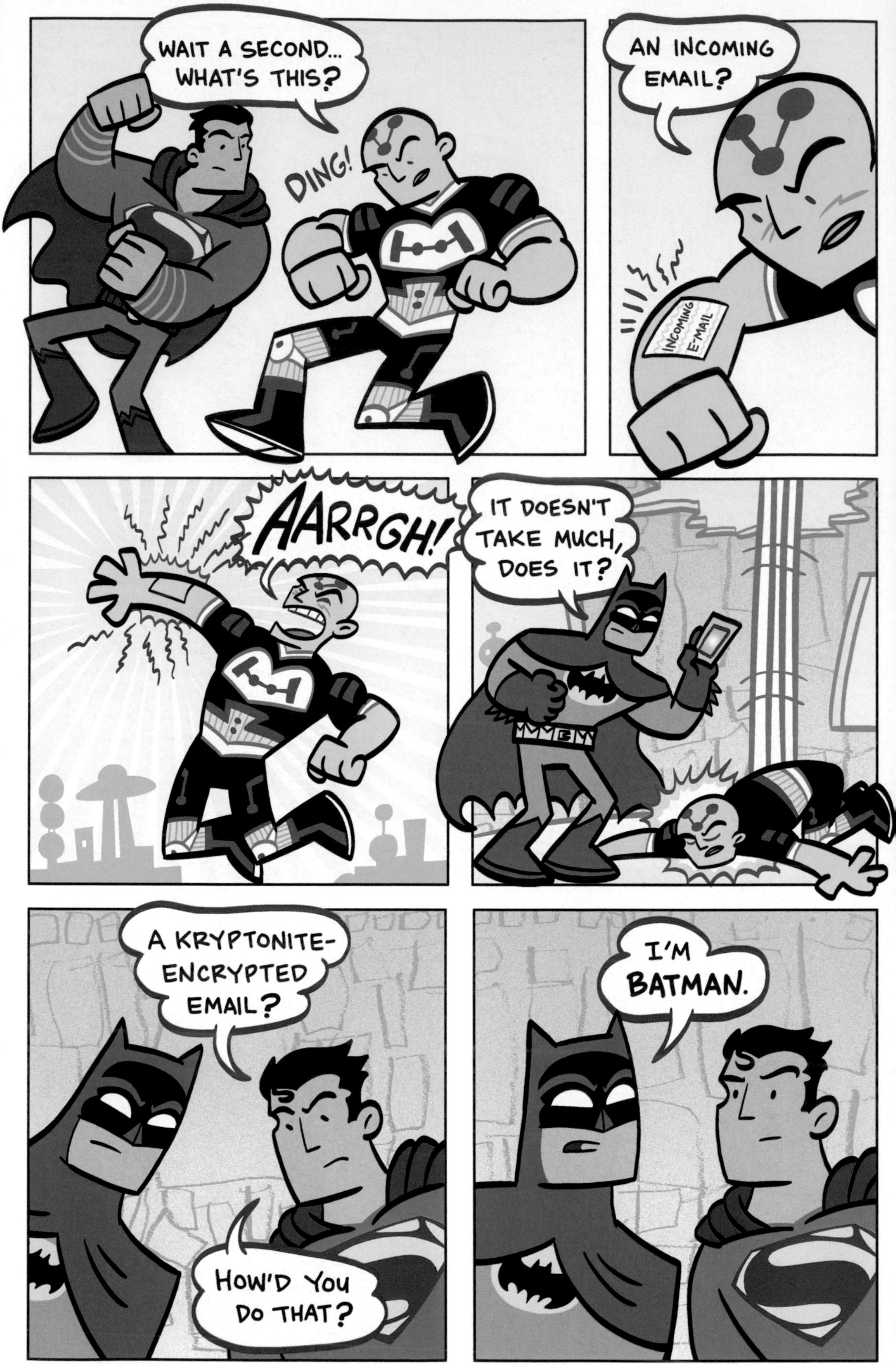
WAIT A SECOND... WHAT'S THIS?
DING!
AN INCOMING EMAIL?
INCOMING E-MAIL
AARRGH!
IT DOESN'T TAKE MUCH, DOES IT?
A KRYPTONITE-ENCRYPTED EMAIL?
HOW'D YOU DO THAT?
I'M BATMAN.

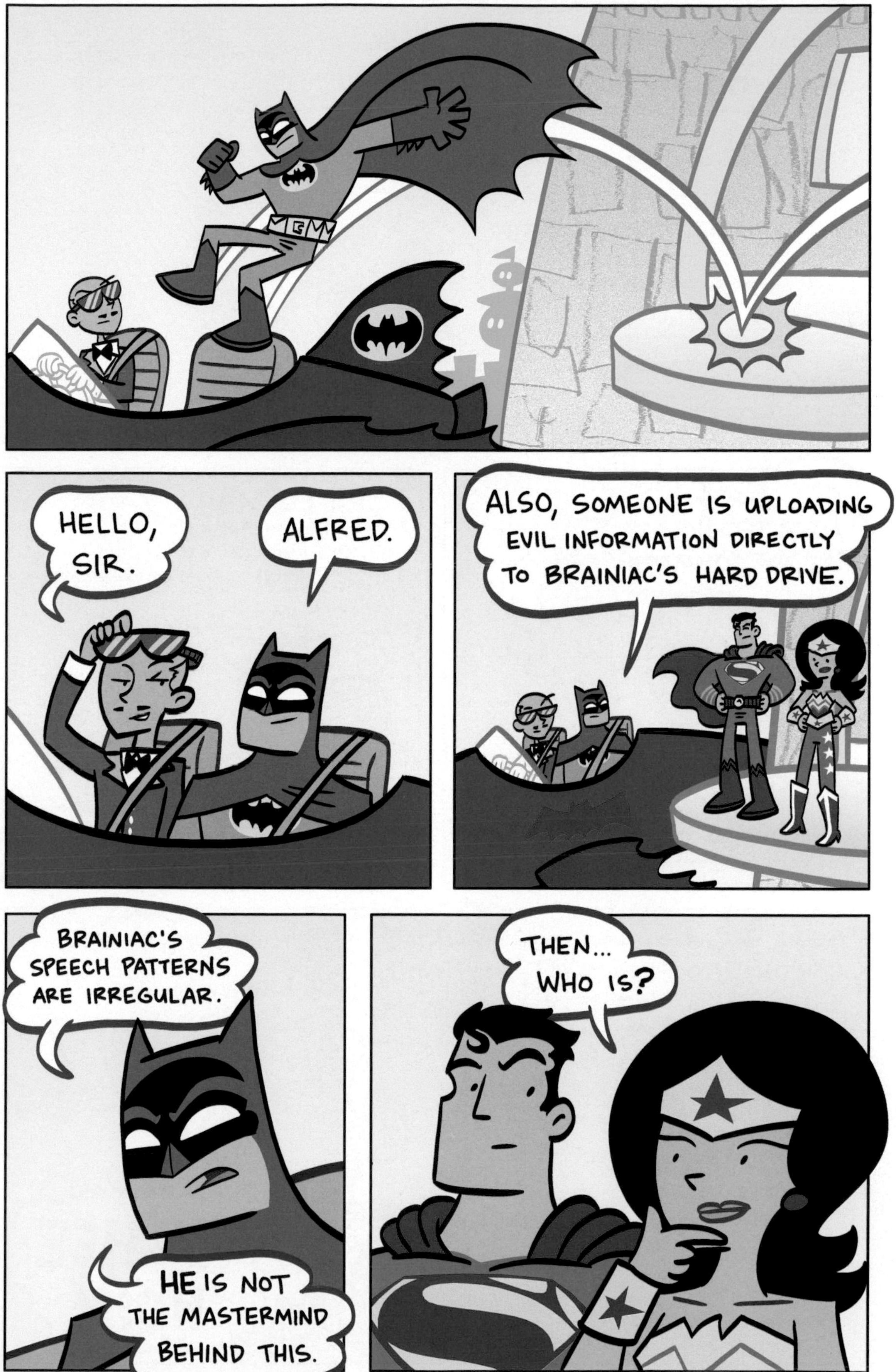
HELLO, SIR.
ALFRED.
ALSO, SOMEONE IS UPLOADING EVIL INFORMATION DIRECTLY TO BRAINIAC'S HARD DRIVE.
BRAINIAC'S SPEECH PATTERNS ARE IRREGULAR.
HE IS NOT THE MASTERMIND BEHIND THIS.
THEN... WHO IS?

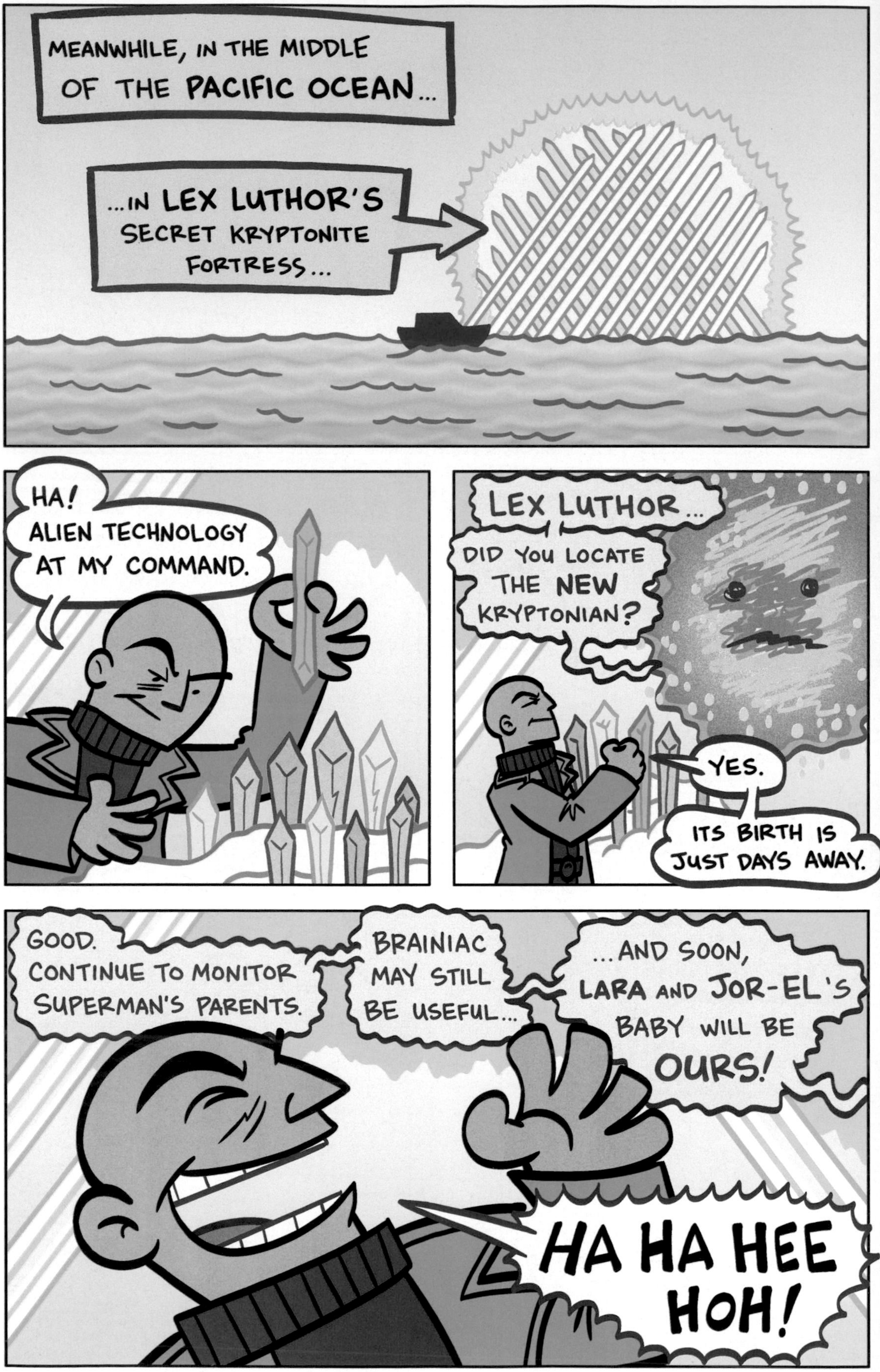
MEANWHILE, IN THE MIDDLE OF THE PACIFIC OCEAN...
...IN LEX LUTHOR'S SECRET KRYPTONITE FORTRESS...
HA! ALIEN TECHNOLOGY AT MY COMMAND.
LEX LUTHOR...
DID YOU LOCATE THE NEW KRYPTONIAN?
YES.
ITS BIRTH IS JUST DAYS AWAY.
GOOD. CONTINUE TO MONITOR SUPERMAN'S PARENTS.
BRAINIAC MAY STILL BE USEFUL...
...AND SOON, LARA AND JOR-EL'S BABY WILL BE OURS!
HA HA HEE HOH!

—WHO'S GONNA SAVE ME?

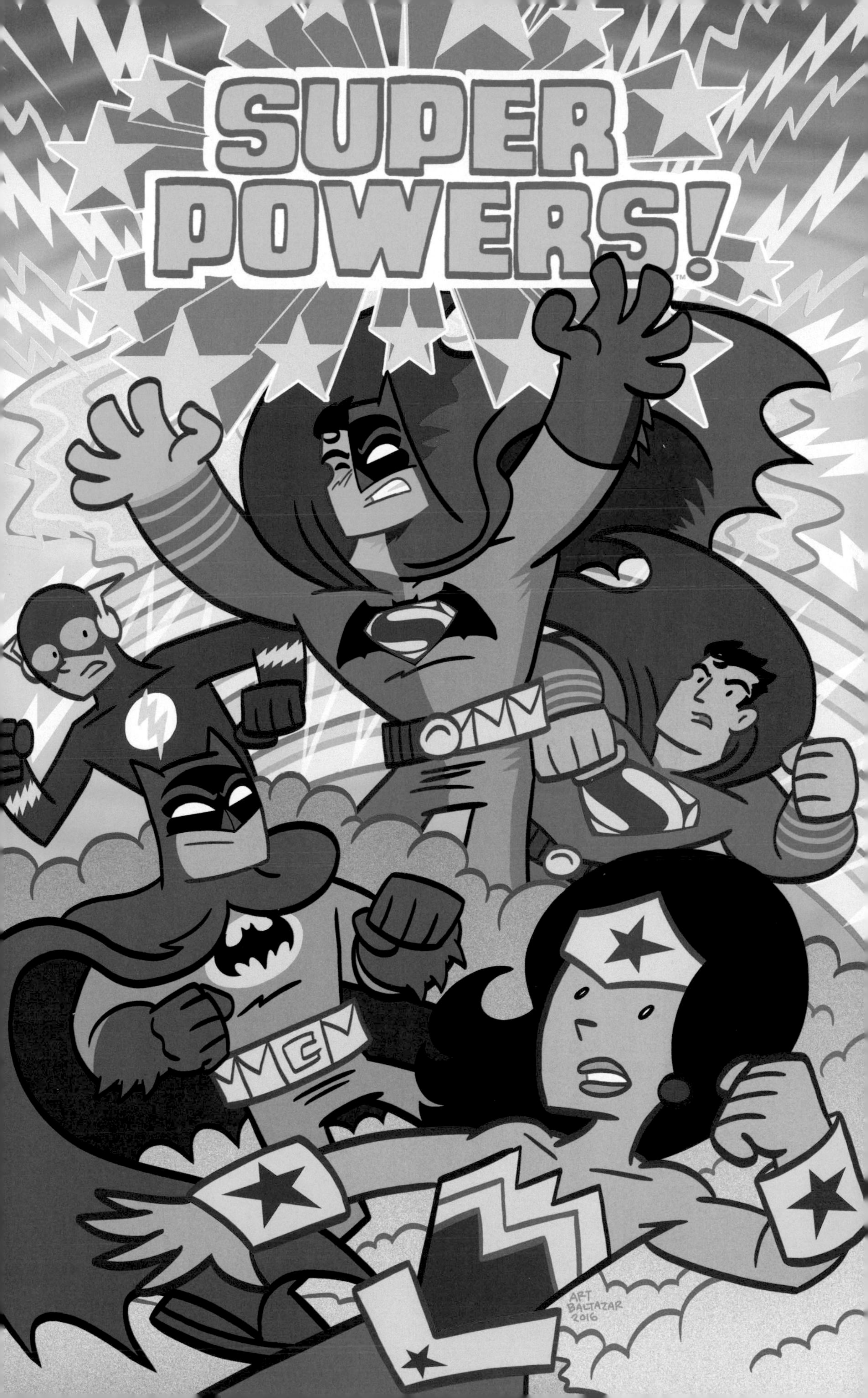
SUPER POWERS!™
ART BALTAZAR 2016

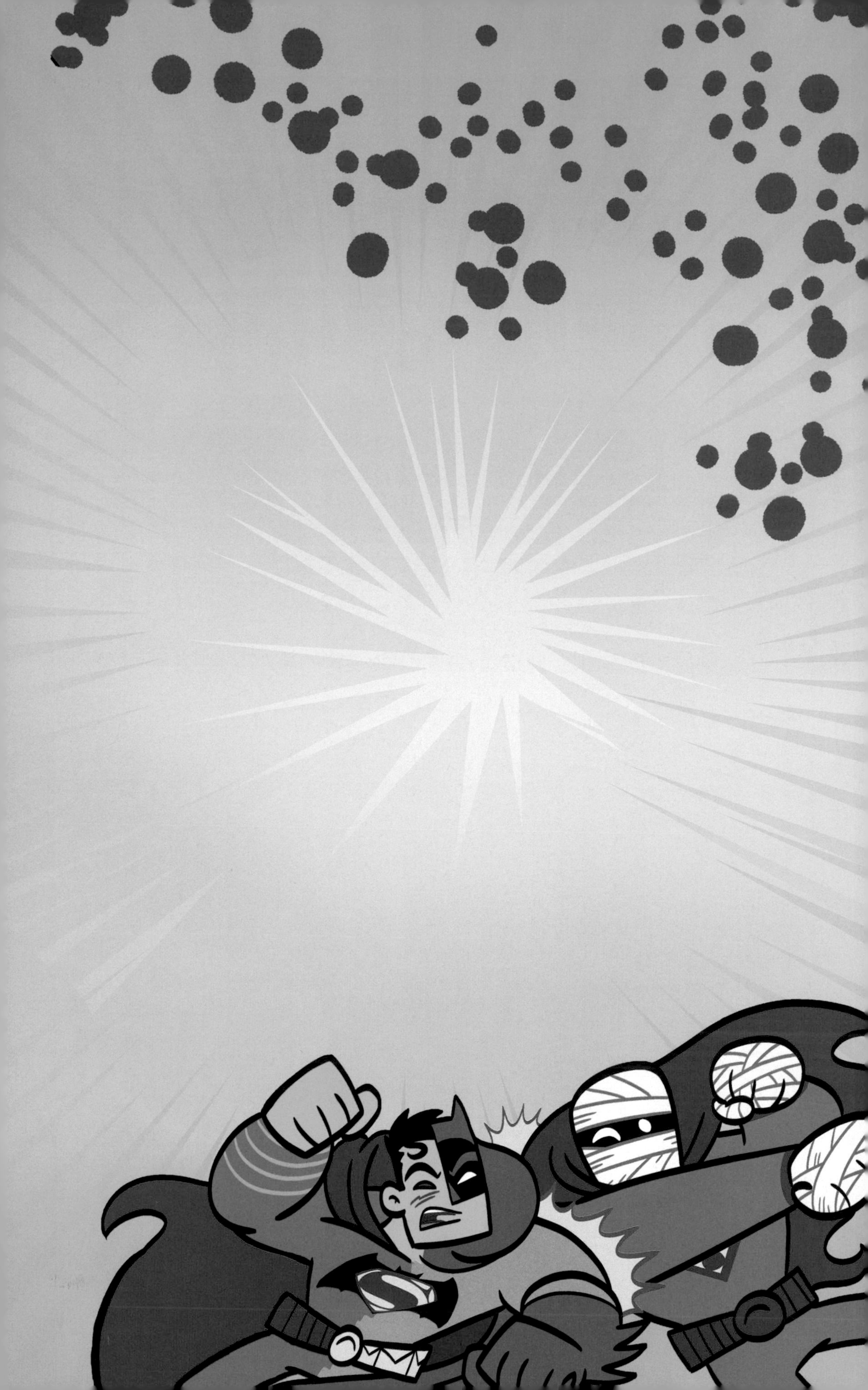

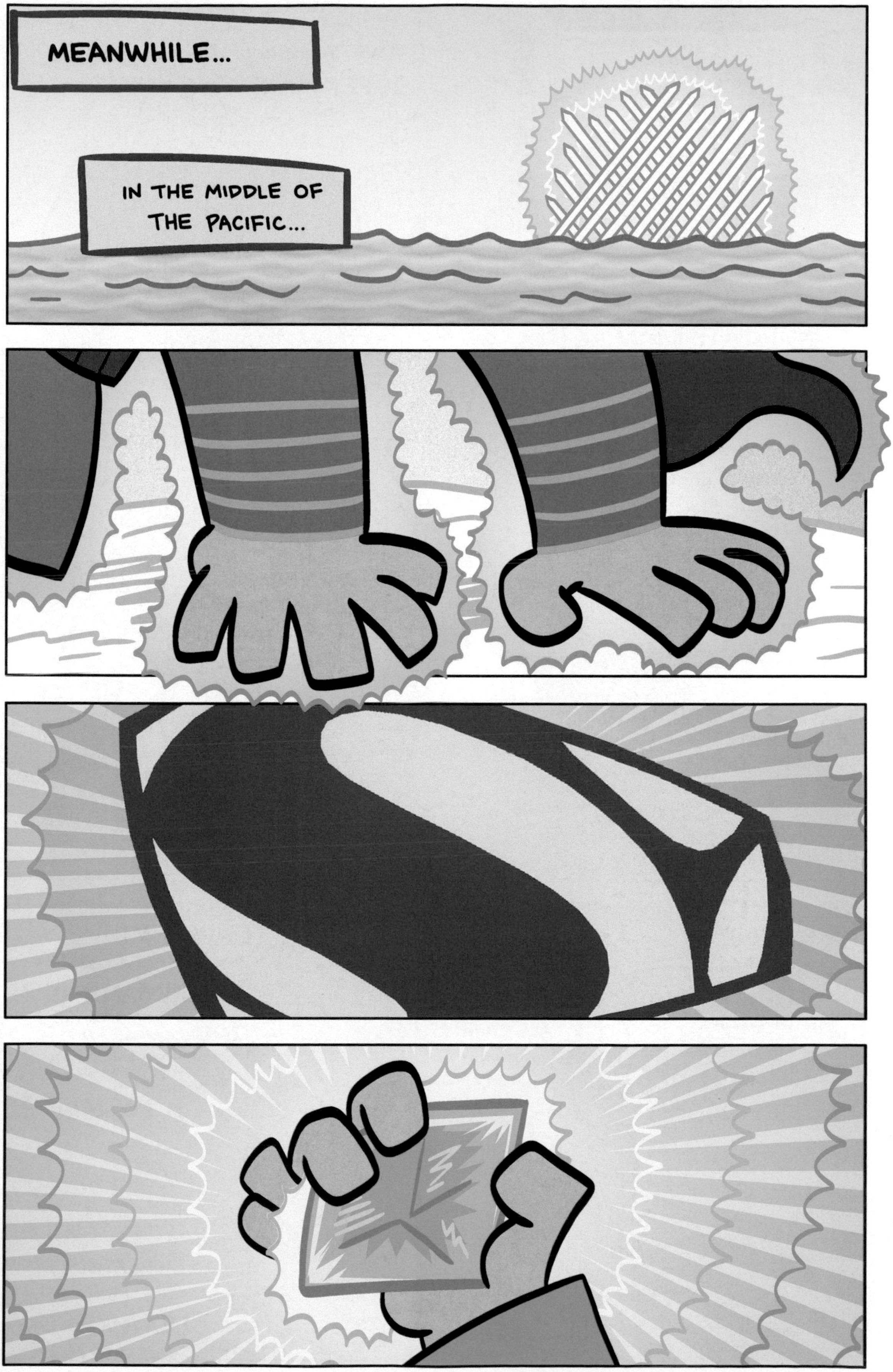
MEANWHILE...
IN THE MIDDLE OF THE PACIFIC...

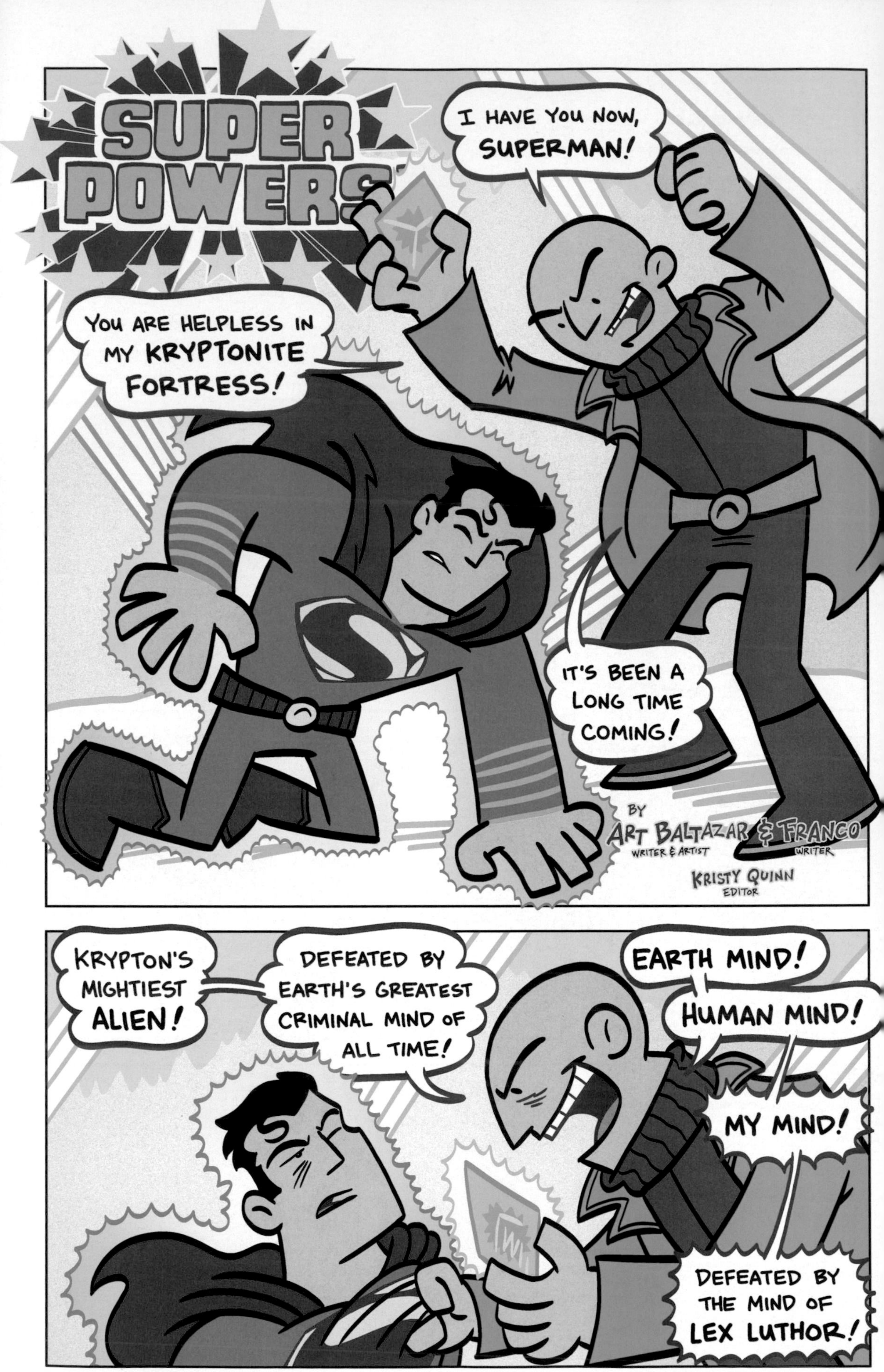
SUPER POWERS
I HAVE YOU NOW, SUPERMAN!
YOU ARE HELPLESS IN MY KRYPTONITE FORTRESS!
IT'S BEEN A LONG TIME COMING!
BY ART BALTAZAR WRITER & ARTIST & FRANCO WRITER
KRISTY QUINN EDITOR
KRYPTON'S MIGHTIEST ALIEN!
DEFEATED BY EARTH'S GREATEST CRIMINAL MIND OF ALL TIME!
EARTH MIND!
HUMAN MIND!
MY MIND!
DEFEATED BY THE MIND OF LEX LUTHOR!

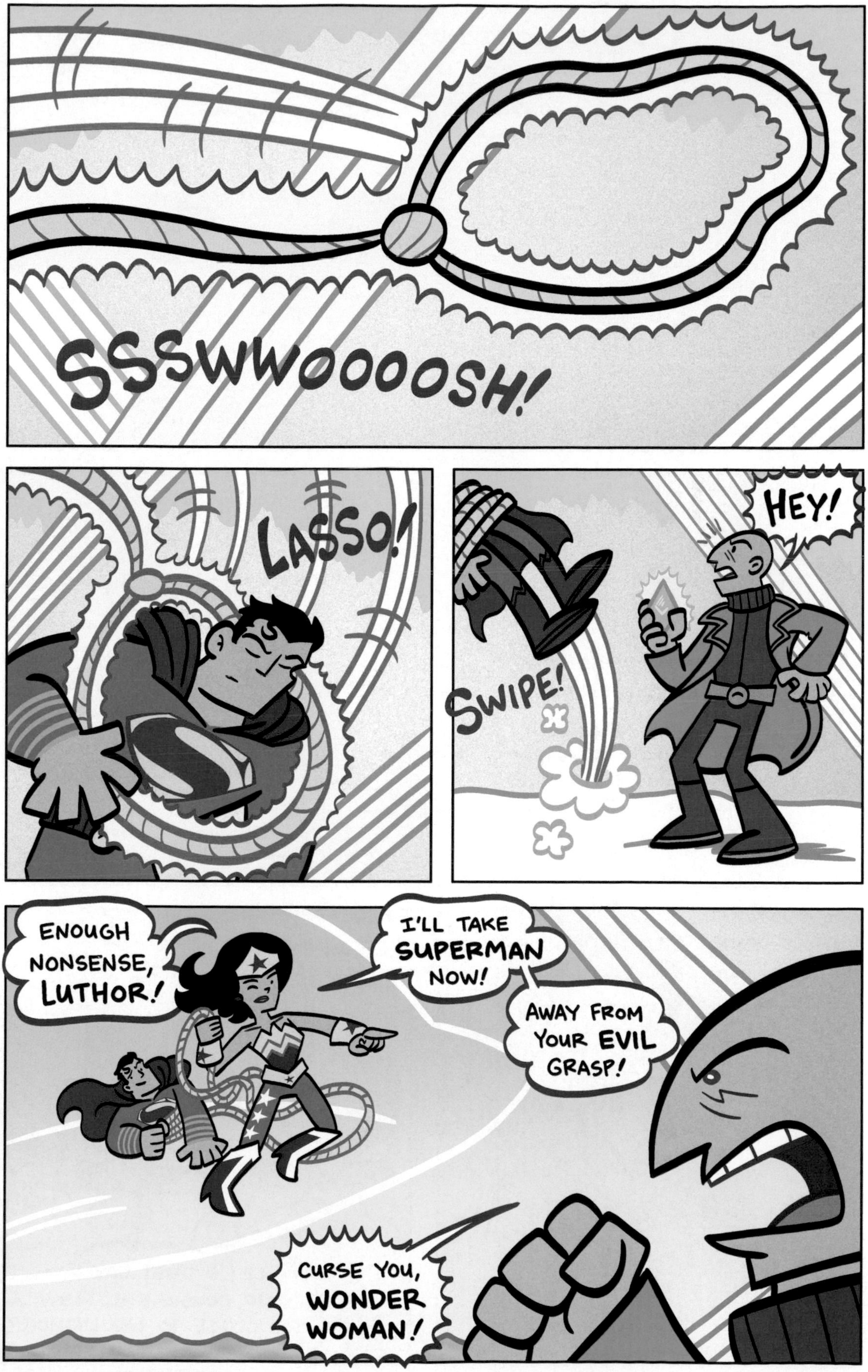
SSSWWOOOOSH!
LASSO!
SWIPE!
HEY!
ENOUGH NONSENSE, LUTHOR!
I'LL TAKE SUPERMAN NOW!
AWAY FROM YOUR EVIL GRASP!
CURSE YOU, WONDER WOMAN!

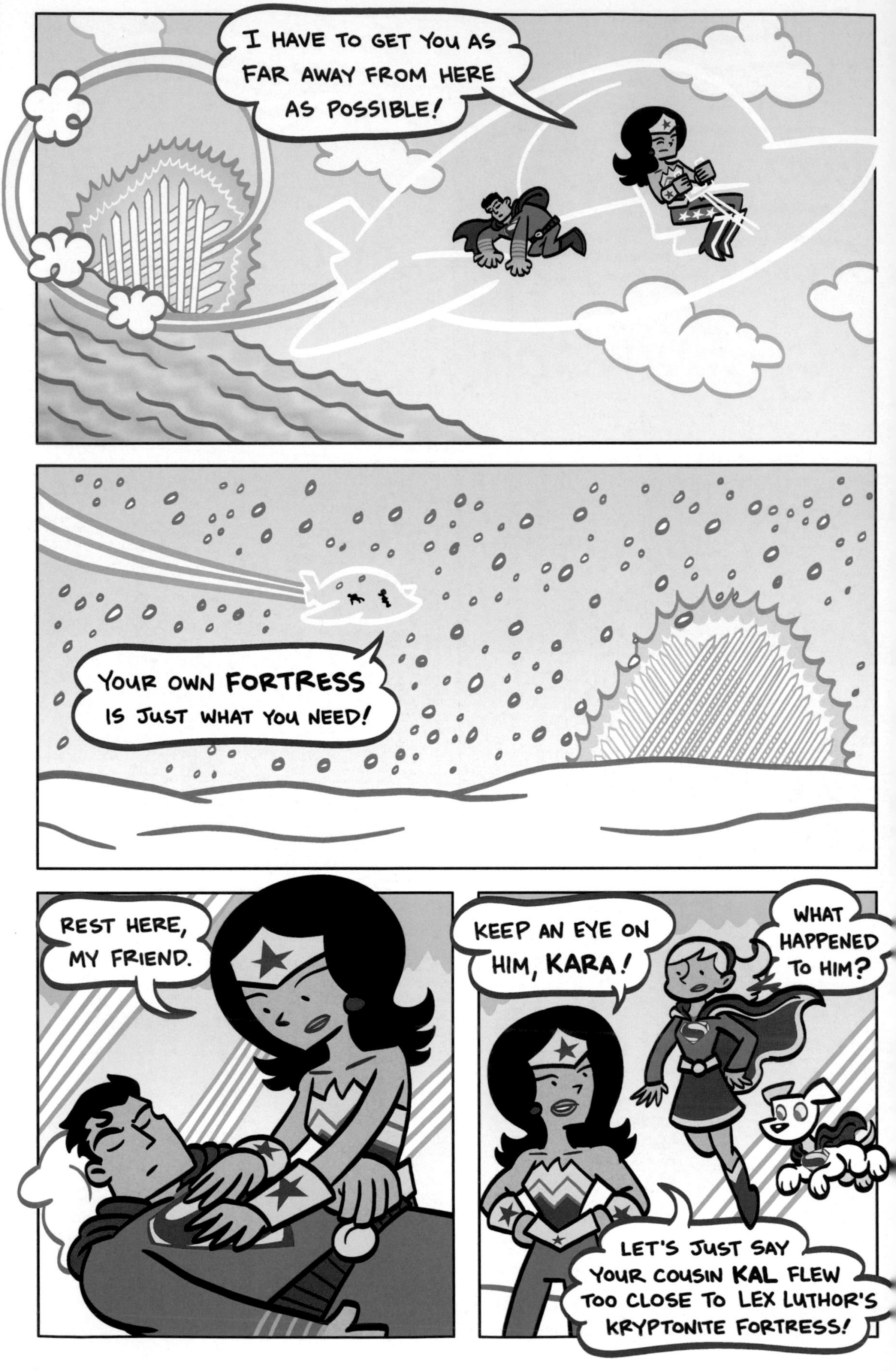
I HAVE TO GET YOU AS FAR AWAY FROM HERE AS POSSIBLE!
YOUR OWN FORTRESS IS JUST WHAT YOU NEED!
REST HERE, MY FRIEND.
KEEP AN EYE ON HIM, KARA!
WHAT HAPPENED TO HIM?
LET'S JUST SAY YOUR COUSIN KAL FLEW TOO CLOSE TO LEX LUTHOR'S KRYPTONITE FORTRESS!

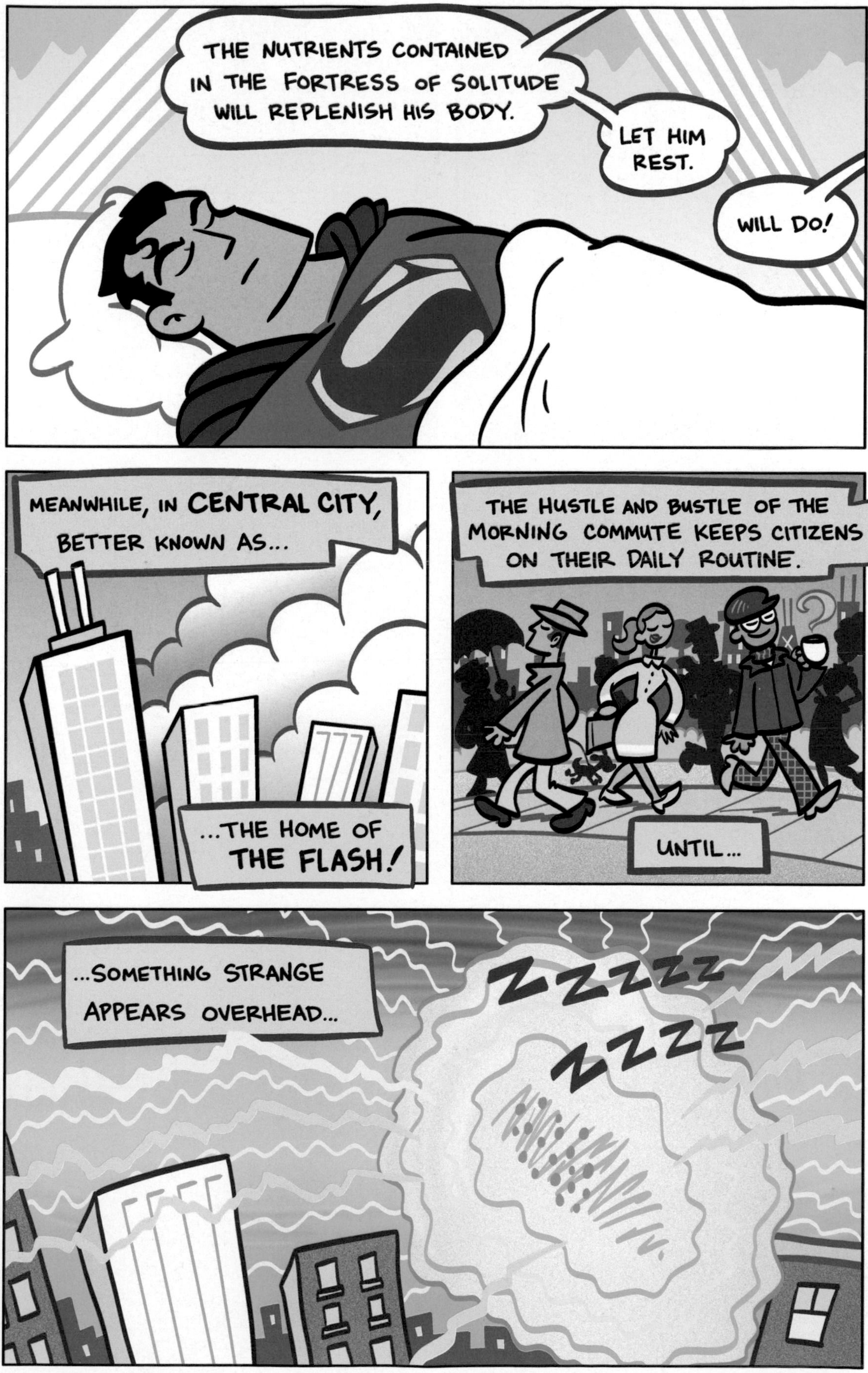
THE NUTRIENTS CONTAINED IN THE FORTRESS OF SOLITUDE WILL REPLENISH HIS BODY.
LET HIM REST.
WILL DO!
MEANWHILE, IN CENTRAL CITY, BETTER KNOWN AS...
...THE HOME OF THE FLASH!
THE HUSTLE AND BUSTLE OF THE MORNING COMMUTE KEEPS CITIZENS ON THEIR DAILY ROUTINE.
UNTIL...
...SOMETHING STRANGE APPEARS OVERHEAD...
ZZZZZ
ZZZZ

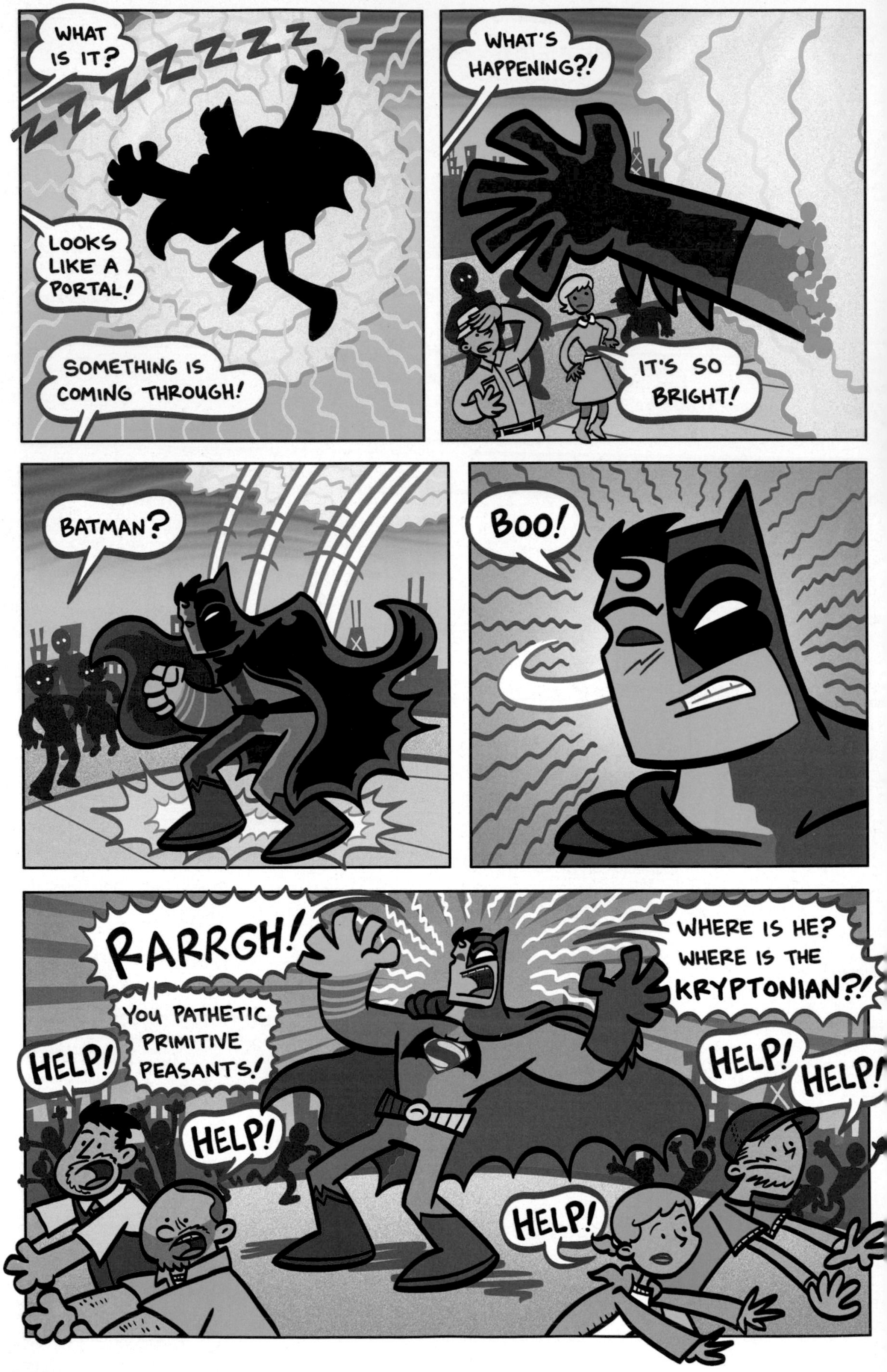
WHAT IS IT?
ZZZZZZZZZ
LOOKS LIKE A PORTAL!
SOMETHING IS COMING THROUGH!
WHAT'S HAPPENING?!
IT'S SO BRIGHT!
BATMAN?
BOO!
RARRGH!
YOU PATHETIC PRIMITIVE PEASANTS!
WHERE IS HE? WHERE IS THE KRYPTONIAN?!
HELP!
HELP!
HELP!
HELP!
HELP!

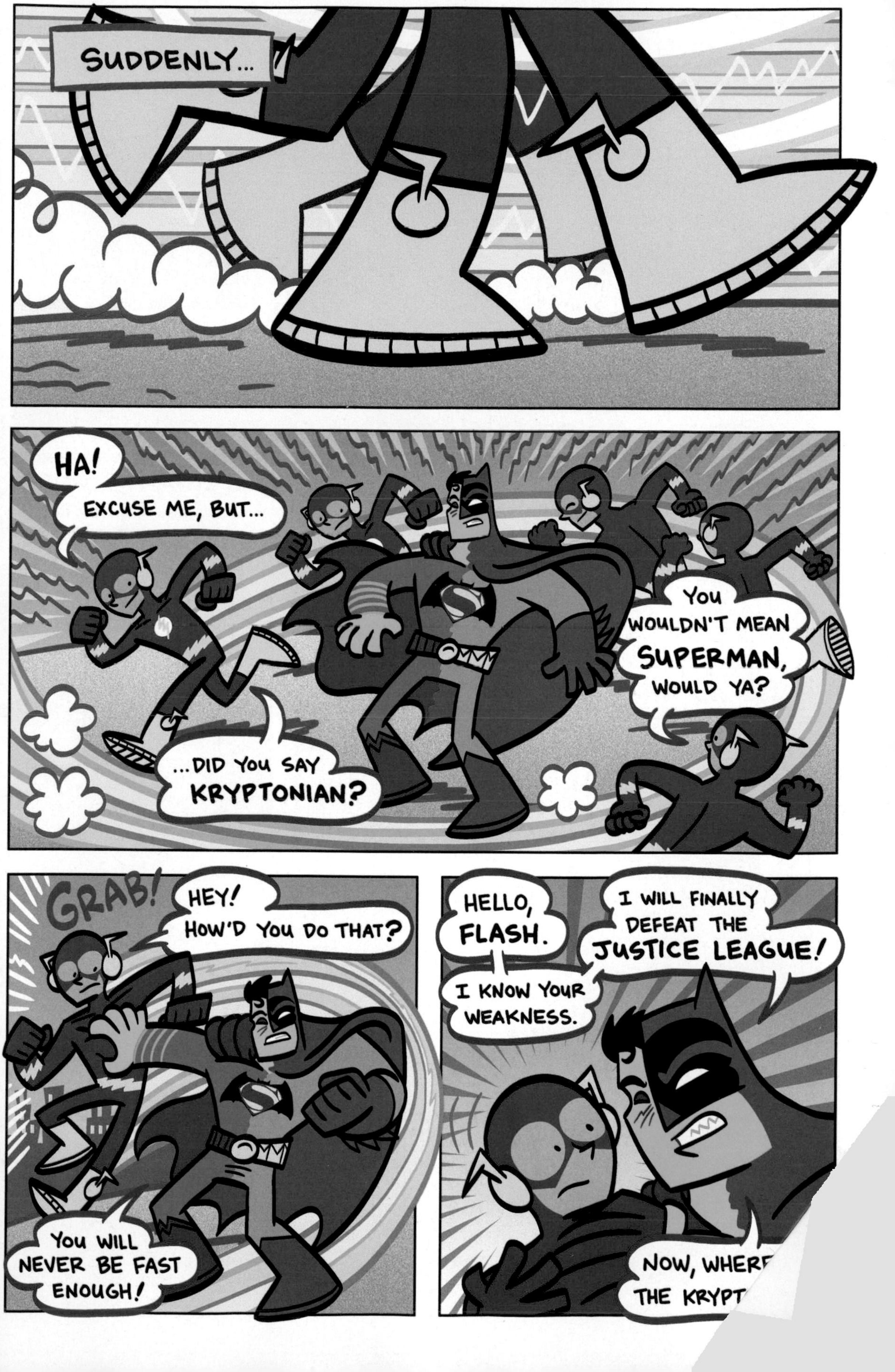
SUDDENLY...
HA!
EXCUSE ME, BUT...
...DID YOU SAY KRYPTONIAN?
YOU WOULDN'T MEAN SUPERMAN, WOULD YA?
GRAB!
HEY! HOW'D YOU DO THAT?
YOU WILL NEVER BE FAST ENOUGH!
HELLO, FLASH.
I KNOW YOUR WEAKNESS.
I WILL FINALLY DEFEAT THE JUSTICE LEAGUE!
NOW, WHERE
THE KRYPT

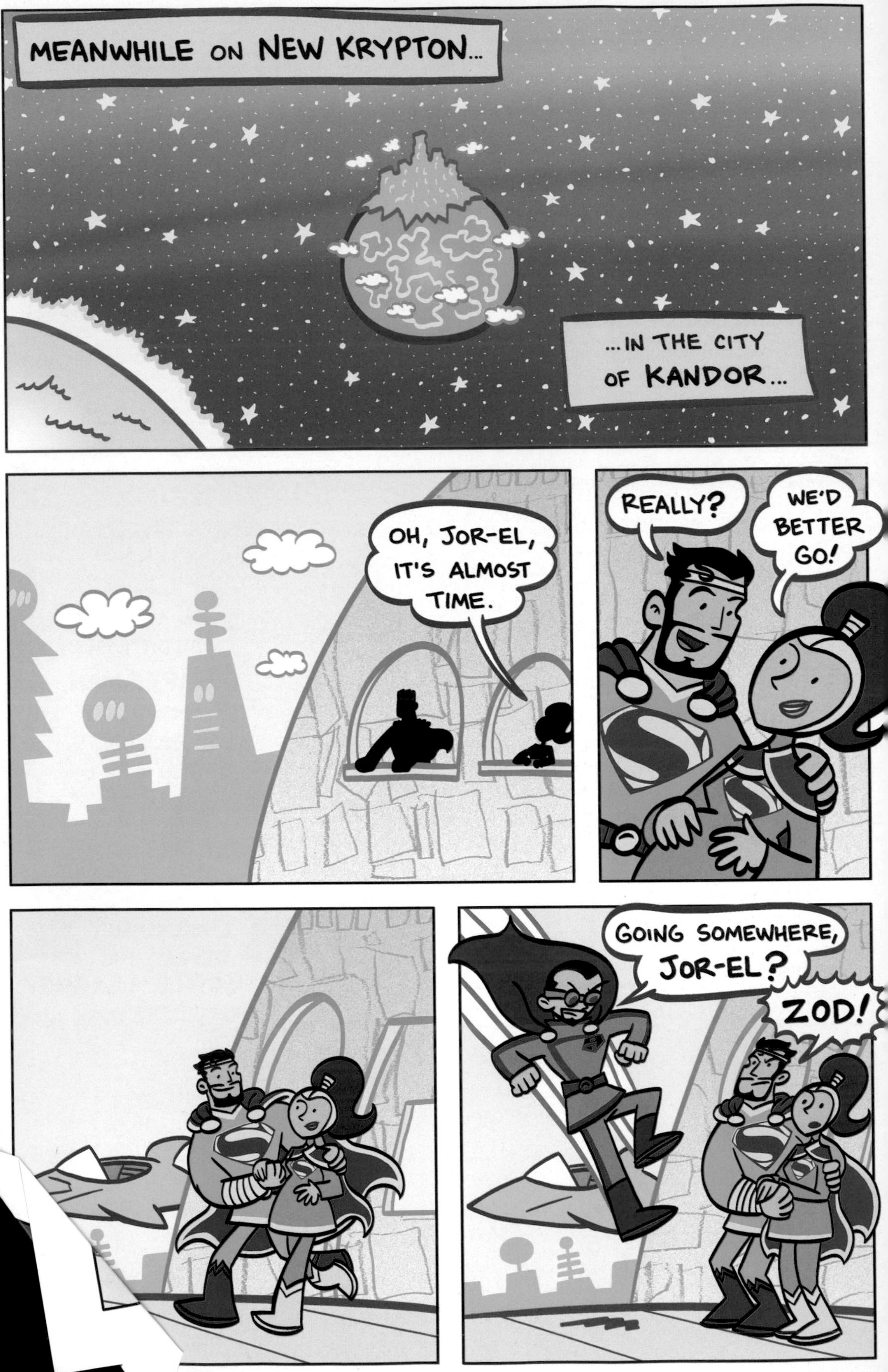
MEANWHILE ON NEW KRYPTON...
...IN THE CITY OF KANDOR...
OH, JOR-EL, IT'S ALMOST TIME.
REALLY?
WE'D BETTER GO!
GOING SOMEWHERE, JOR-EL?
ZOD!

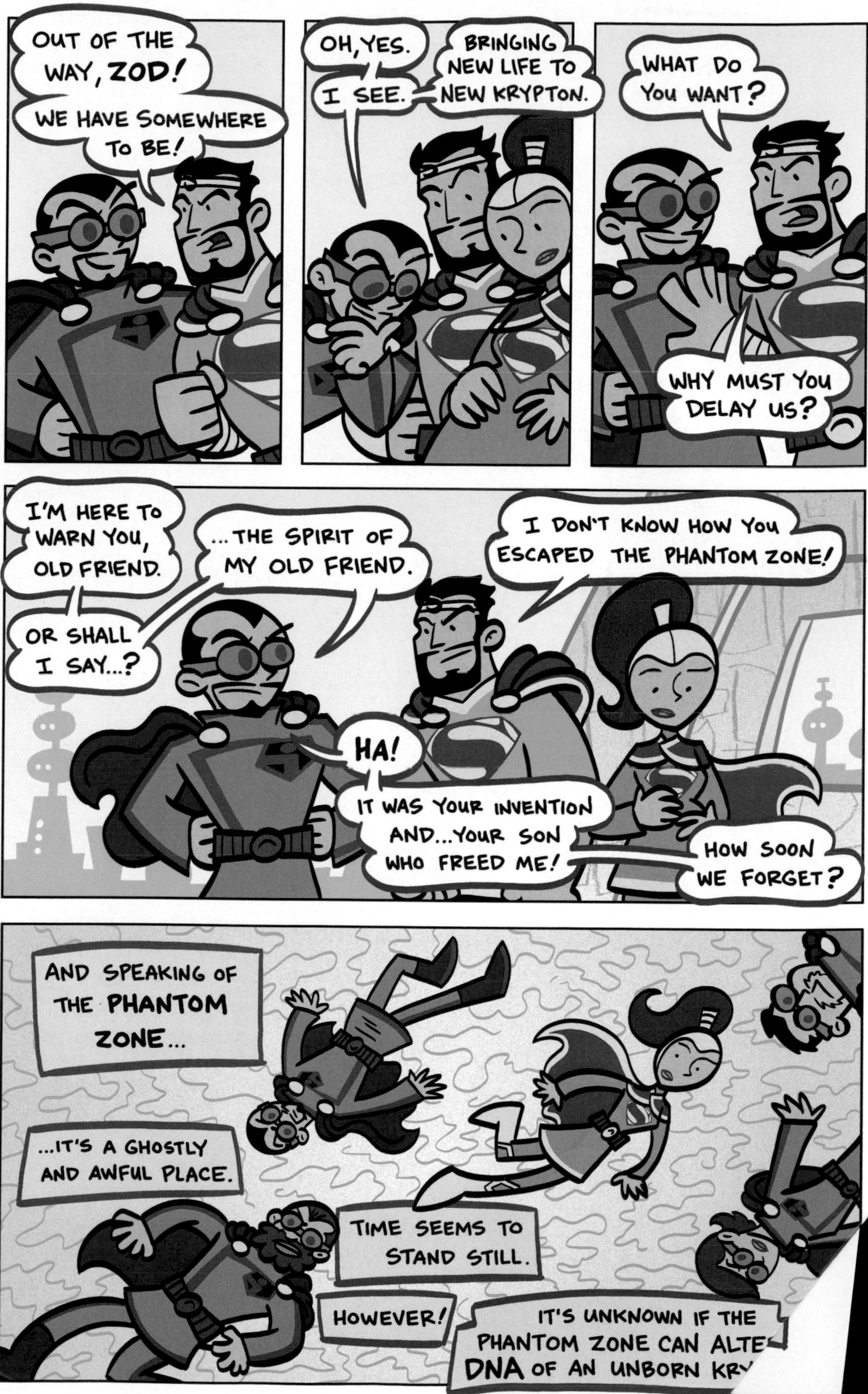
OUT OF THE WAY, ZOD!
WE HAVE SOMEWHERE TO BE!
OH, YES.
I SEE.
BRINGING NEW LIFE TO NEW KRYPTON.
WHAT DO YOU WANT?
WHY MUST YOU DELAY US?
I'M HERE TO WARN YOU, OLD FRIEND.
OR SHALL I SAY...?
...THE SPIRIT OF MY OLD FRIEND.
I DON'T KNOW HOW YOU ESCAPED THE PHANTOM ZONE!
HA!
IT WAS YOUR INVENTION AND...YOUR SON WHO FREED ME!
HOW SOON WE FORGET?
AND SPEAKING OF THE PHANTOM ZONE...
...IT'S A GHOSTLY AND AWFUL PLACE.
TIME SEEMS TO STAND STILL.
HOWEVER!
IT'S UNKNOWN IF THE PHANTOM ZONE CAN ALTE
DNA OF AN UNBORN KRY

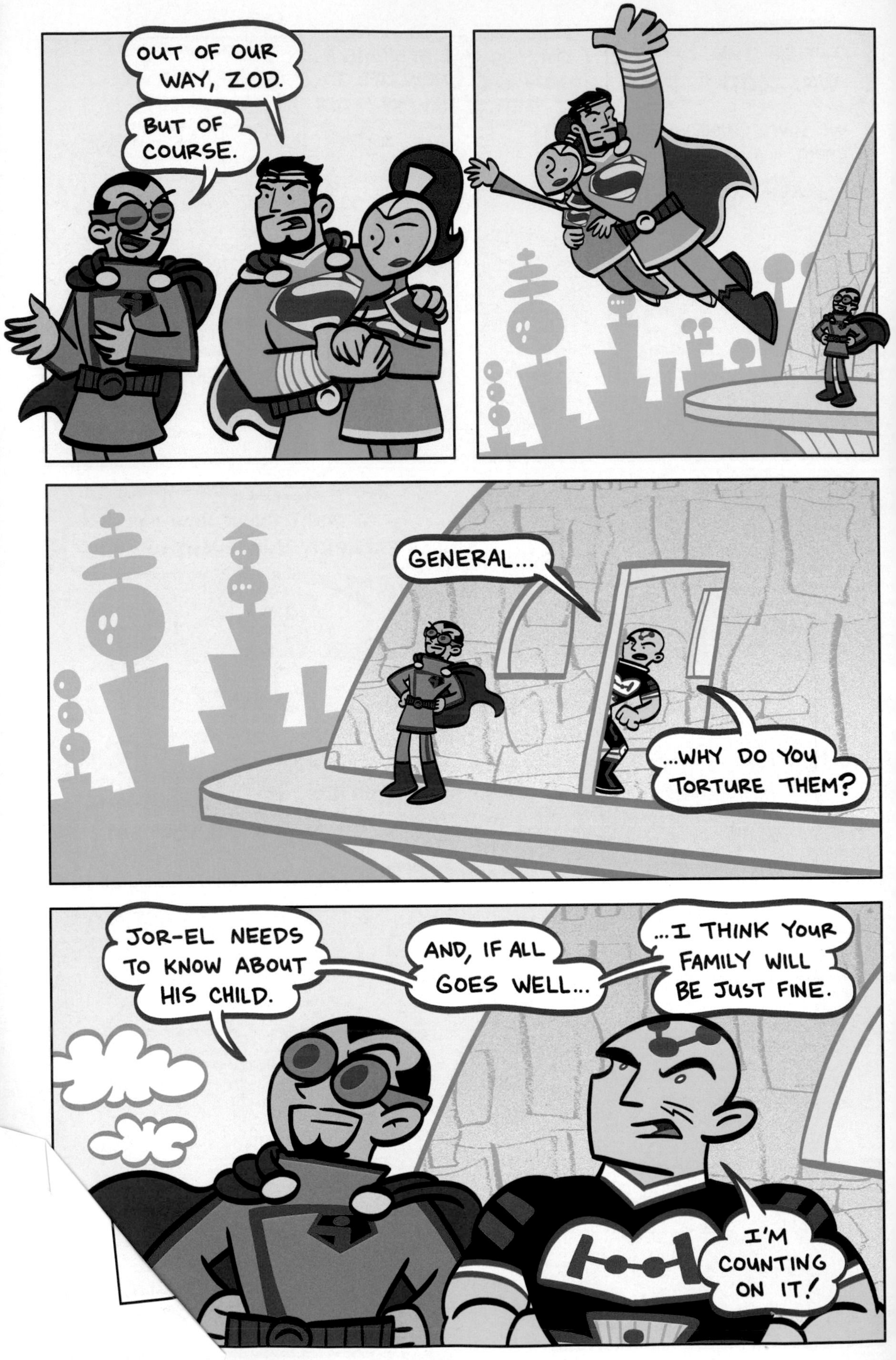
OUT OF OUR WAY, ZOD.
BUT OF COURSE.
GENERAL...
...WHY DO YOU TORTURE THEM?
JOR-EL NEEDS TO KNOW ABOUT HIS CHILD.
AND, IF ALL GOES WELL...
...I THINK YOUR FAMILY WILL BE JUST FINE.
I'M COUNTING ON IT!

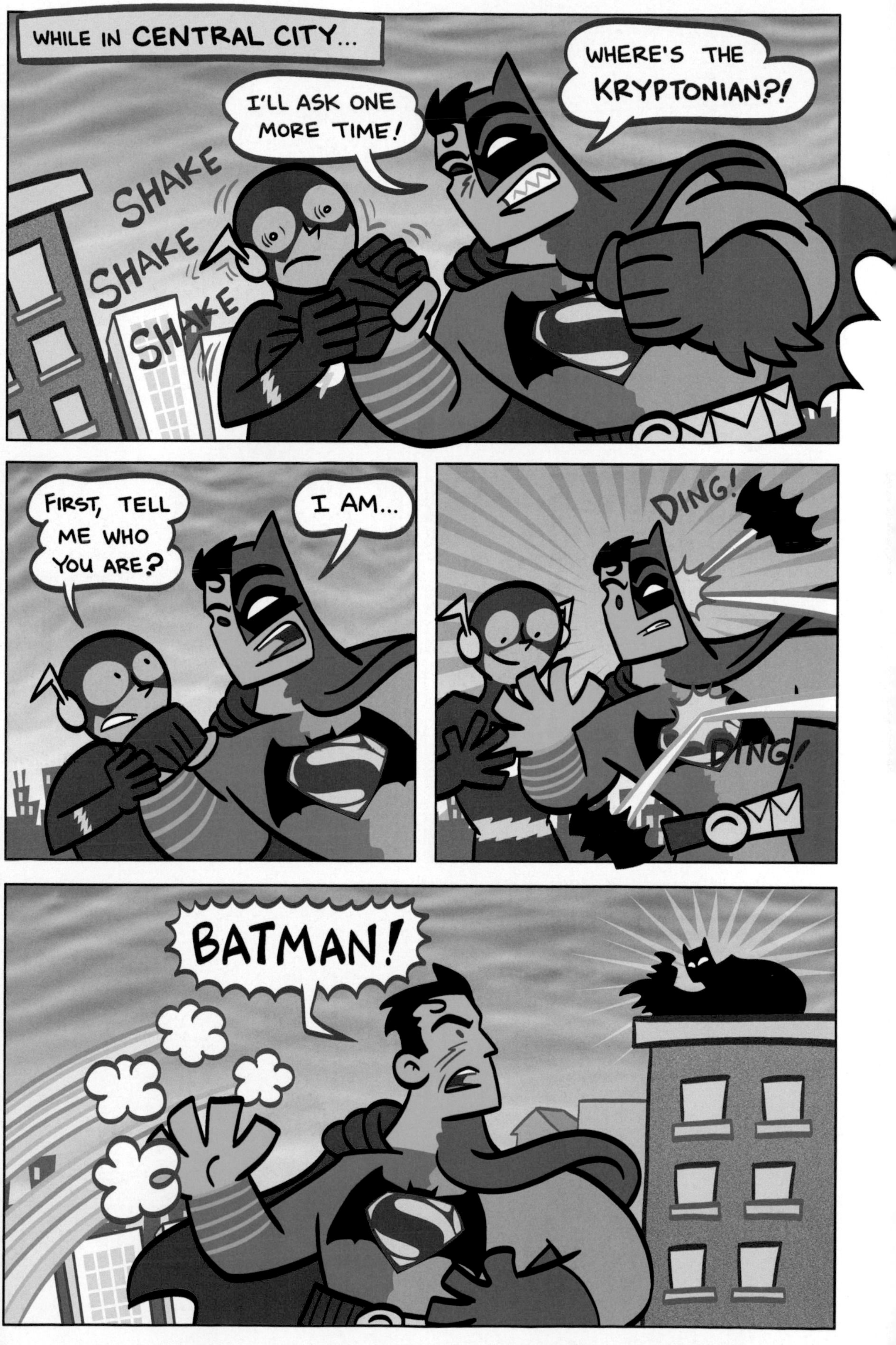
WHILE IN CENTRAL CITY...
I'LL ASK ONE MORE TIME!
WHERE'S THE KRYPTONIAN?!
SHAKE
SHAKE
SHAKE
FIRST, TELL ME WHO YOU ARE?
I AM...
DING!
DING!
BATMAN!

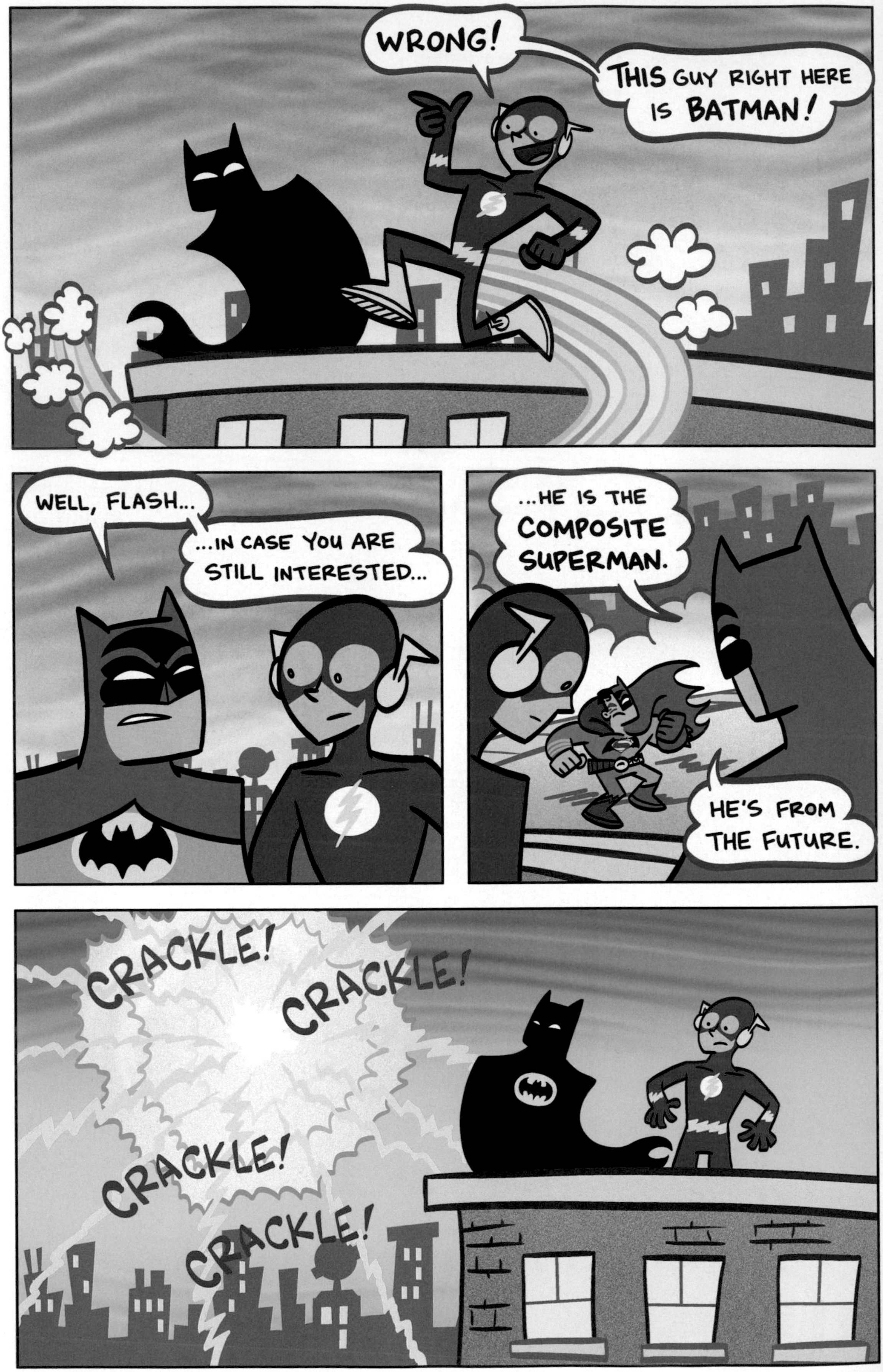
WRONG!
THIS GUY RIGHT HERE IS BATMAN!
WELL, FLASH...
...IN CASE YOU ARE STILL INTERESTED...
...HE IS THE COMPOSITE SUPERMAN.
HE'S FROM THE FUTURE.
CRACKLE!
CRACKLE!
CRACKLE!
CRACKLE!

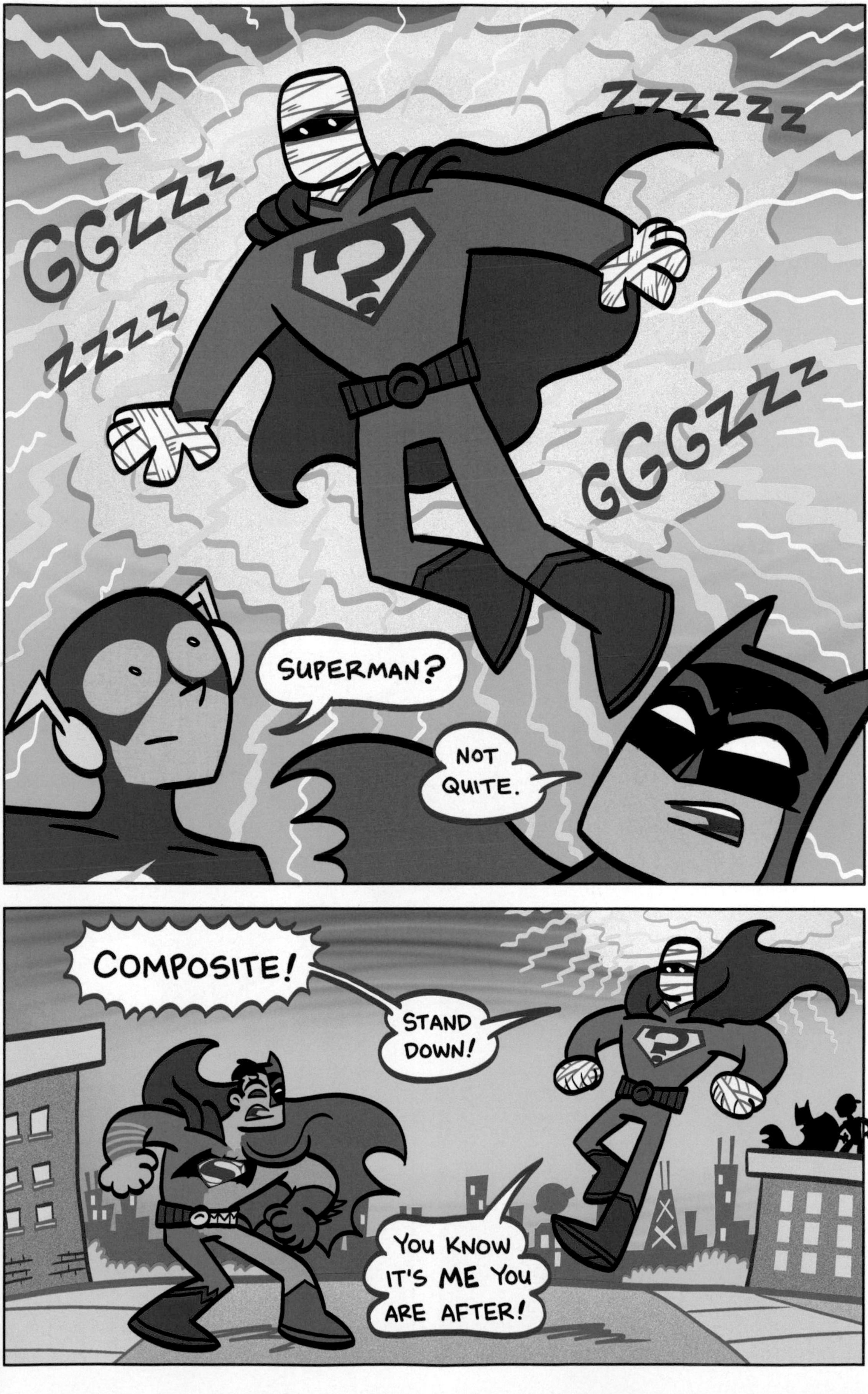
GGZZZZ
ZZZZZZZ
ZZZZ
GGGZZZZ
SUPERMAN?
NOT QUITE.
COMPOSITE!
STAND DOWN!
YOU KNOW IT'S ME YOU ARE AFTER!

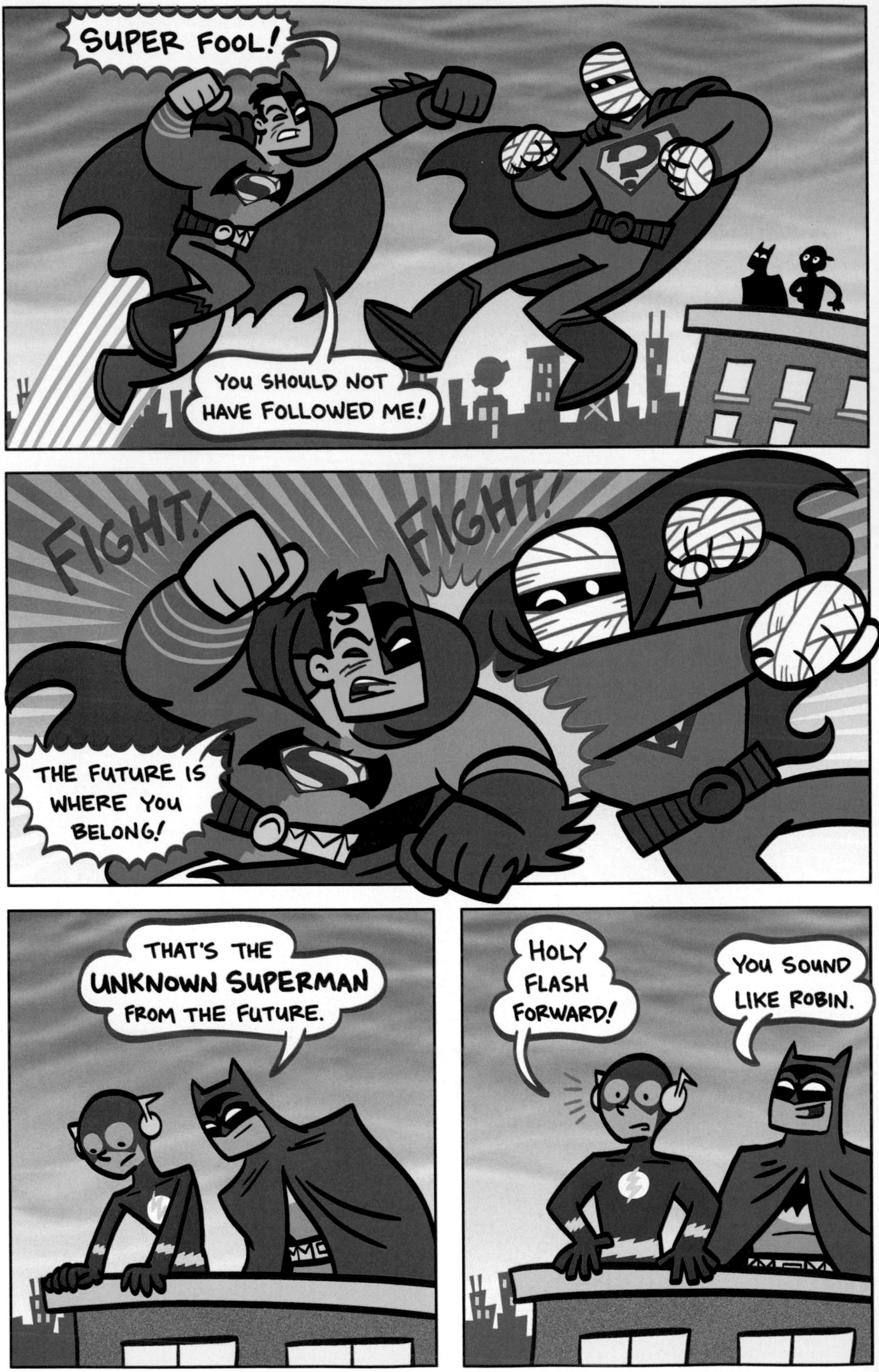
SUPER FOOL!
YOU SHOULD NOT HAVE FOLLOWED ME!
FIGHT!
FIGHT!
THE FUTURE IS WHERE YOU BELONG!
THAT'S THE UNKNOWN SUPERMAN FROM THE FUTURE.
HOLY FLASH FORWARD!
YOU SOUND LIKE ROBIN.

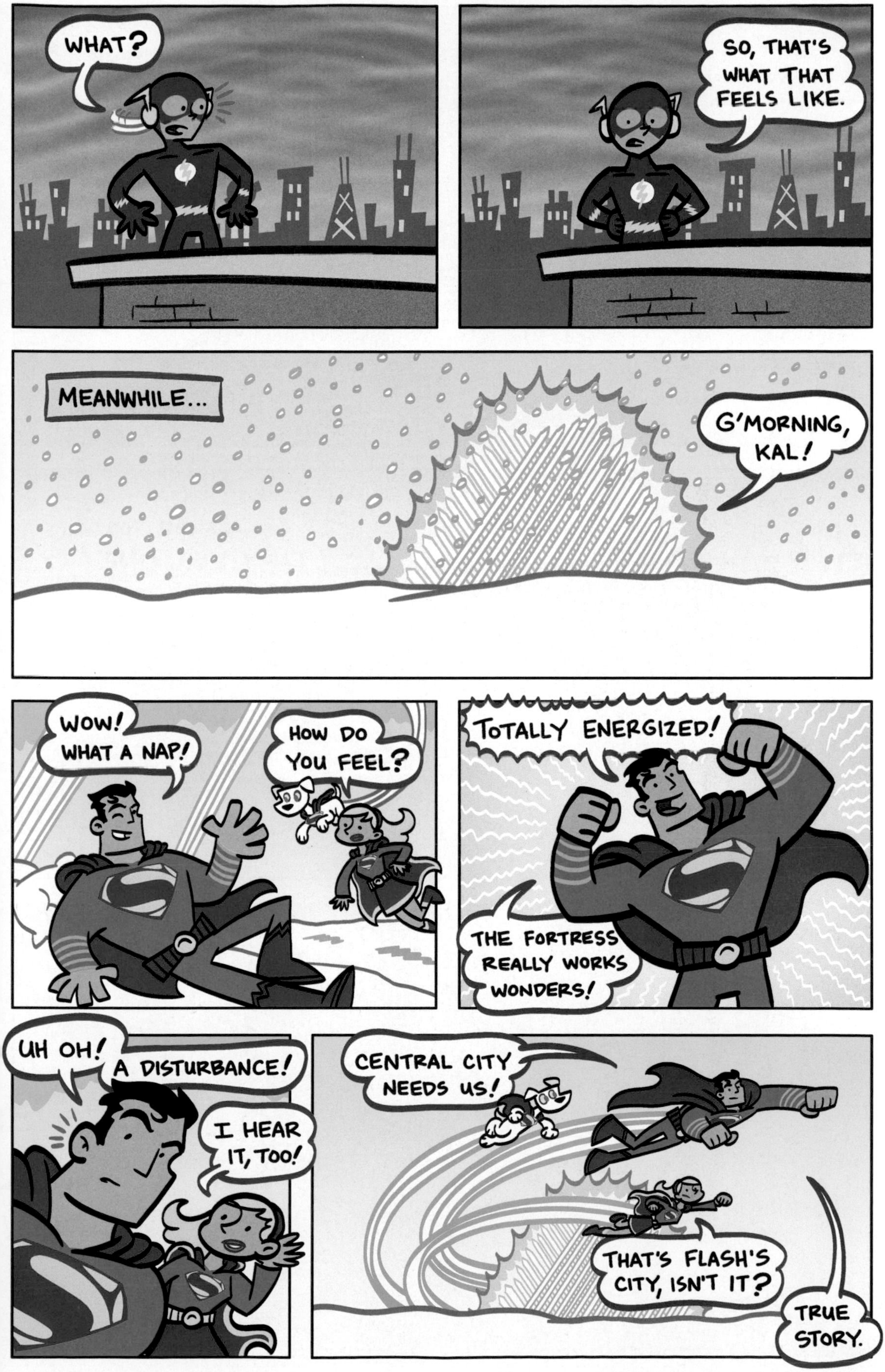
WHAT?
SO, THAT'S WHAT THAT FEELS LIKE.
MEANWHILE...
G'MORNING, KAL!
WOW! WHAT A NAP!
HOW DO YOU FEEL?
TOTALLY ENERGIZED!
THE FORTRESS REALLY WORKS WONDERS!
UH OH!
A DISTURBANCE!
I HEAR IT, TOO!
CENTRAL CITY NEEDS US!
THAT'S FLASH'S CITY, ISN'T IT?
TRUE STORY.

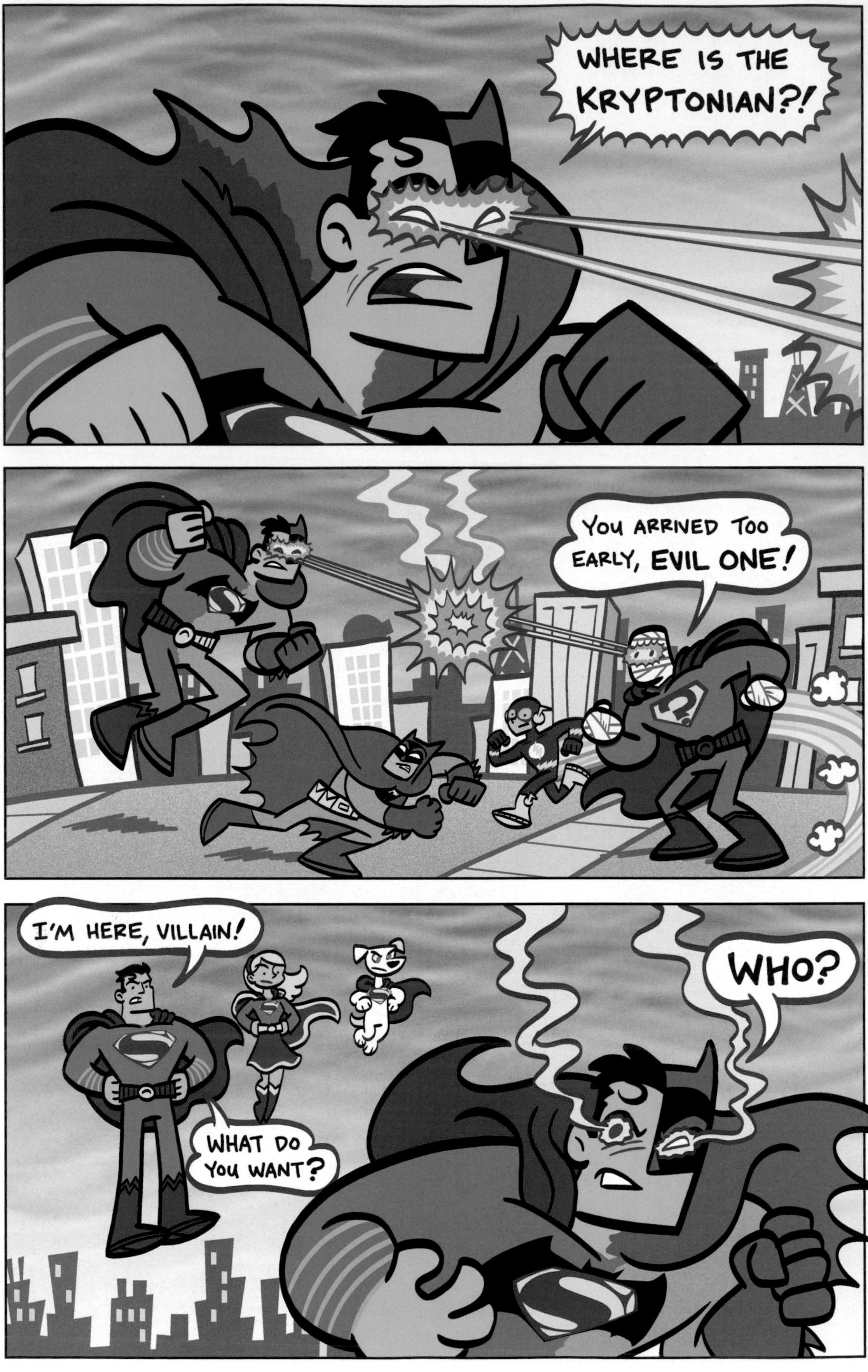
WHERE IS THE KRYPTONIAN?!
YOU ARRIVED TOO EARLY, EVIL ONE!
I'M HERE, VILLAIN!
WHO?
WHAT DO YOU WANT?

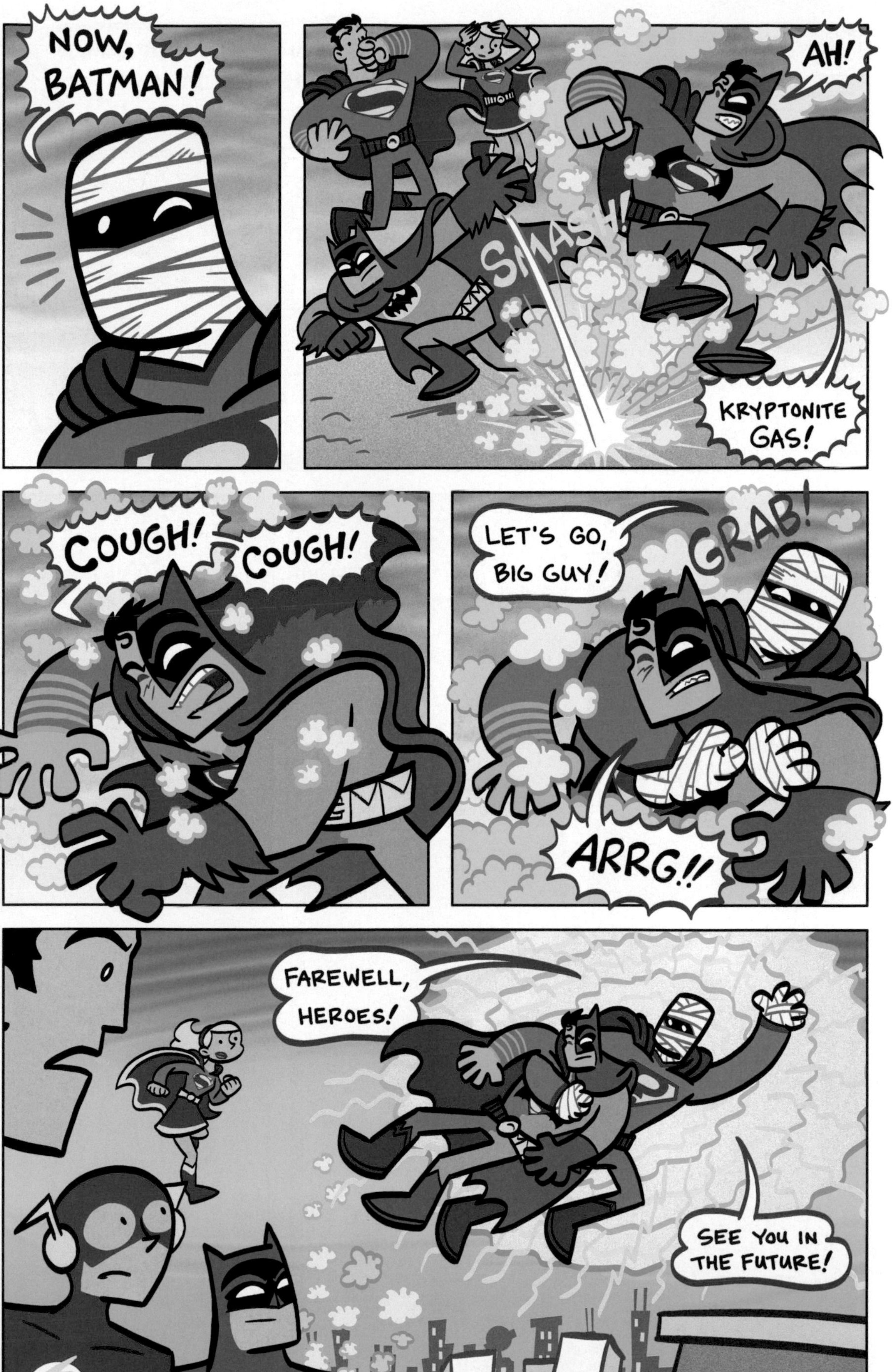
NOW, BATMAN!
AH!
SMASH!
KRYPTONITE GAS!
COUGH! COUGH!
LET'S GO, BIG GUY!
GRAB!
ARRG!!
FAREWELL, HEROES!
SEE YOU IN THE FUTURE!

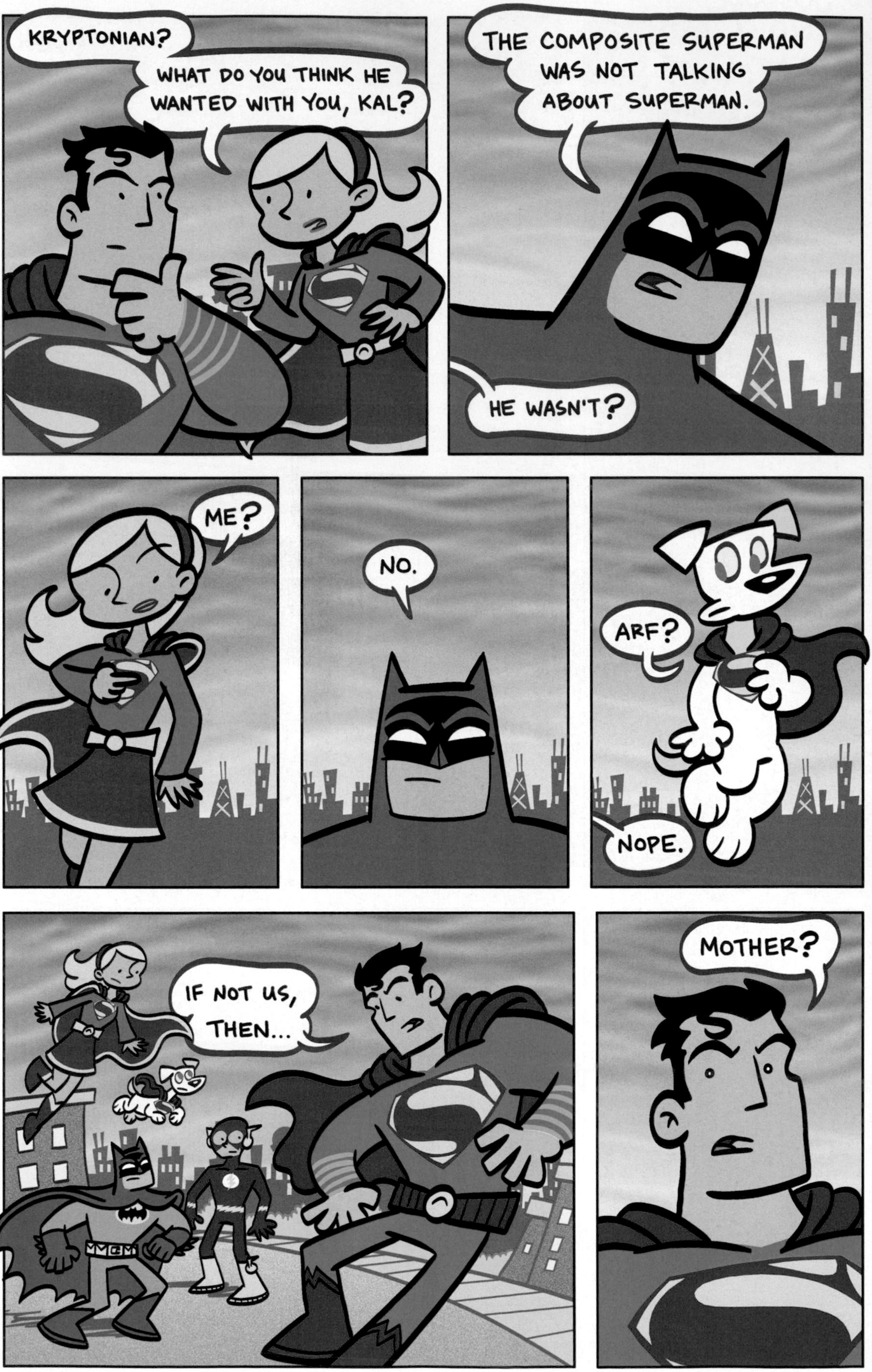
KRYPTONIAN?
WHAT DO YOU THINK HE WANTED WITH YOU, KAL?
THE COMPOSITE SUPERMAN WAS NOT TALKING ABOUT SUPERMAN.
HE WASN'T?
ME?
NO.
ARF?
NOPE.
IF NOT US, THEN...
MOTHER?

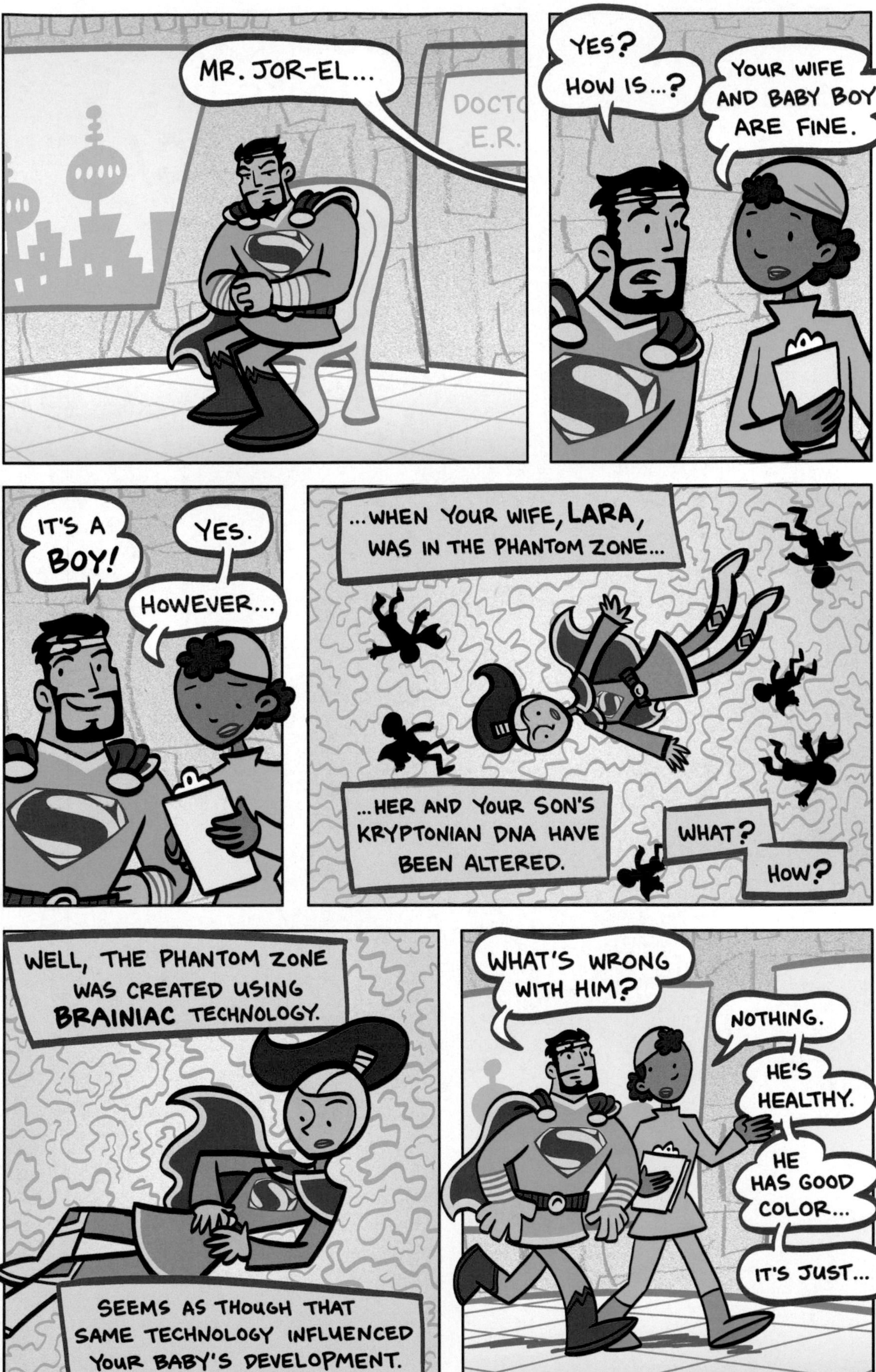
DOCTO
E.R.
MR. JOR-EL...
YES?
HOW IS...?
YOUR WIFE AND BABY BOY ARE FINE.
IT'S A BOY!
YES.
HOWEVER...
...WHEN YOUR WIFE, LARA, WAS IN THE PHANTOM ZONE...
...HER AND YOUR SON'S KRYPTONIAN DNA HAVE BEEN ALTERED.
WHAT?
HOW?
WELL, THE PHANTOM ZONE WAS CREATED USING BRAINIAC TECHNOLOGY.
SEEMS AS THOUGH THAT SAME TECHNOLOGY INFLUENCED YOUR BABY'S DEVELOPMENT.
WHAT'S WRONG WITH HIM?
NOTHING.
HE'S HEALTHY.
HE HAS GOOD COLOR...
IT'S JUST...

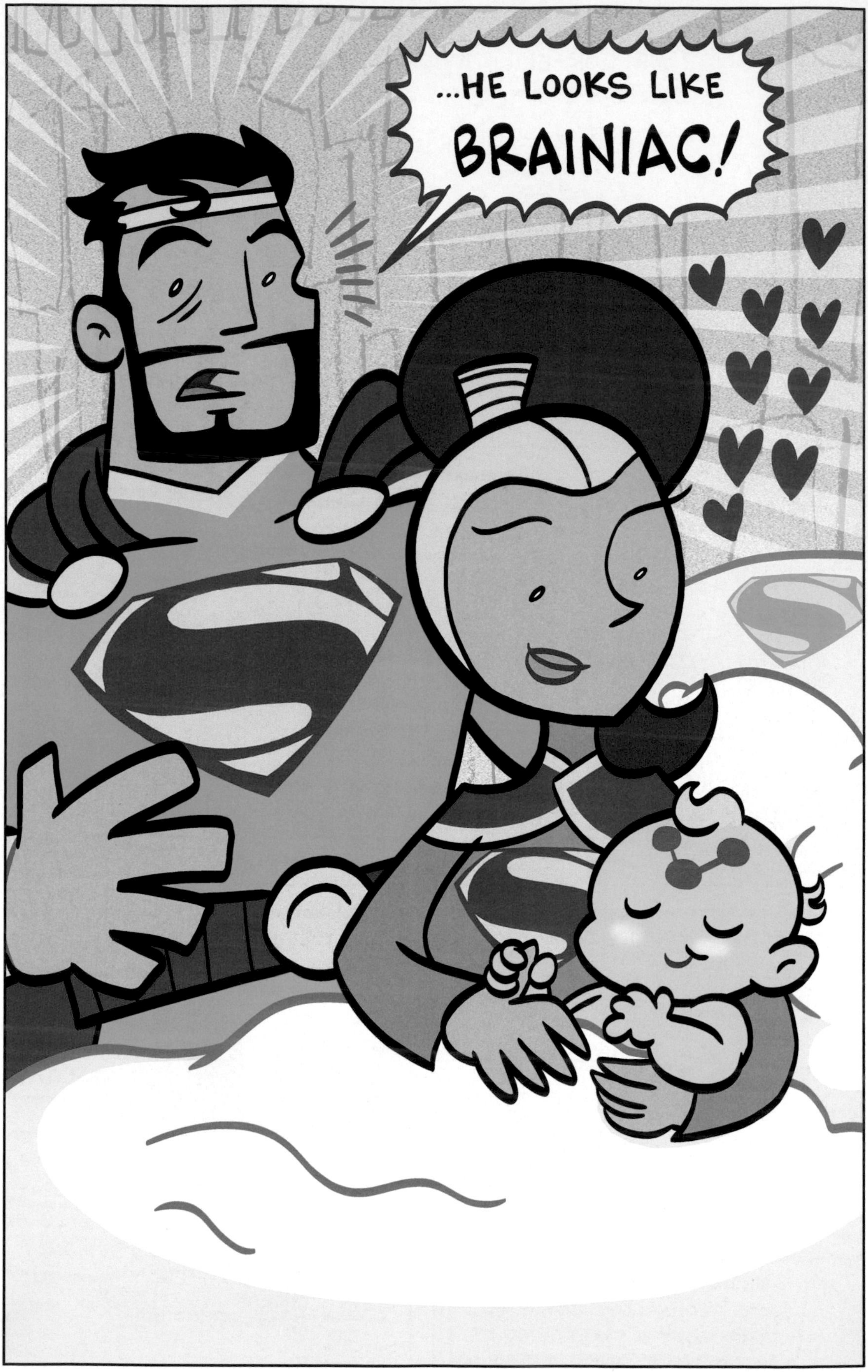
...HE LOOKS LIKE BRAINIAC!

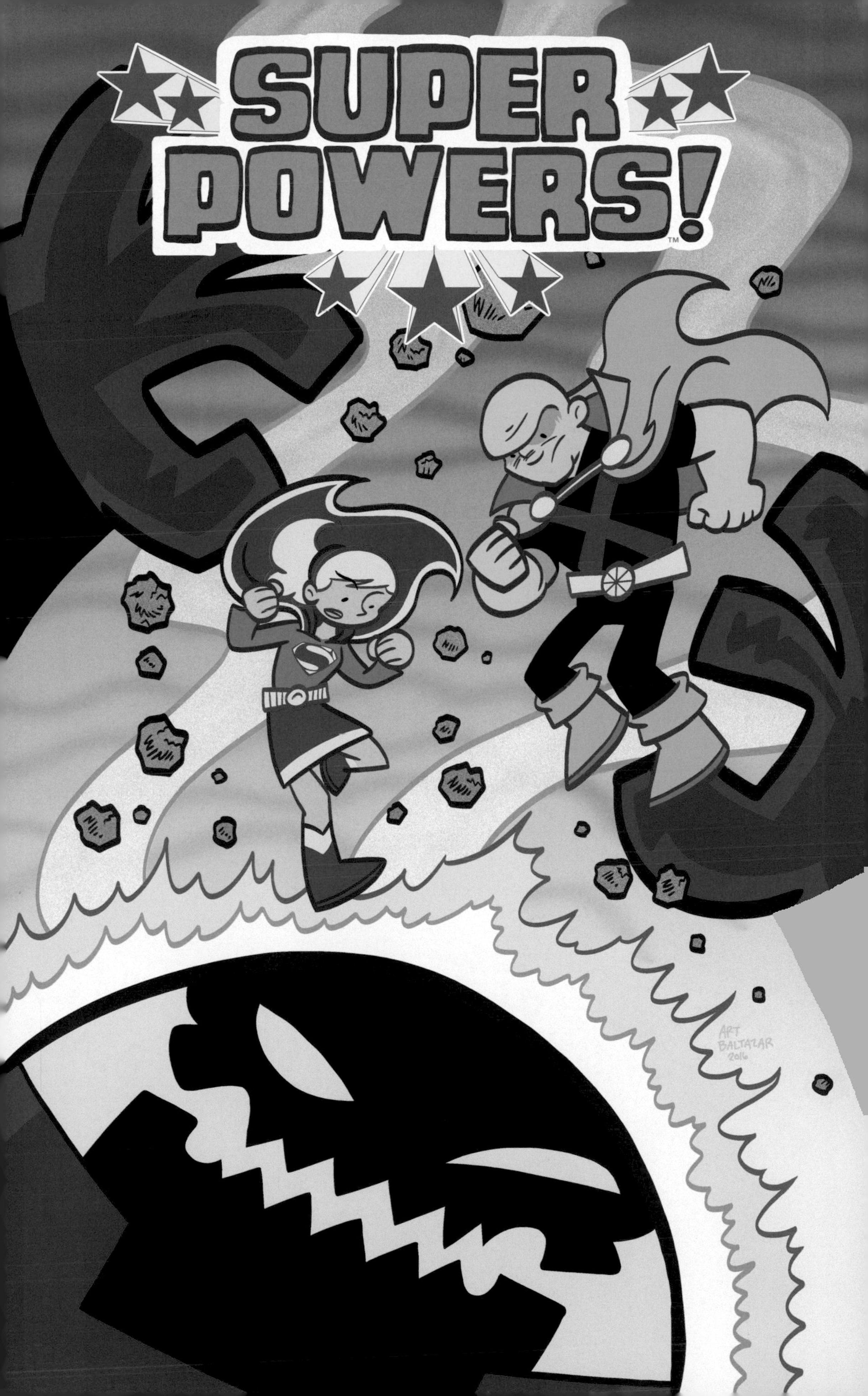
SUPER POWERS!™
ART BALTAZAR 2016

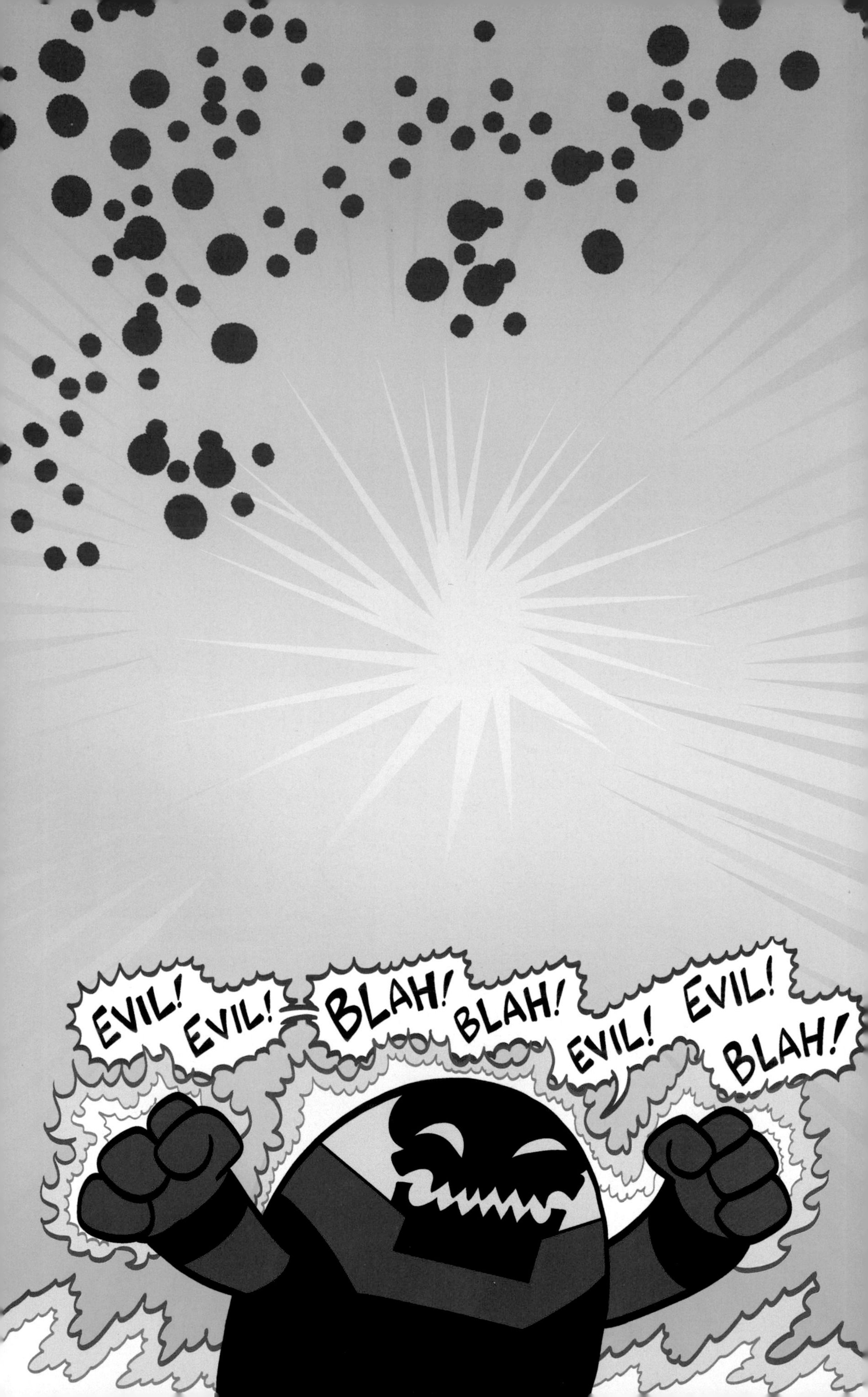
EVIL! EVIL!
BLAH! BLAH!
EVIL! EVIL! BLAH!

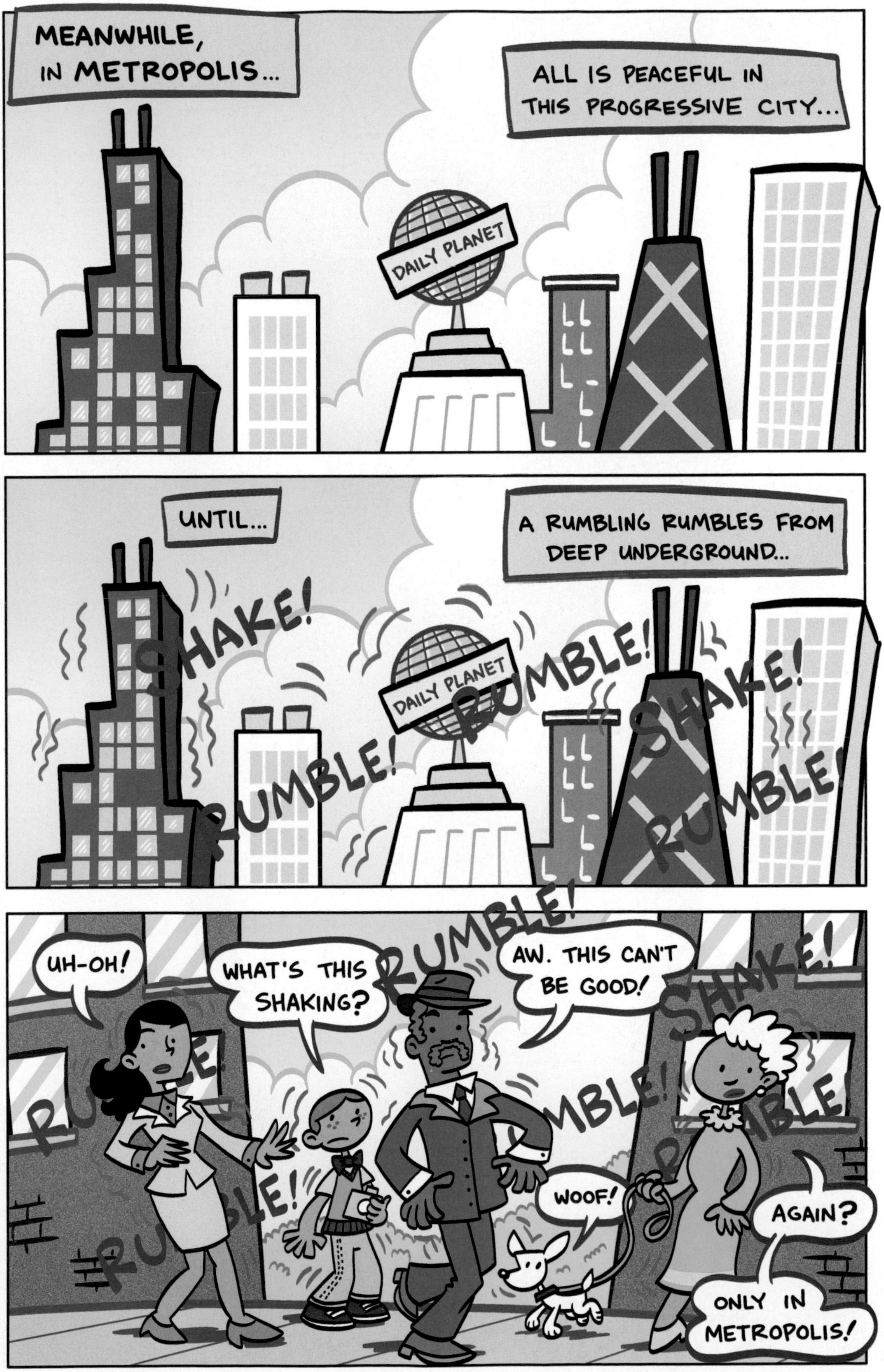
MEANWHILE, IN METROPOLIS...
ALL IS PEACEFUL IN THIS PROGRESSIVE CITY...
DAILY PLANET
UNTIL...
A RUMBLING RUMBLES FROM DEEP UNDERGROUND...
SHAKE!
DAILY PLANET
RUMBLE!
RUMBLE!
SHAKE!
RUMBLE!
UH-OH!
WHAT'S THIS SHAKING?
RUMBLE!
AW. THIS CAN'T BE GOOD!
SHAKE!
WOOF!
AGAIN?
ONLY IN METROPOLIS!

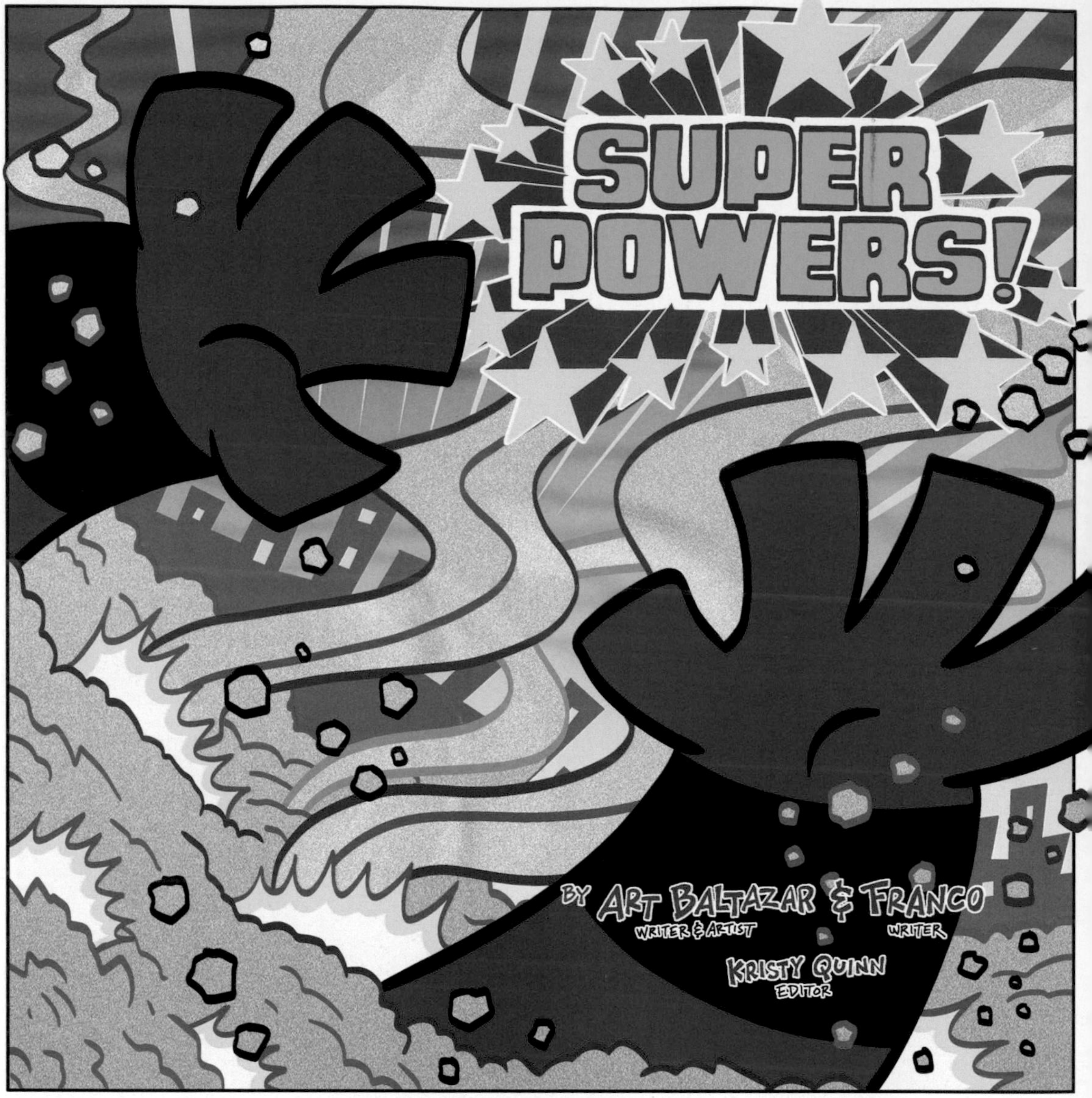
SUPER POWERS!
BY ART BALTAZAR & FRANCO
WRITER & ARTIST
WRITER
KRISTY QUINN
EDITOR

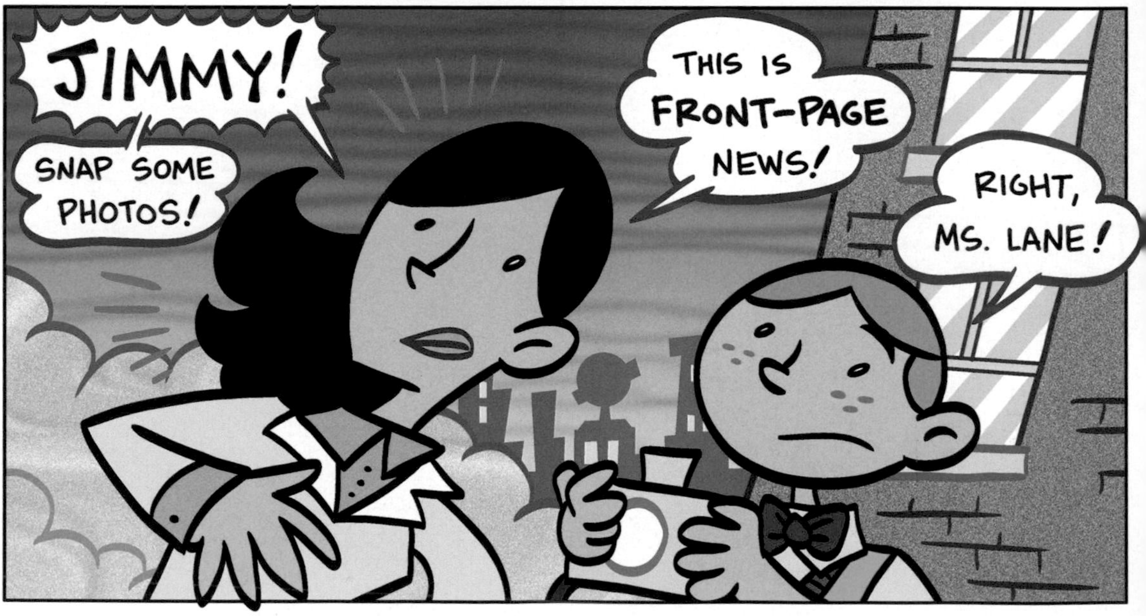
JIMMY!
SNAP SOME PHOTOS!
THIS IS FRONT-PAGE NEWS!
RIGHT, MS. LANE!

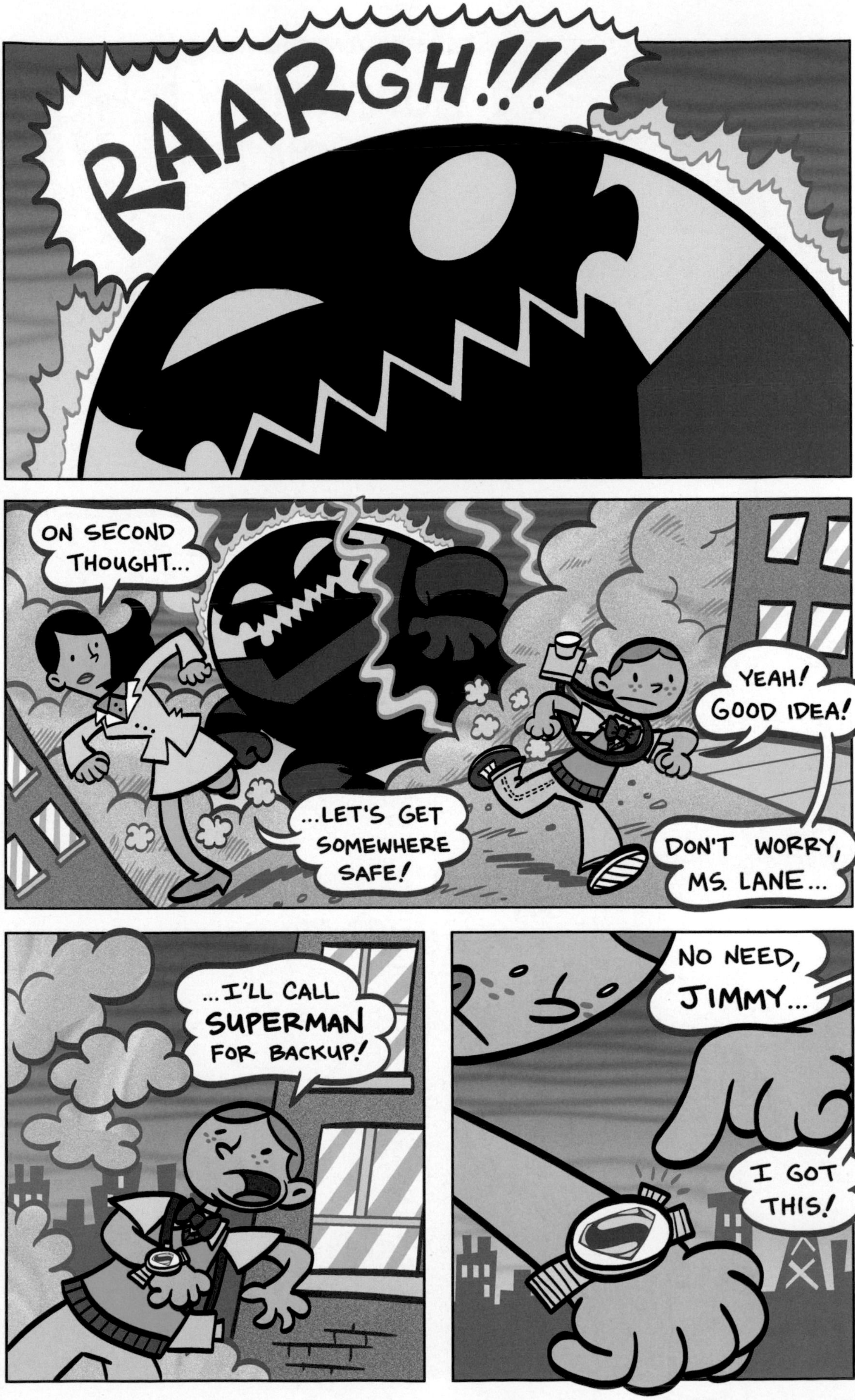
RAARGH!!!
ON SECOND THOUGHT...
...LET'S GET SOMEWHERE SAFE!
DON'T WORRY, MS. LANE...
YEAH! GOOD IDEA!
...I'LL CALL SUPERMAN FOR BACKUP!
NO NEED, JIMMY...
I GOT THIS!

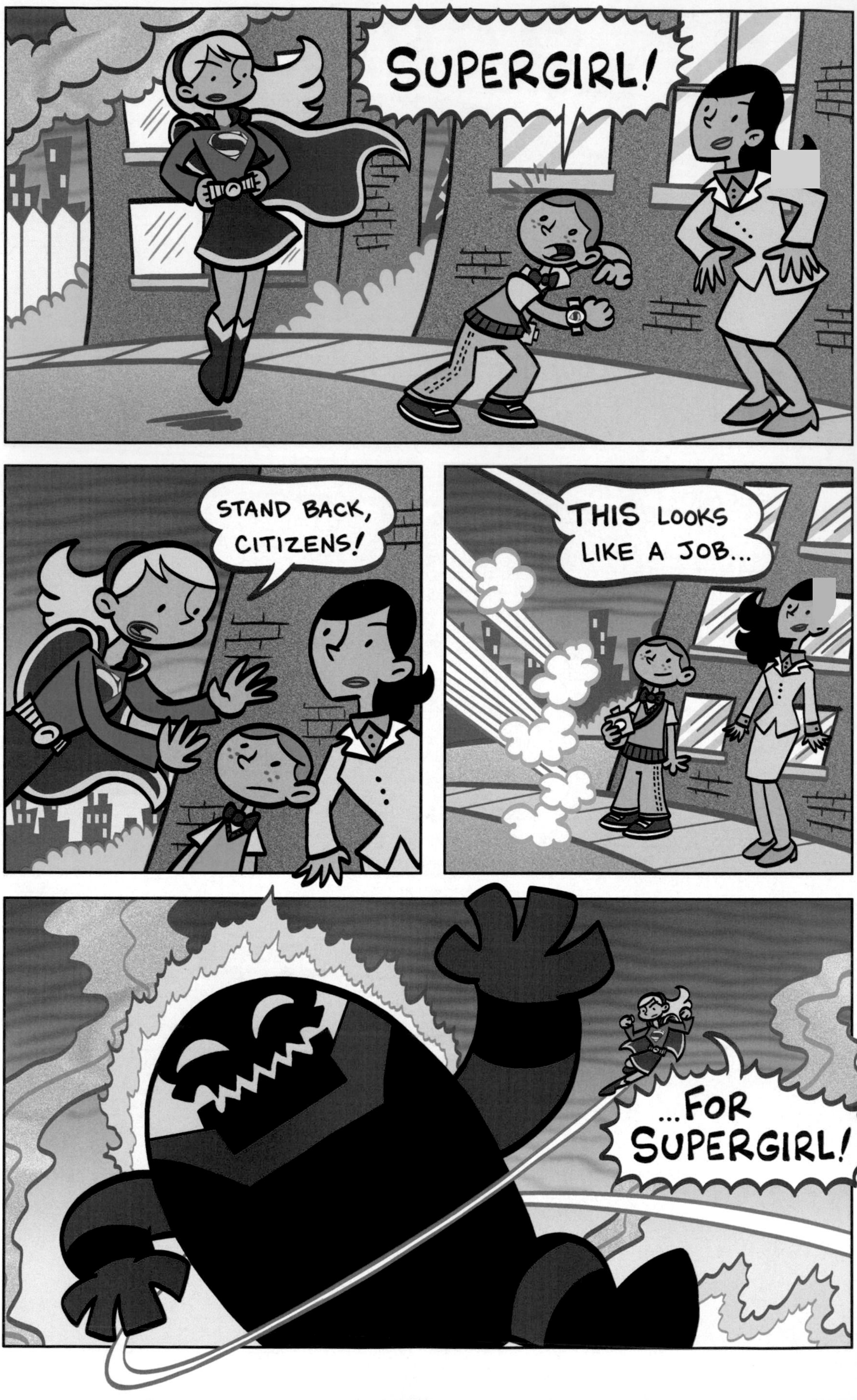
SUPERGIRL!
STAND BACK, CITIZENS!
THIS LOOKS LIKE A JOB...
...FOR SUPERGIRL!

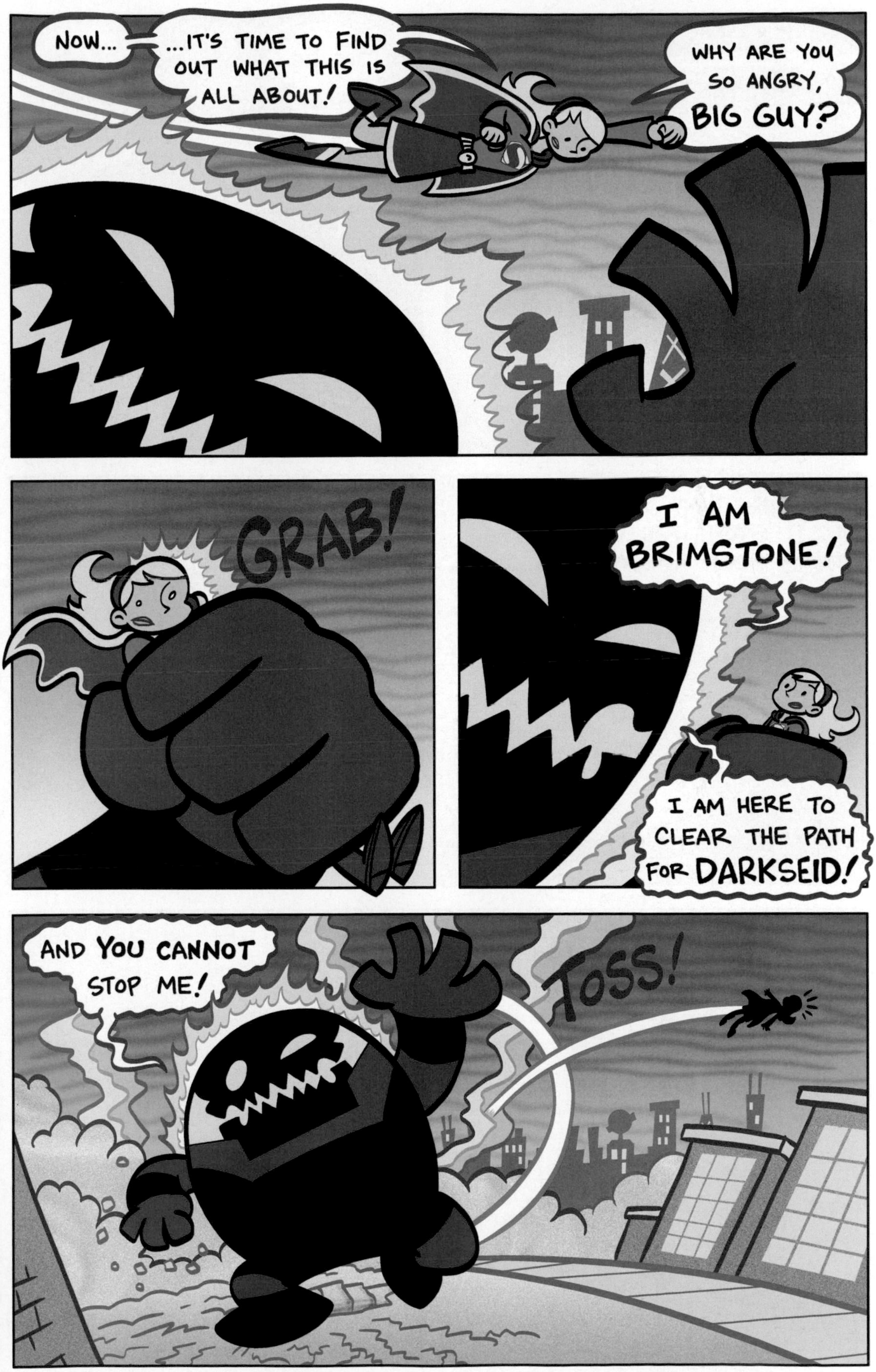
NOW...
...IT'S TIME TO FIND OUT WHAT THIS IS ALL ABOUT!
WHY ARE YOU SO ANGRY, BIG GUY?
GRAB!
I AM BRIMSTONE!
I AM HERE TO CLEAR THE PATH FOR DARKSEID!
AND YOU CANNOT STOP ME!
TOSS!

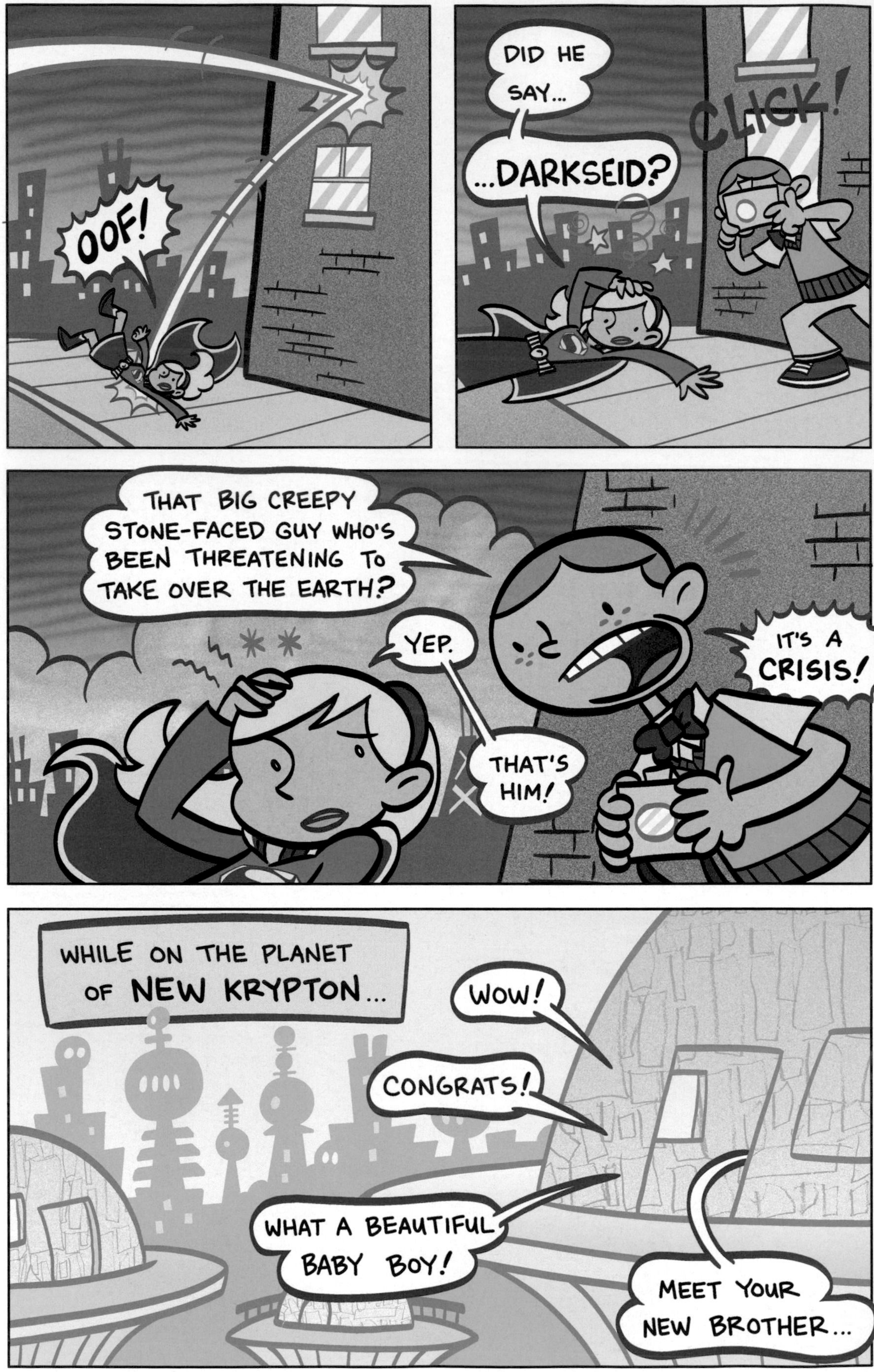
OOF!
DID HE SAY...
...DARKSEID?
CLICK!
THAT BIG CREEPY STONE-FACED GUY WHO'S BEEN THREATENING TO TAKE OVER THE EARTH?
YEP.
THAT'S HIM!
IT'S A CRISIS!
WHILE ON THE PLANET OF NEW KRYPTON...
WOW!
CONGRATS!
WHAT A BEAUTIFUL BABY BOY!
MEET YOUR NEW BROTHER...

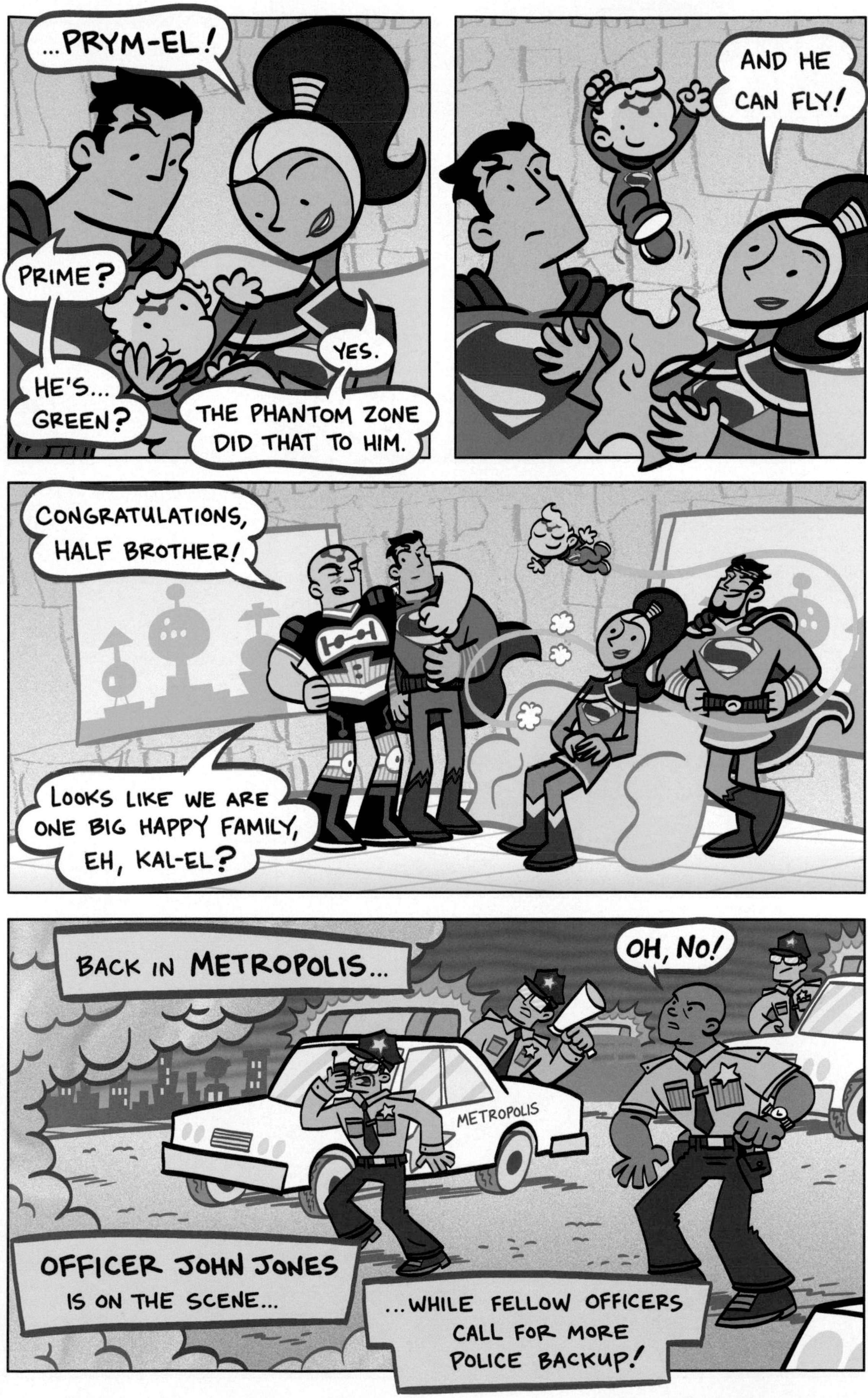
...PRYM-EL!
PRIME?
HE'S... GREEN?
YES.
THE PHANTOM ZONE DID THAT TO HIM.
AND HE CAN FLY!
CONGRATULATIONS, HALF BROTHER!
LOOKS LIKE WE ARE ONE BIG HAPPY FAMILY, EH, KAL-EL?
BACK IN METROPOLIS...
OH, NO!
METROPOLIS
OFFICER JOHN JONES IS ON THE SCENE...
...WHILE FELLOW OFFICERS CALL FOR MORE POLICE BACKUP!

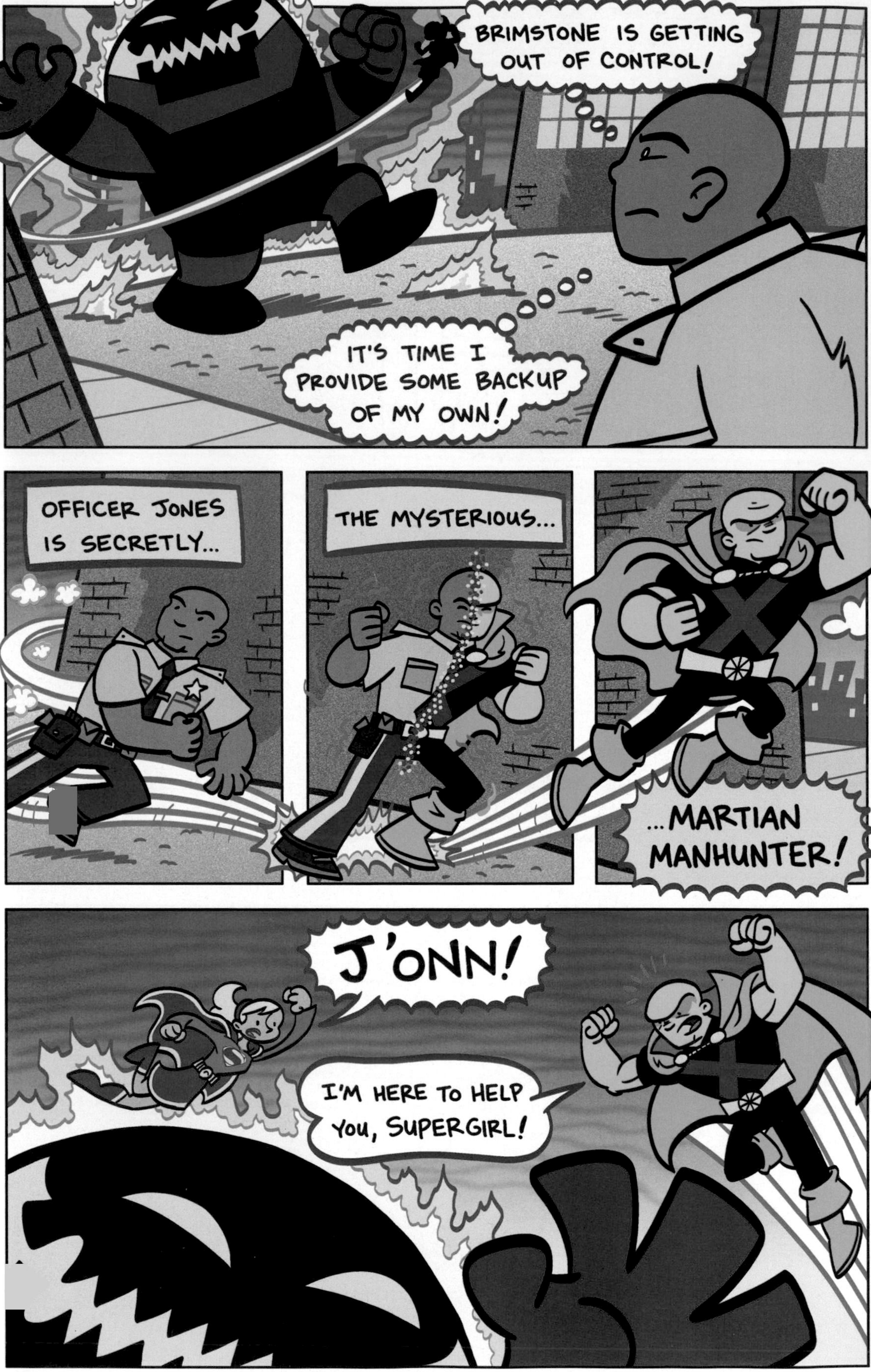
BRIMSTONE IS GETTING OUT OF CONTROL!
IT'S TIME I PROVIDE SOME BACKUP OF MY OWN!
OFFICER JONES IS SECRETLY...
THE MYSTERIOUS...
...MARTIAN MANHUNTER!
J'ONN!
I'M HERE TO HELP YOU, SUPERGIRL!

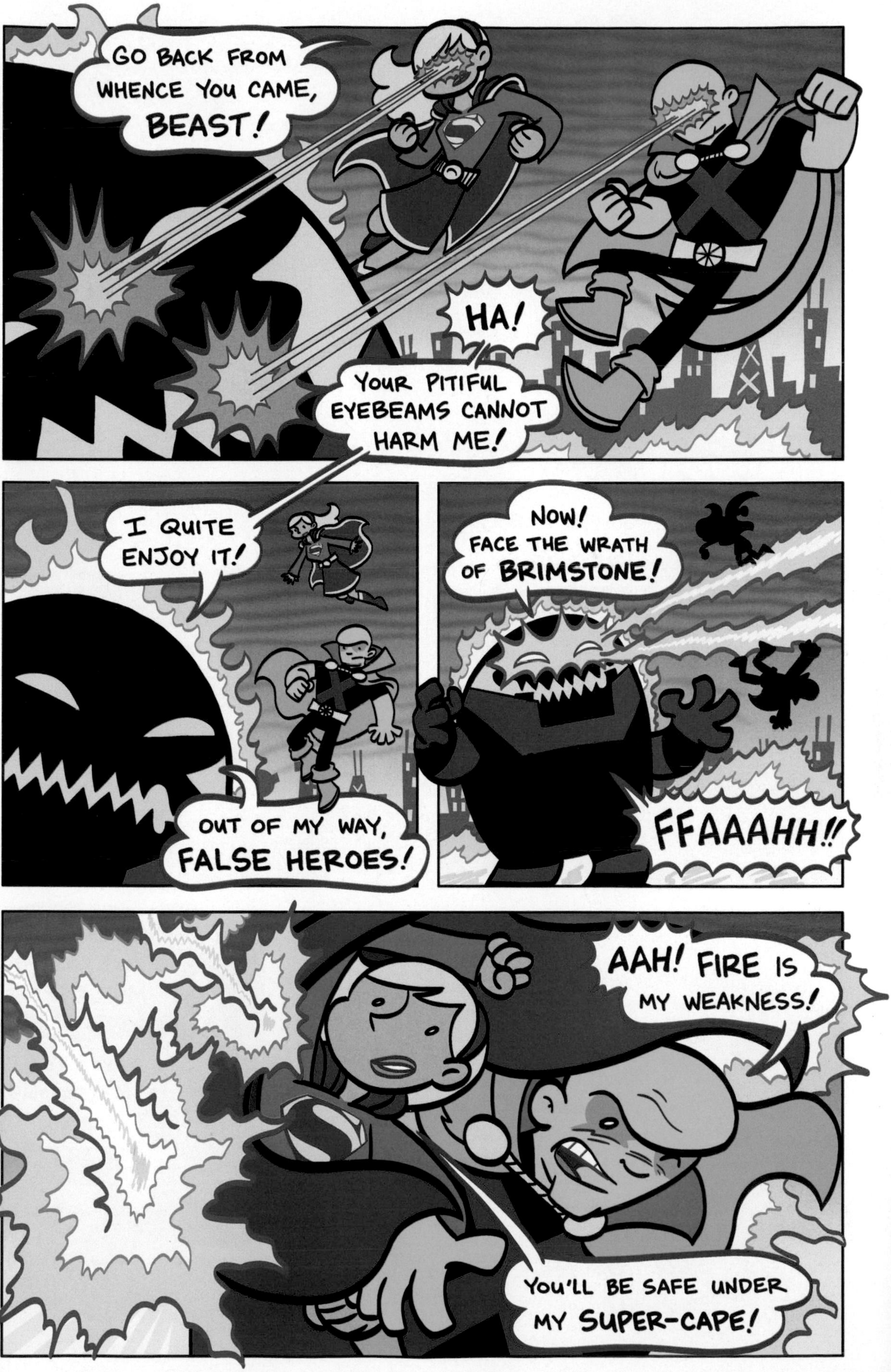
GO BACK FROM WHENCE YOU CAME, BEAST!
HA!
YOUR PITIFUL EYEBEAMS CANNOT HARM ME!
I QUITE ENJOY IT!
OUT OF MY WAY, FALSE HEROES!
NOW! FACE THE WRATH OF BRIMSTONE!
FFAAAHH!!
AAH! FIRE IS MY WEAKNESS!
YOU'LL BE SAFE UNDER MY SUPER-CAPE!

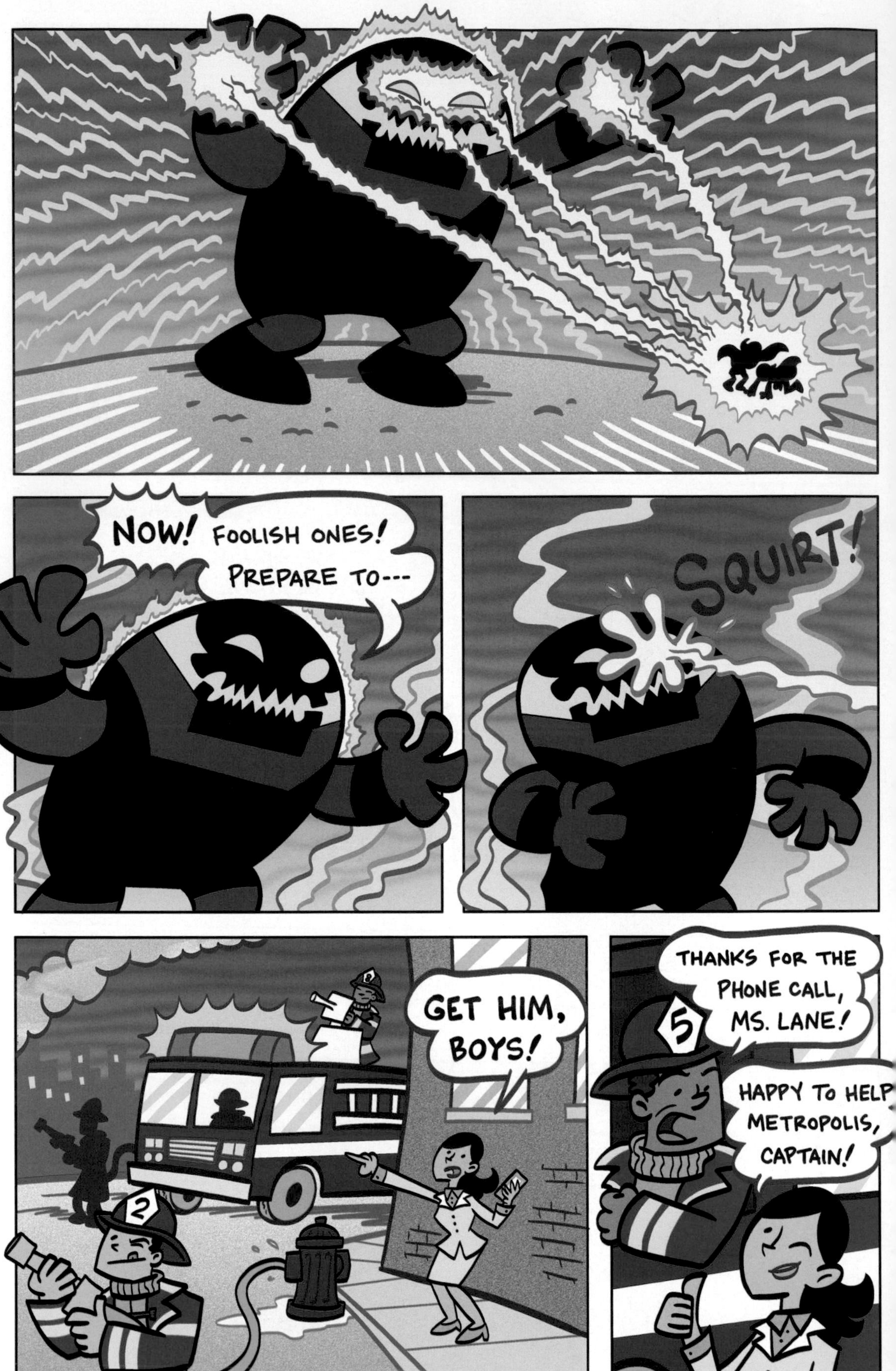
NOW! FOOLISH ONES! PREPARE TO---
SQUIRT!
GET HIM, BOYS!
THANKS FOR THE PHONE CALL, MS. LANE!
HAPPY TO HELP METROPOLIS, CAPTAIN!

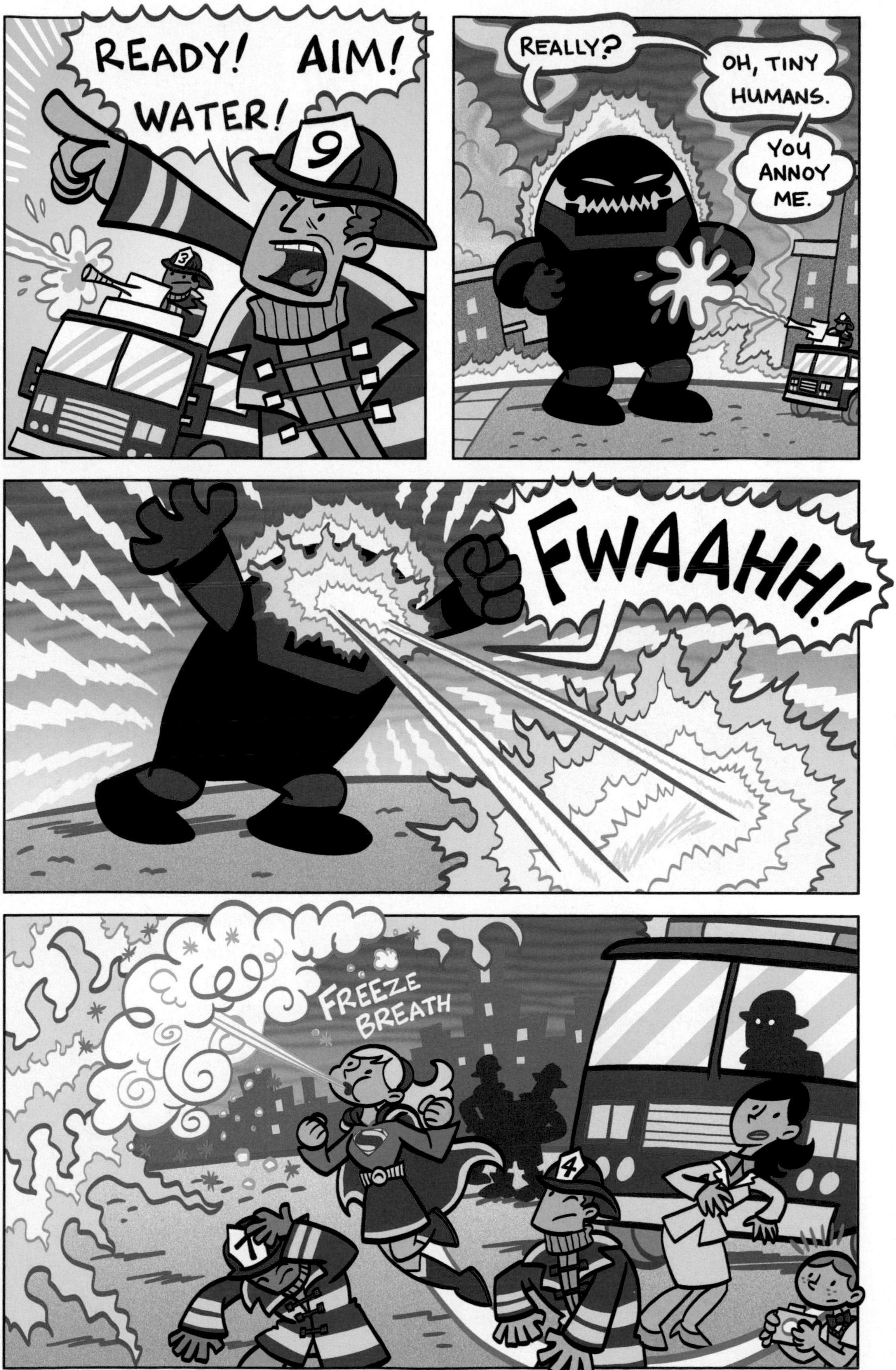
READY! AIM! WATER!
REALLY?
OH, TINY HUMANS.
YOU ANNOY ME.
FWAAHH!
FREEZE BREATH

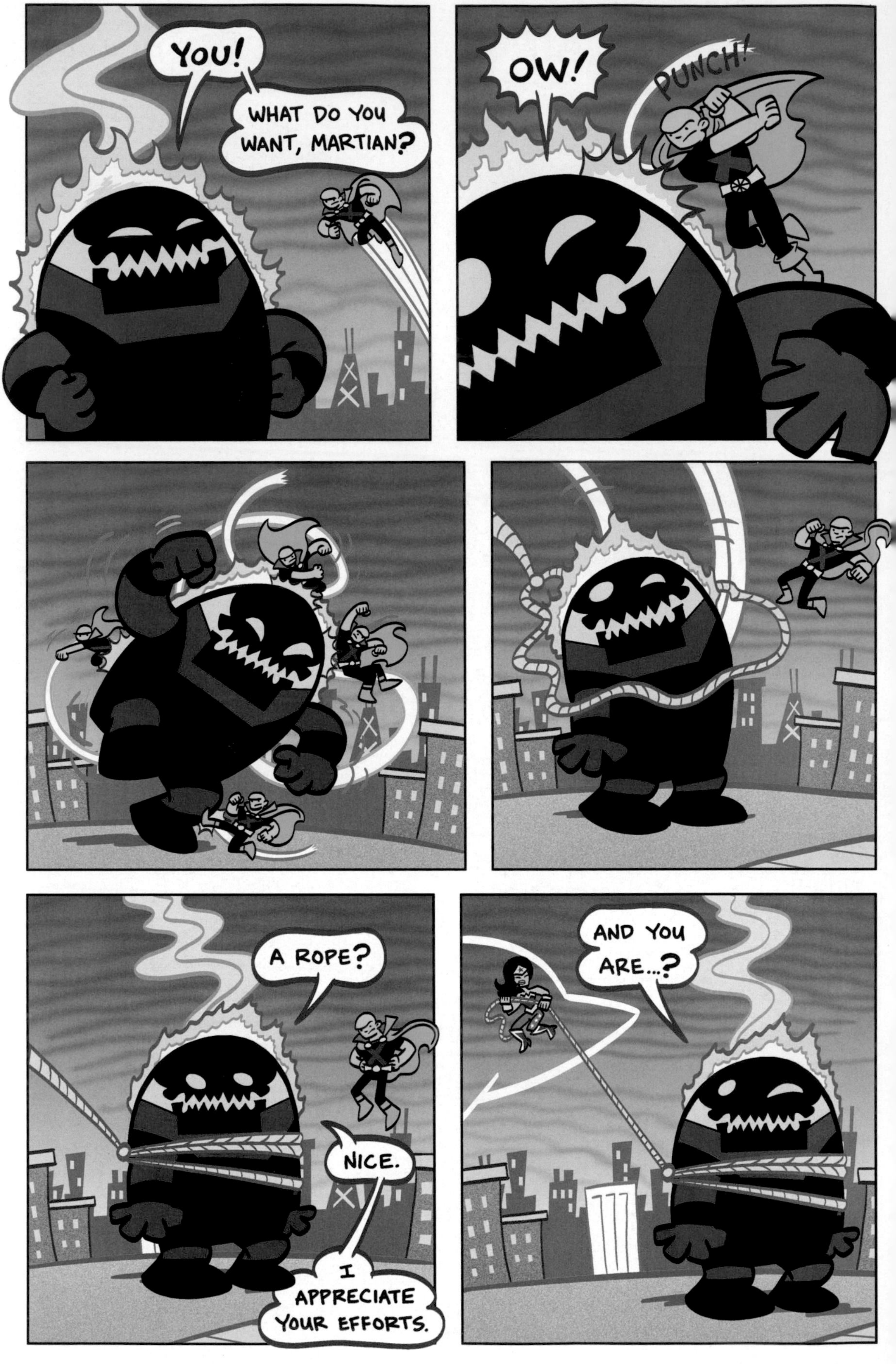
YOU!
WHAT DO YOU WANT, MARTIAN?
OW!
PUNCH!
A ROPE?
NICE.
I APPRECIATE YOUR EFFORTS.
AND YOU ARE...?

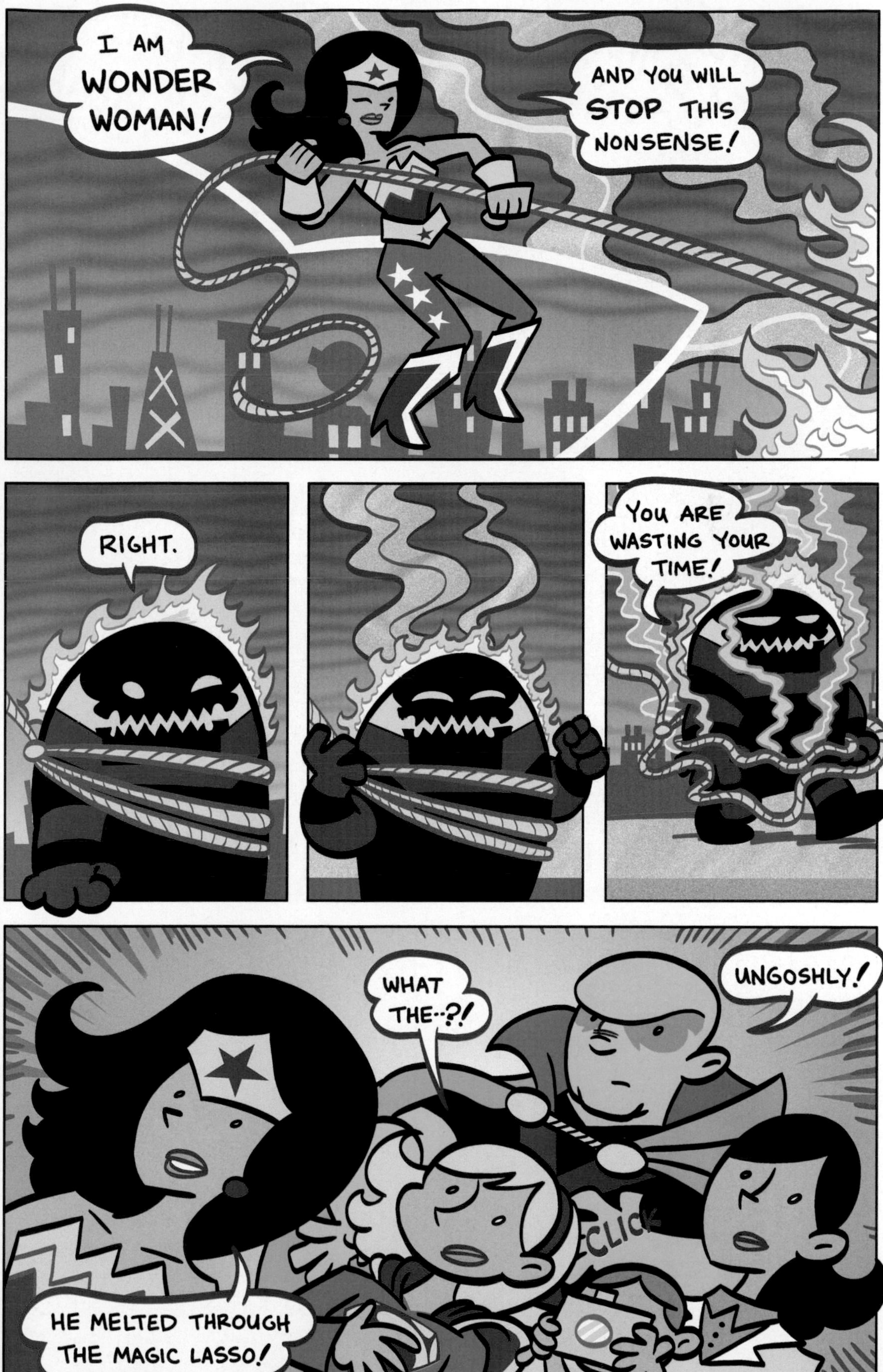
I AM WONDER WOMAN!
AND YOU WILL STOP THIS NONSENSE!
RIGHT.
YOU ARE WASTING YOUR TIME!
WHAT THE--?!
UNGOSHLY!
CLICK
HE MELTED THROUGH THE MAGIC LASSO!

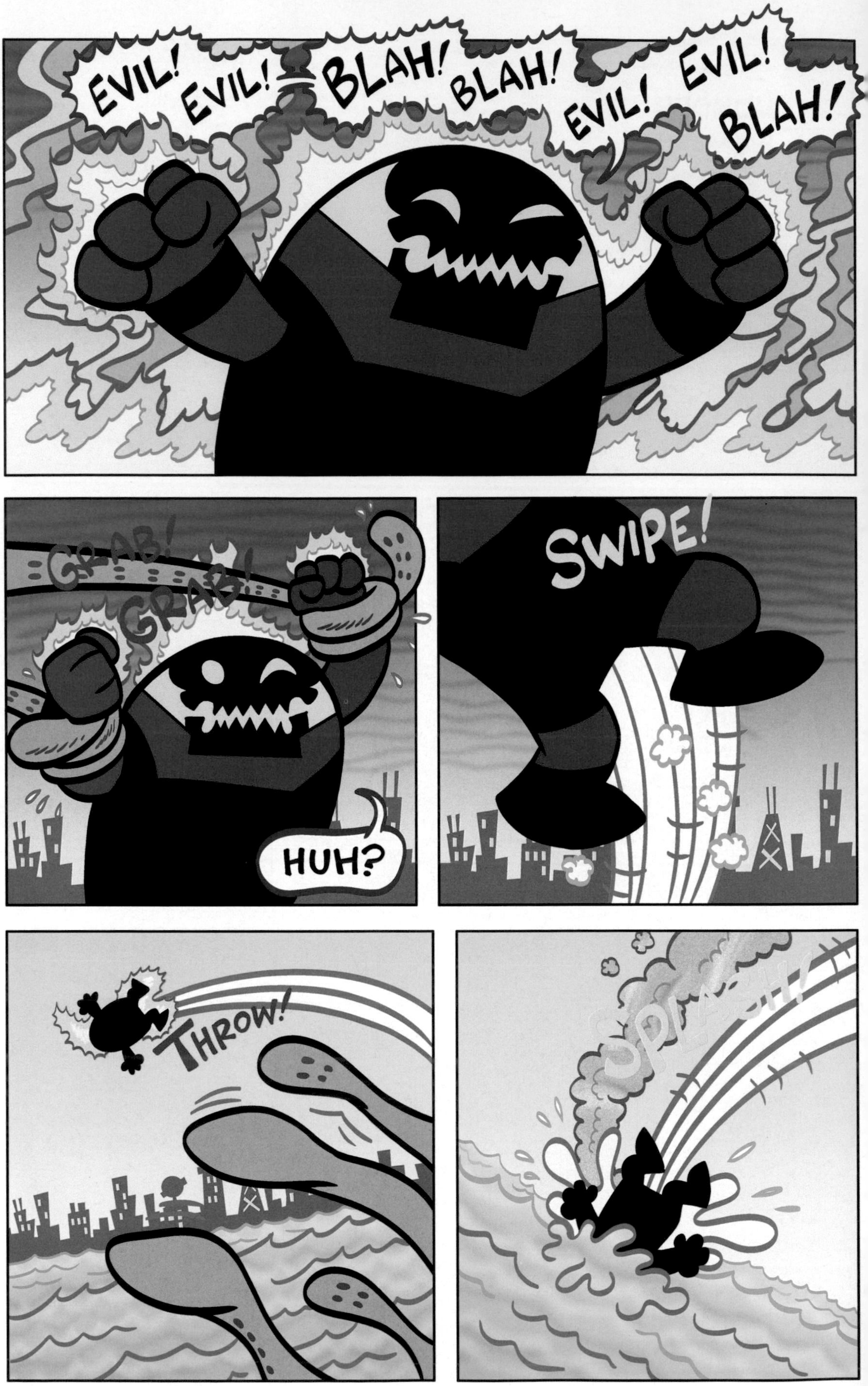
EVIL! EVIL! BLAH! BLAH! EVIL! EVIL! BLAH!
GRAB! GRAB!
HUH?
SWIPE!
THROW!
SPLASH!

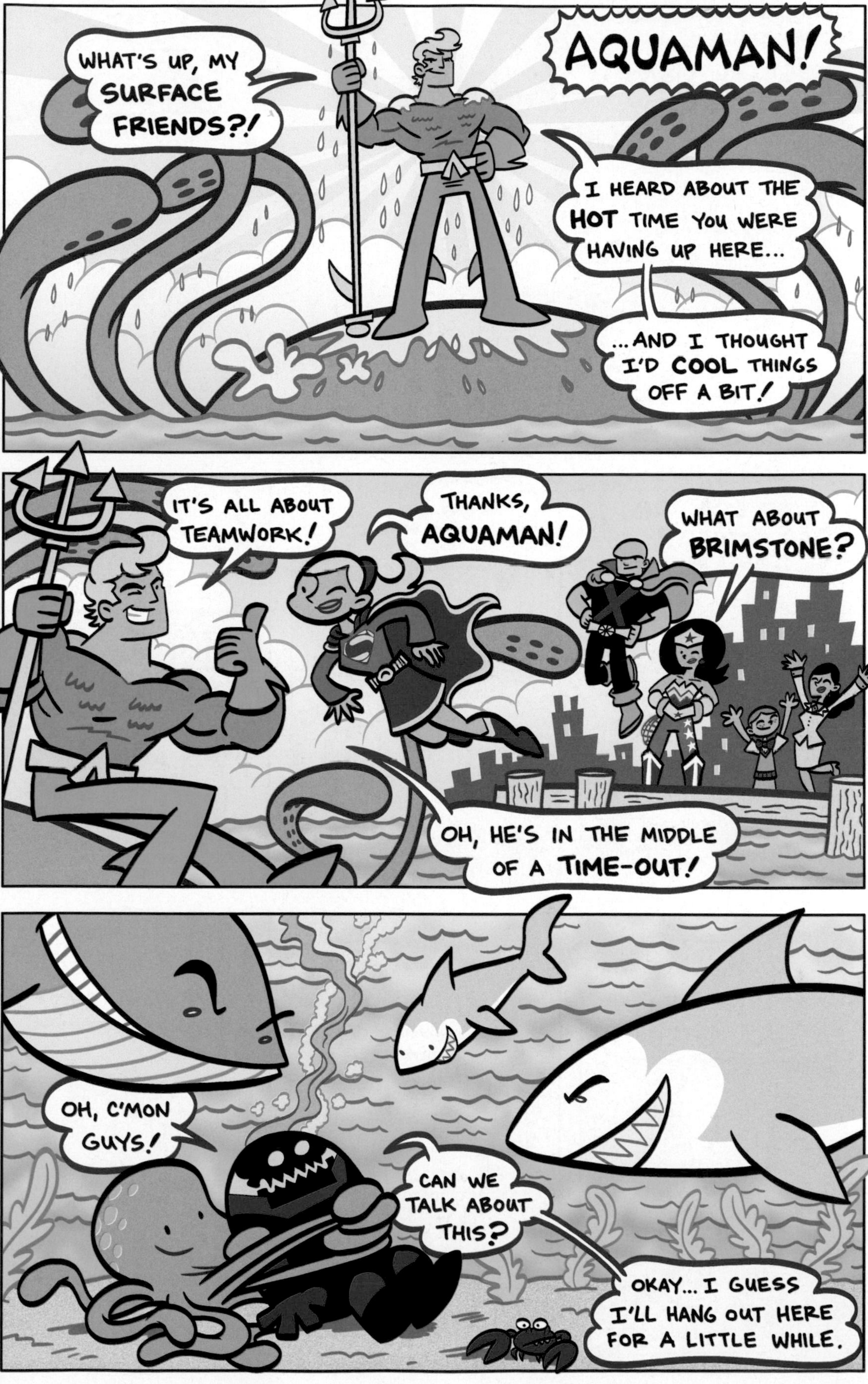
WHAT'S UP, MY SURFACE FRIENDS?!
AQUAMAN!
I HEARD ABOUT THE HOT TIME YOU WERE HAVING UP HERE...
...AND I THOUGHT I'D COOL THINGS OFF A BIT!
IT'S ALL ABOUT TEAMWORK!
THANKS, AQUAMAN!
WHAT ABOUT BRIMSTONE?
OH, HE'S IN THE MIDDLE OF A TIME-OUT!
OH, C'MON GUYS!
CAN WE TALK ABOUT THIS?
OKAY... I GUESS I'LL HANG OUT HERE FOR A LITTLE WHILE.

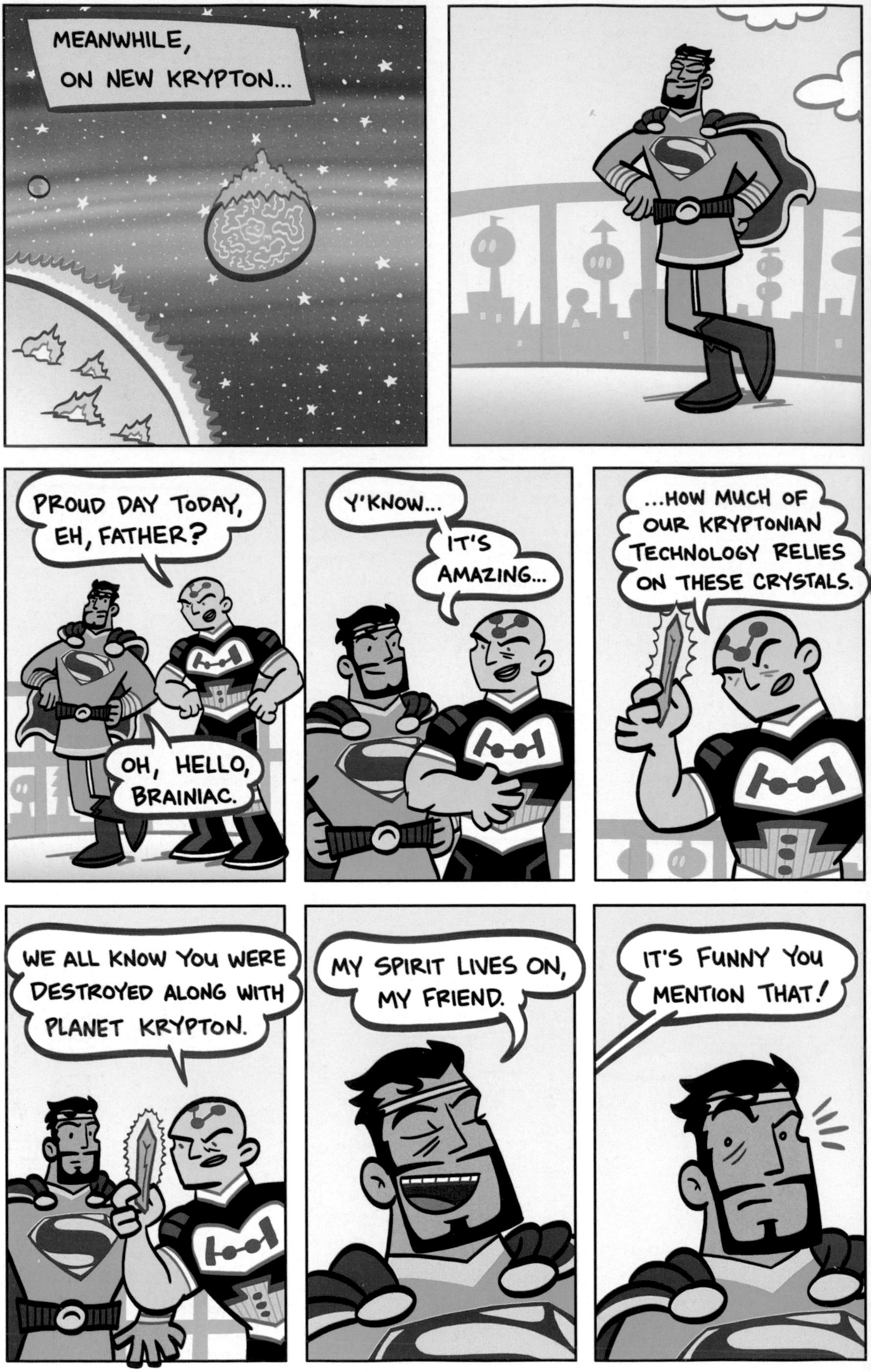
MEANWHILE, ON NEW KRYPTON...
PROUD DAY TODAY, EH, FATHER?
OH, HELLO, BRAINIAC.
Y'KNOW...
IT'S AMAZING...
...HOW MUCH OF OUR KRYPTONIAN TECHNOLOGY RELIES ON THESE CRYSTALS.
WE ALL KNOW YOU WERE DESTROYED ALONG WITH PLANET KRYPTON.
MY SPIRIT LIVES ON, MY FRIEND.
IT'S FUNNY YOU MENTION THAT!

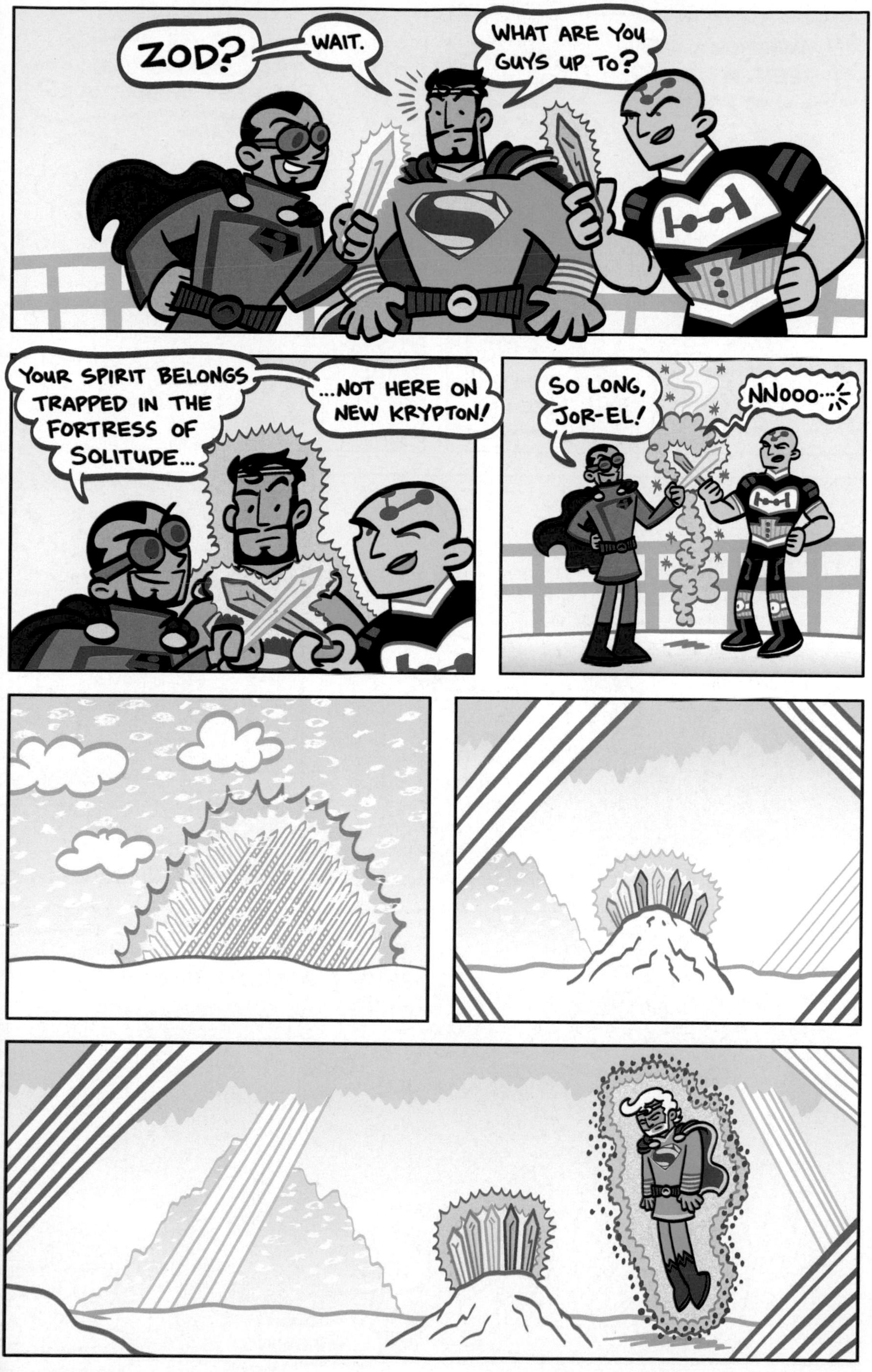
ZOD?
WAIT.
WHAT ARE YOU GUYS UP TO?
YOUR SPIRIT BELONGS TRAPPED IN THE FORTRESS OF SOLITUDE...
...NOT HERE ON NEW KRYPTON!
SO LONG, JOR-EL!
NNOOO...

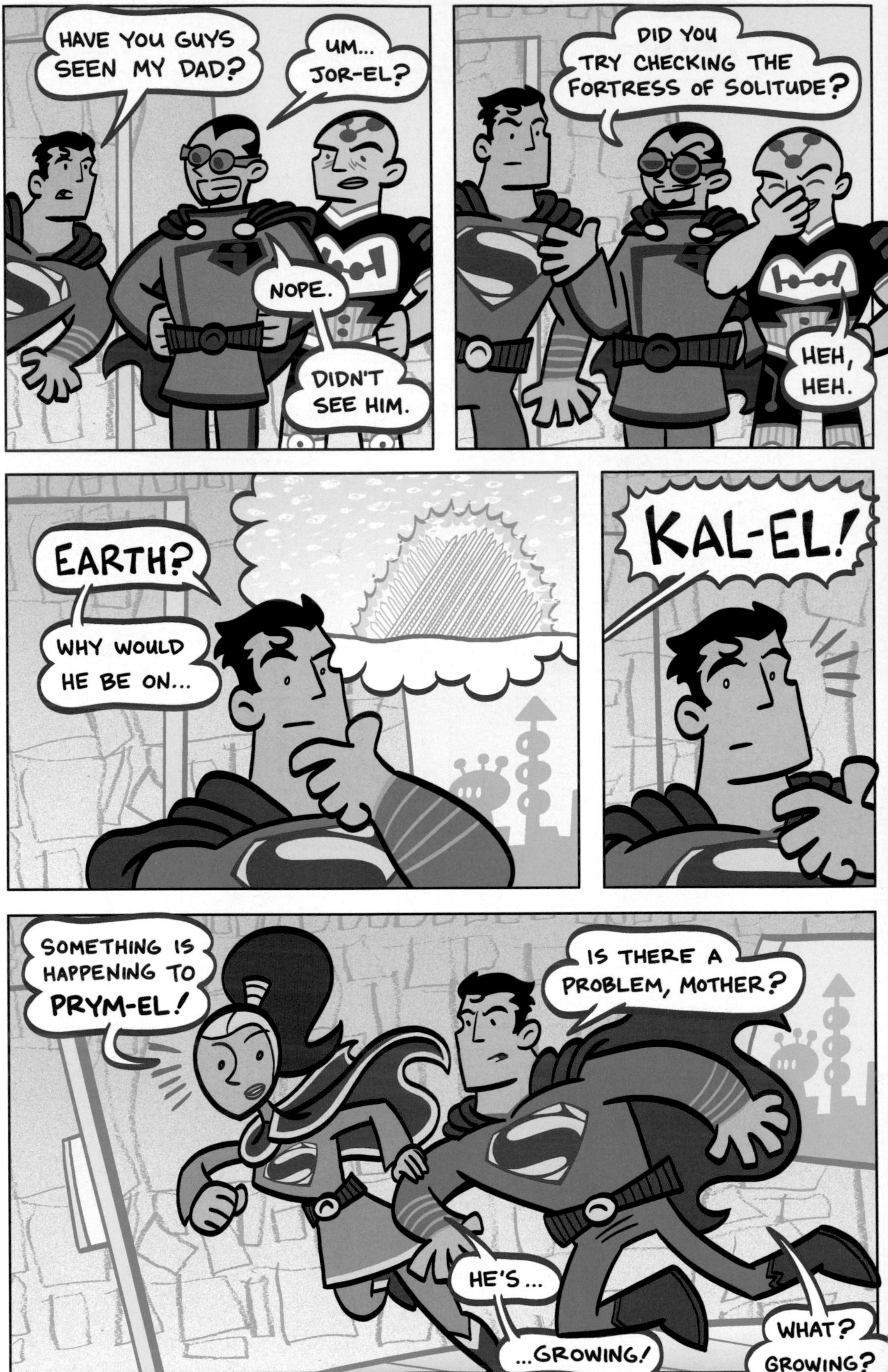
HAVE YOU GUYS SEEN MY DAD?
UM... JOR-EL?
NOPE.
DIDN'T SEE HIM.
DID YOU TRY CHECKING THE FORTRESS OF SOLITUDE?
HEH, HEH.
EARTH?
WHY WOULD HE BE ON...
KAL-EL!
SOMETHING IS HAPPENING TO PRYM-EL!
IS THERE A PROBLEM, MOTHER?
HE'S ...
...GROWING!
WHAT? GROWING?

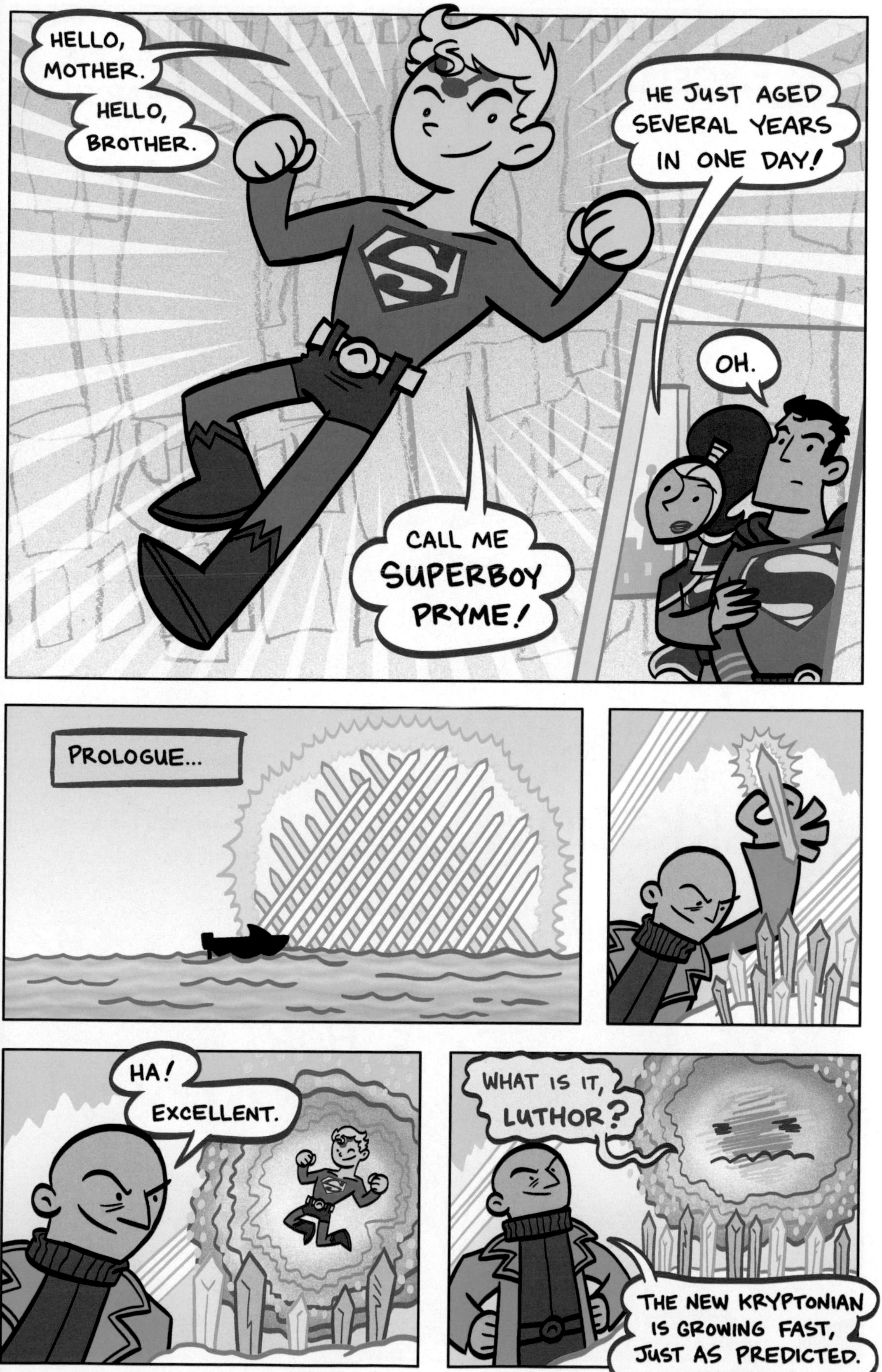
HELLO, MOTHER.
HELLO, BROTHER.
HE JUST AGED SEVERAL YEARS IN ONE DAY!
OH.
CALL ME SUPERBOY PRYME!
PROLOGUE...
HA! EXCELLENT.
WHAT IS IT, LUTHOR?
THE NEW KRYPTONIAN IS GROWING FAST, JUST AS PREDICTED.

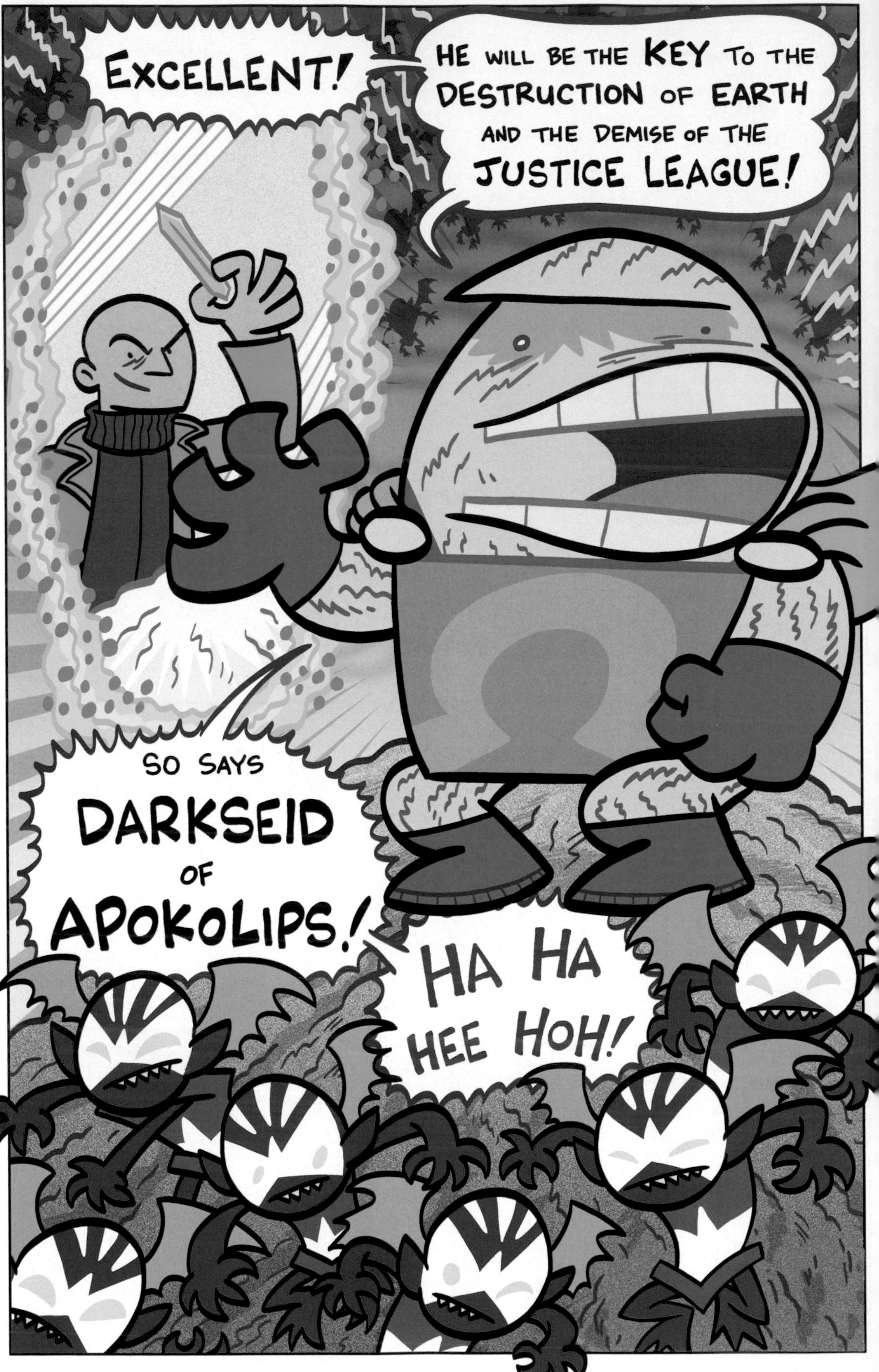
EXCELLENT!
HE WILL BE THE KEY TO THE DESTRUCTION OF EARTH AND THE DEMISE OF THE JUSTICE LEAGUE!
SO SAYS DARKSEID OF APOKOLIPS!
HA HA HEE HOH!

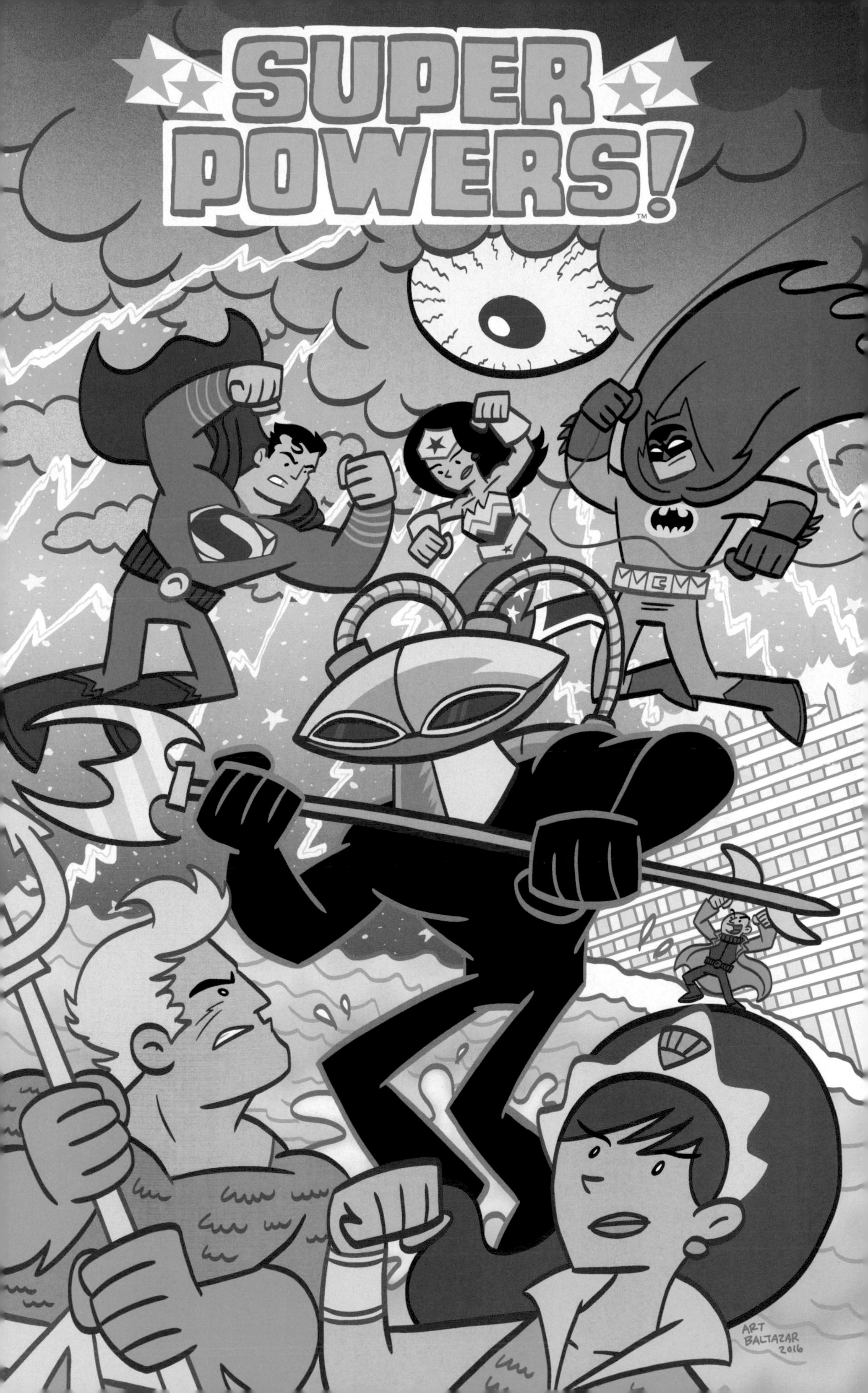
SUPER POWERS!™
ART BALTAZAR 2016

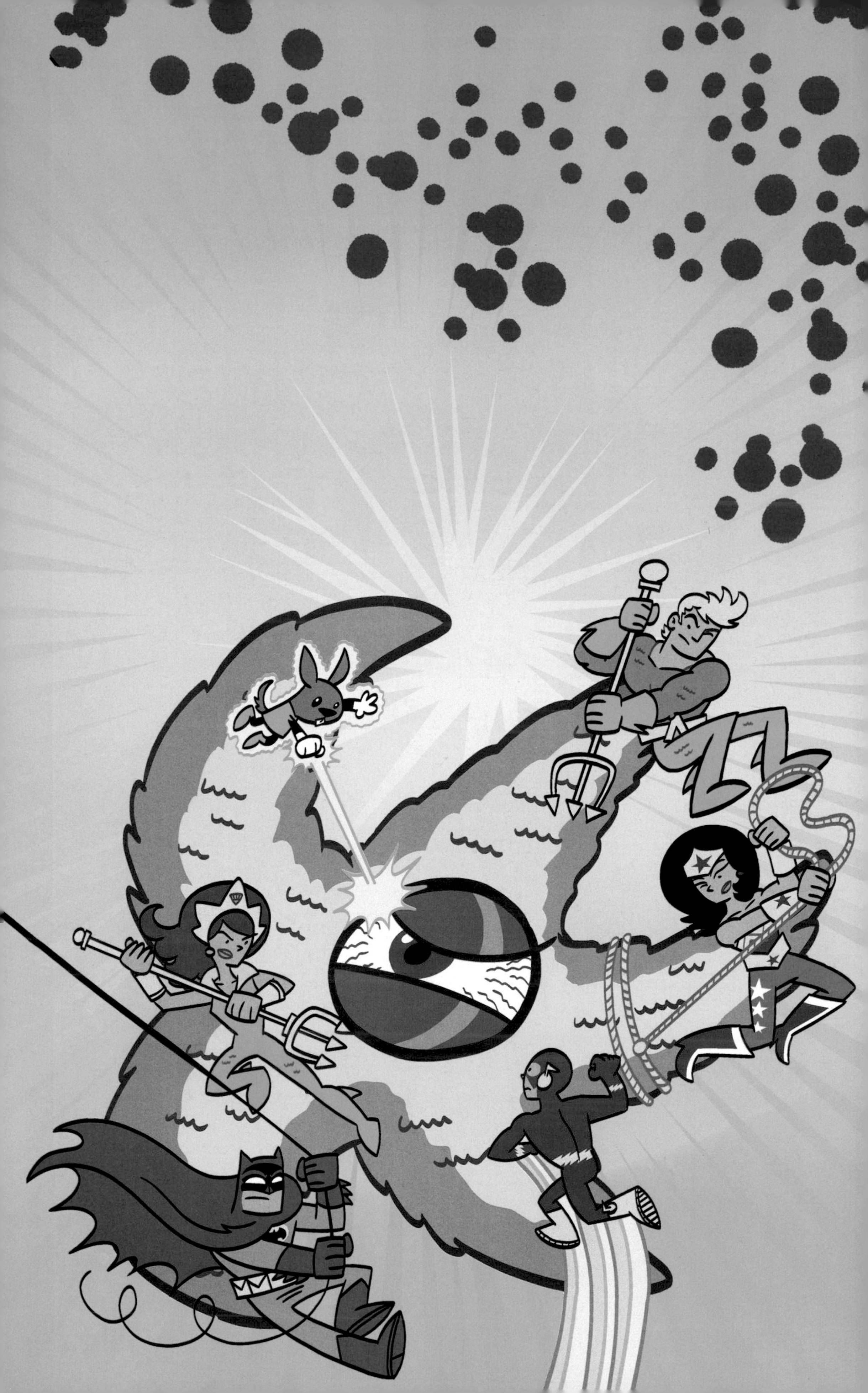

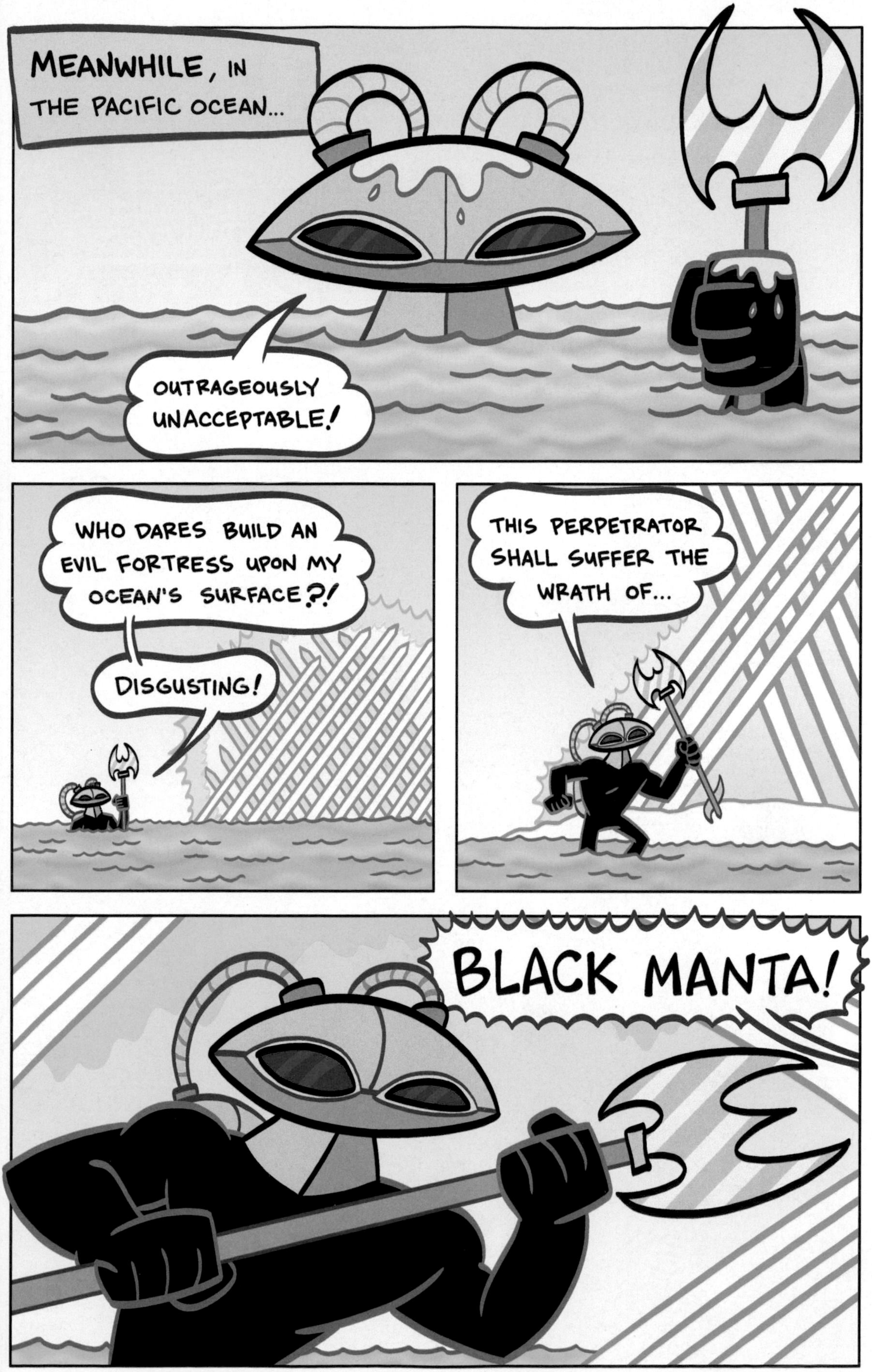
MEANWHILE, IN THE PACIFIC OCEAN...
OUTRAGEOUSLY UNACCEPTABLE!
WHO DARES BUILD AN EVIL FORTRESS UPON MY OCEAN'S SURFACE?!
DISGUSTING!
THIS PERPETRATOR SHALL SUFFER THE WRATH OF...
BLACK MANTA!

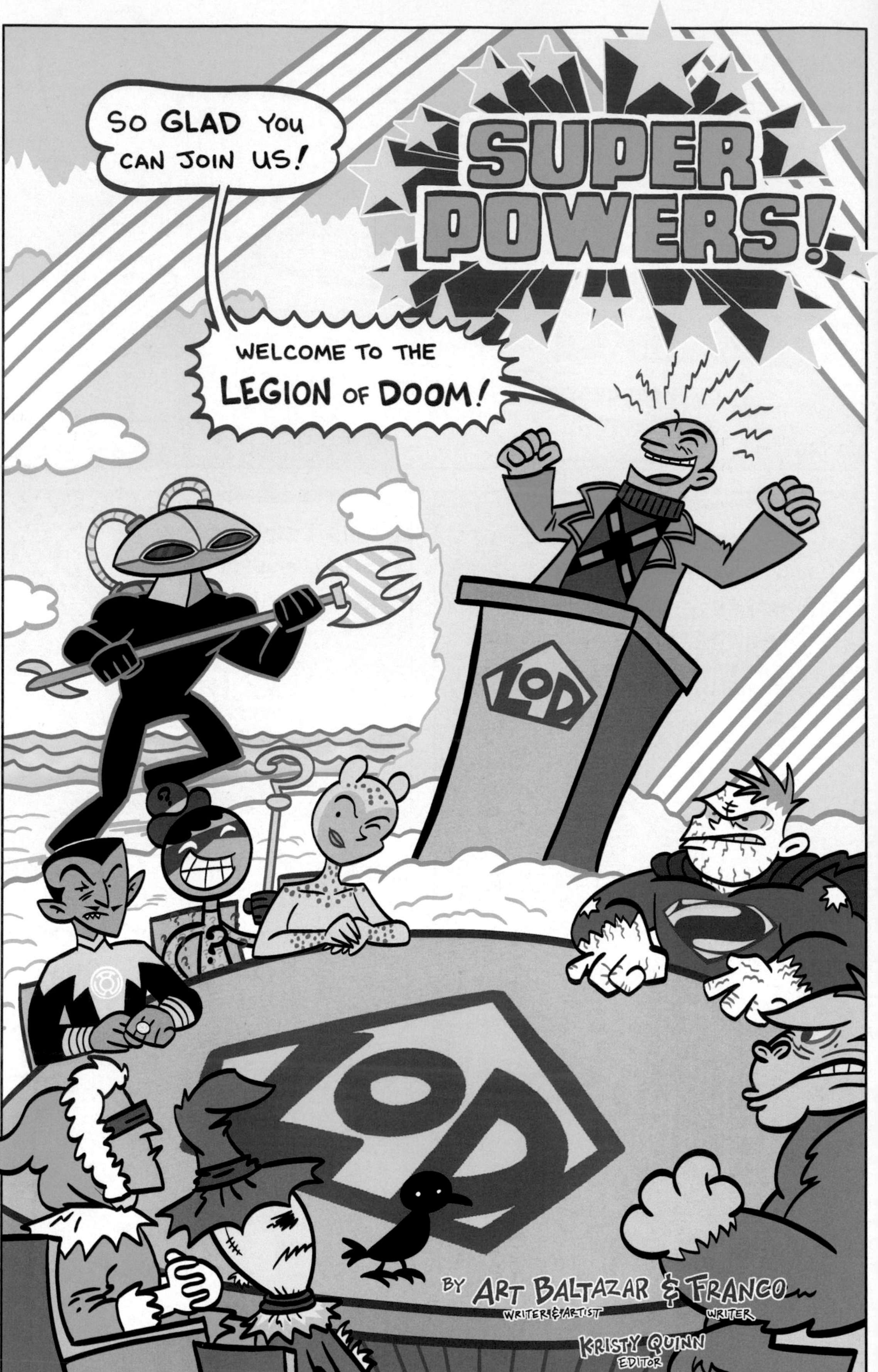
SUPER POWERS!
SO GLAD YOU CAN JOIN US!
WELCOME TO THE LEGION OF DOOM!
BY ART BALTAZAR WRITER & ARTIST & FRANCO WRITER
KRISTY QUINN EDITOR

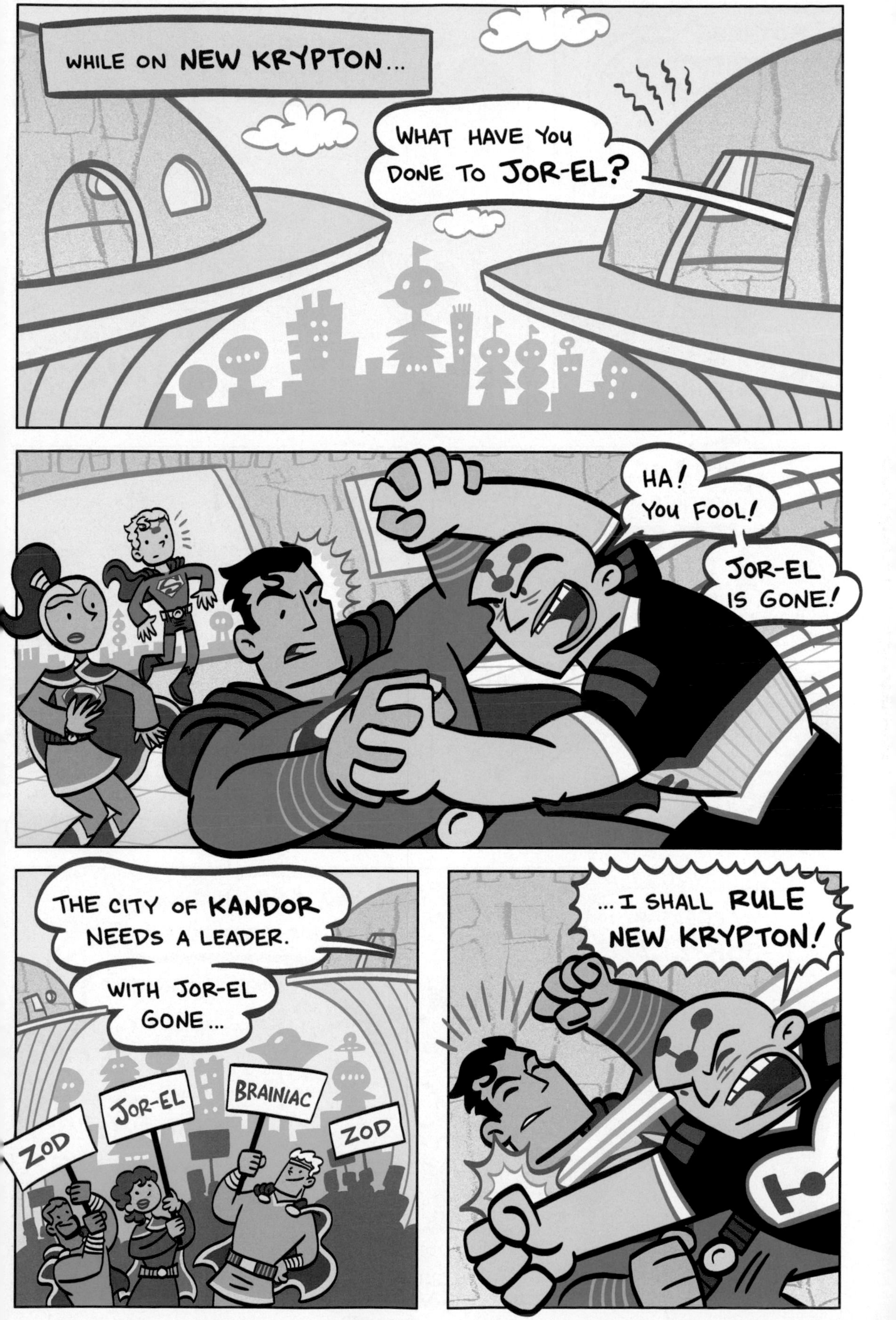
WHILE ON NEW KRYPTON...
WHAT HAVE YOU DONE TO JOR-EL?
HA! YOU FOOL!
JOR-EL IS GONE!
THE CITY OF KANDOR NEEDS A LEADER.
WITH JOR-EL GONE...
ZOD
JOR-EL
BRAINIAC
ZOD
...I SHALL RULE NEW KRYPTON!

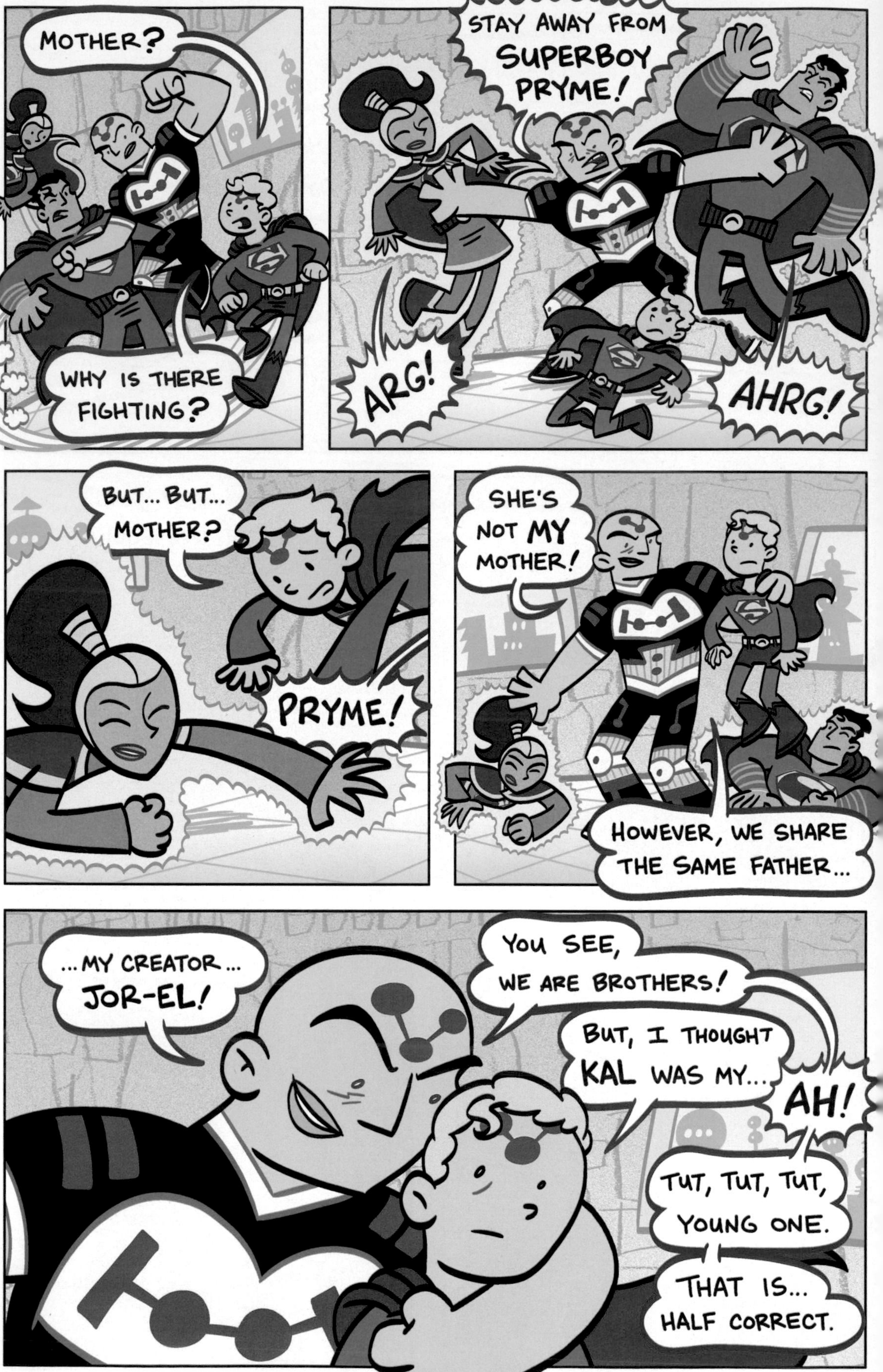
MOTHER?
WHY IS THERE FIGHTING?
STAY AWAY FROM SUPERBOY PRYME!
ARG!
AHRG!
BUT... BUT... MOTHER?
PRYME!
SHE'S NOT MY MOTHER!
HOWEVER, WE SHARE THE SAME FATHER...
...MY CREATOR... JOR-EL!
YOU SEE, WE ARE BROTHERS!
BUT, I THOUGHT KAL WAS MY...
AH!
TUT, TUT, TUT, YOUNG ONE.
THAT IS... HALF CORRECT.

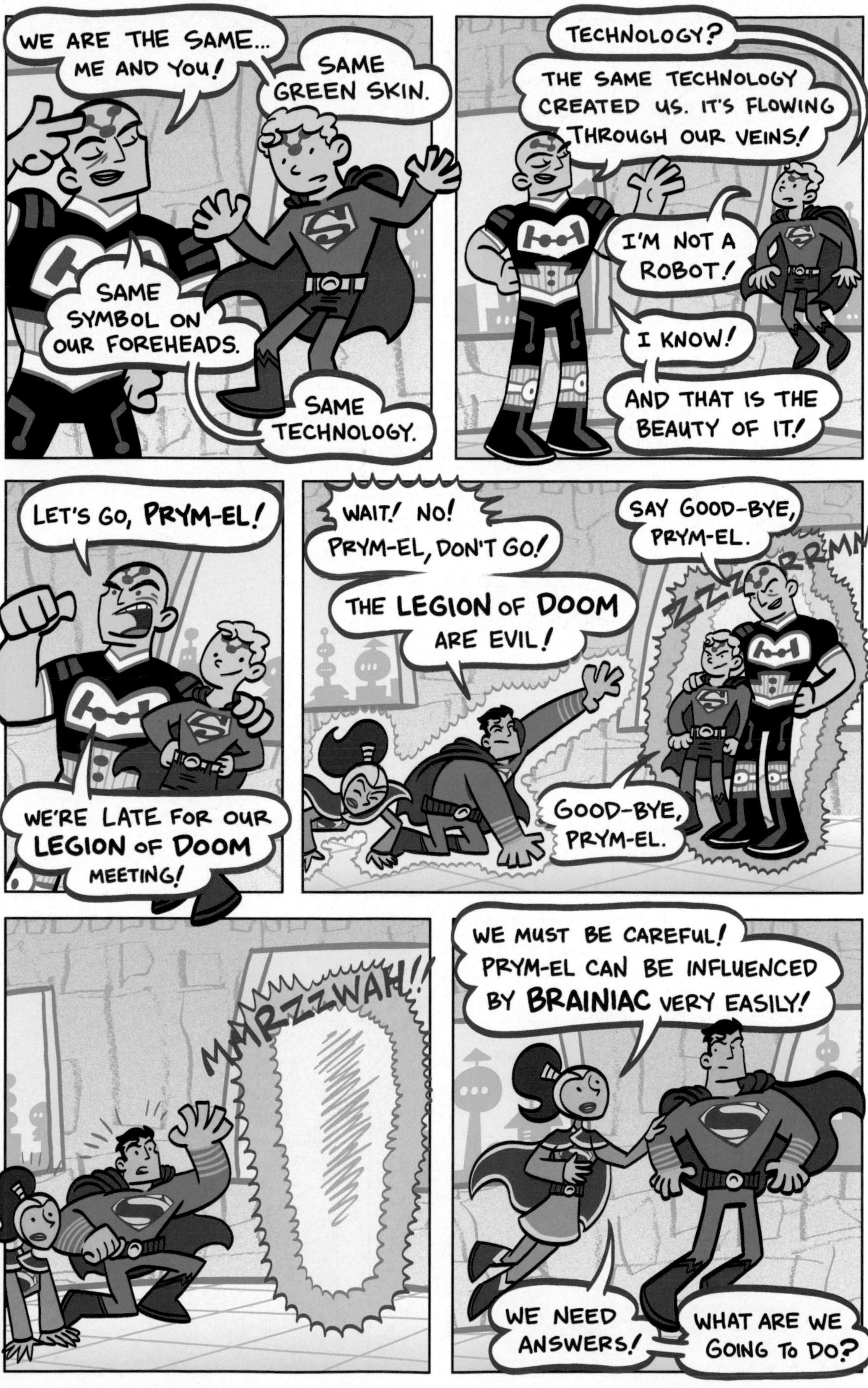
WE ARE THE SAME... ME AND YOU!
SAME GREEN SKIN.
SAME SYMBOL ON OUR FOREHEADS.
SAME TECHNOLOGY.
TECHNOLOGY?
THE SAME TECHNOLOGY CREATED US. IT'S FLOWING THROUGH OUR VEINS!
I'M NOT A ROBOT!
I KNOW!
AND THAT IS THE BEAUTY OF IT!
LET'S GO, PRYM-EL!
WE'RE LATE FOR OUR LEGION OF DOOM MEETING!
WAIT! NO! PRYM-EL, DON'T GO!
THE LEGION OF DOOM ARE EVIL!
SAY GOOD-BYE, PRYM-EL.
ZZZRRMM
GOOD-BYE, PRYM-EL.
MMRZZWAH!!
WE MUST BE CAREFUL! PRYM-EL CAN BE INFLUENCED BY BRAINIAC VERY EASILY!
WE NEED ANSWERS!
WHAT ARE WE GOING TO DO?

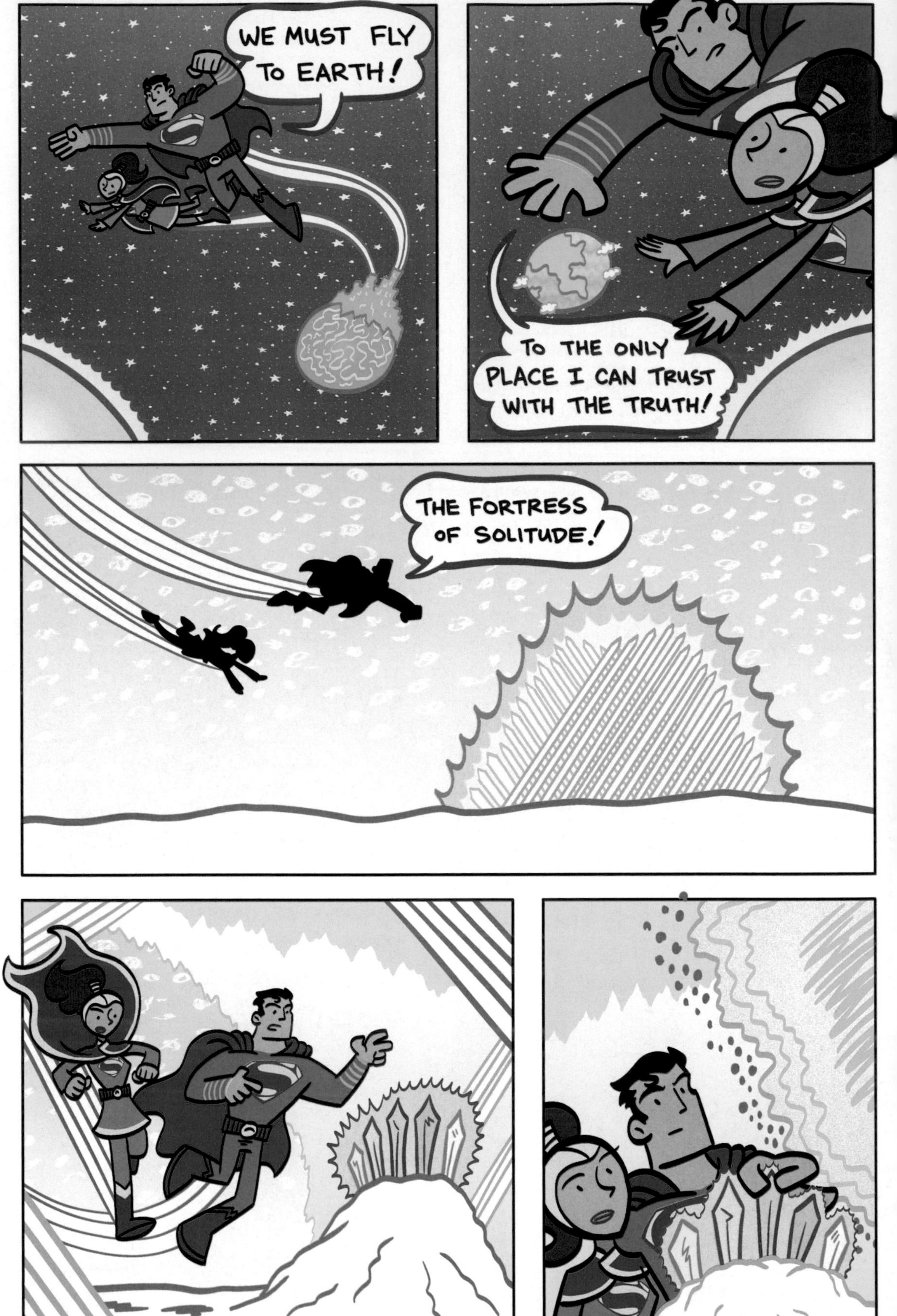
WE MUST FLY TO EARTH!
TO THE ONLY PLACE I CAN TRUST WITH THE TRUTH!
THE FORTRESS OF SOLITUDE!

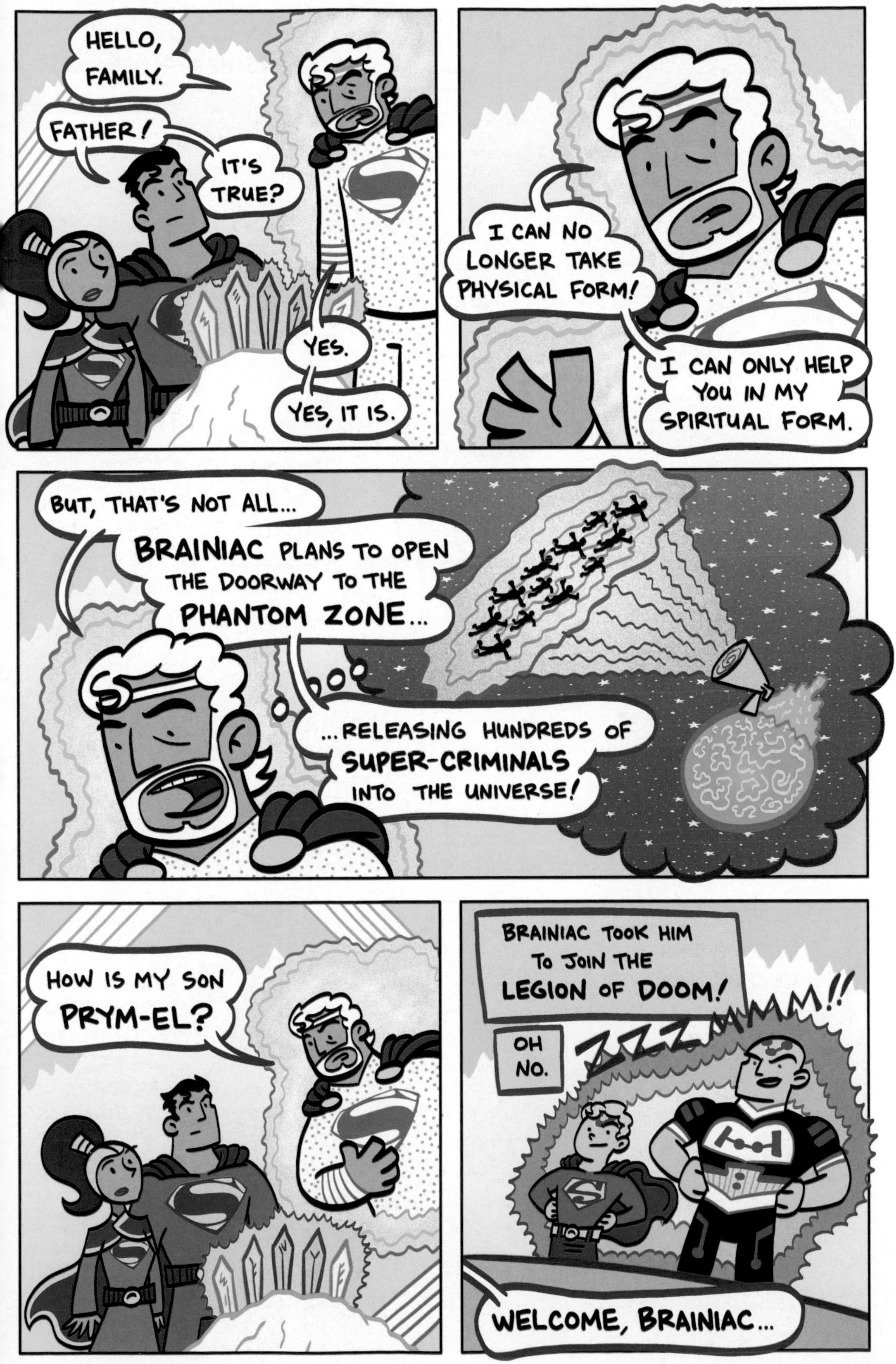
HELLO, FAMILY.
FATHER!
IT'S TRUE?
YES.
YES, IT IS.
I CAN NO LONGER TAKE PHYSICAL FORM!
I CAN ONLY HELP YOU IN MY SPIRITUAL FORM.
BUT, THAT'S NOT ALL...
BRAINIAC PLANS TO OPEN THE DOORWAY TO THE PHANTOM ZONE...
...RELEASING HUNDREDS OF SUPER-CRIMINALS INTO THE UNIVERSE!
HOW IS MY SON PRYM-EL?
BRAINIAC TOOK HIM TO JOIN THE LEGION OF DOOM!
OH NO.
ZZZMMM!!
WELCOME, BRAINIAC...

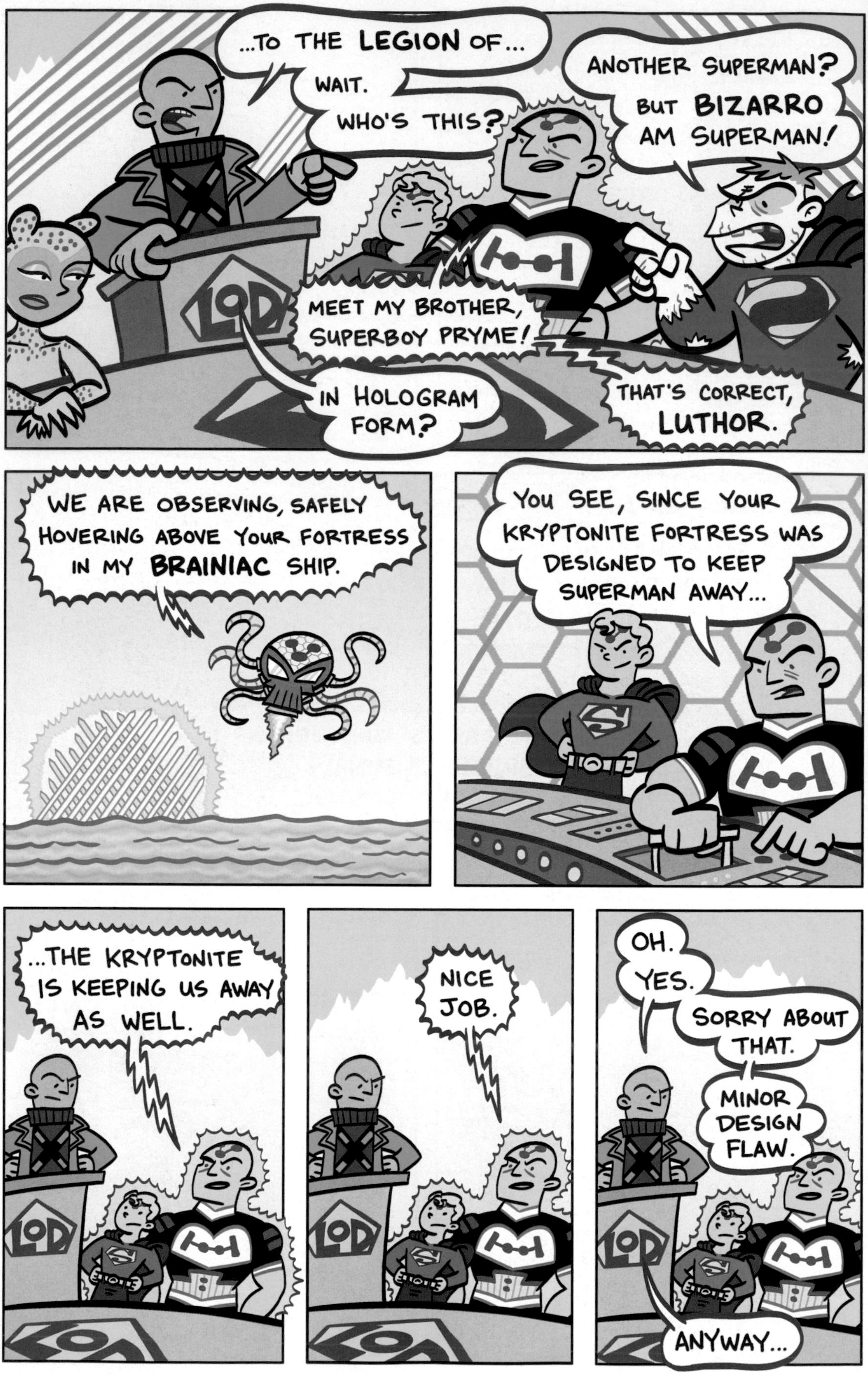
...TO THE LEGION OF...
WAIT.
WHO'S THIS?
ANOTHER SUPERMAN?
BUT BIZARRO AM SUPERMAN!
MEET MY BROTHER, SUPERBOY PRYME!
IN HOLOGRAM FORM?
THAT'S CORRECT, LUTHOR.
WE ARE OBSERVING, SAFELY HOVERING ABOVE YOUR FORTRESS IN MY BRAINIAC SHIP.
YOU SEE, SINCE YOUR KRYPTONITE FORTRESS WAS DESIGNED TO KEEP SUPERMAN AWAY...
...THE KRYPTONITE IS KEEPING US AWAY AS WELL.
NICE JOB.
OH.
YES.
SORRY ABOUT THAT.
MINOR DESIGN FLAW.
ANYWAY...

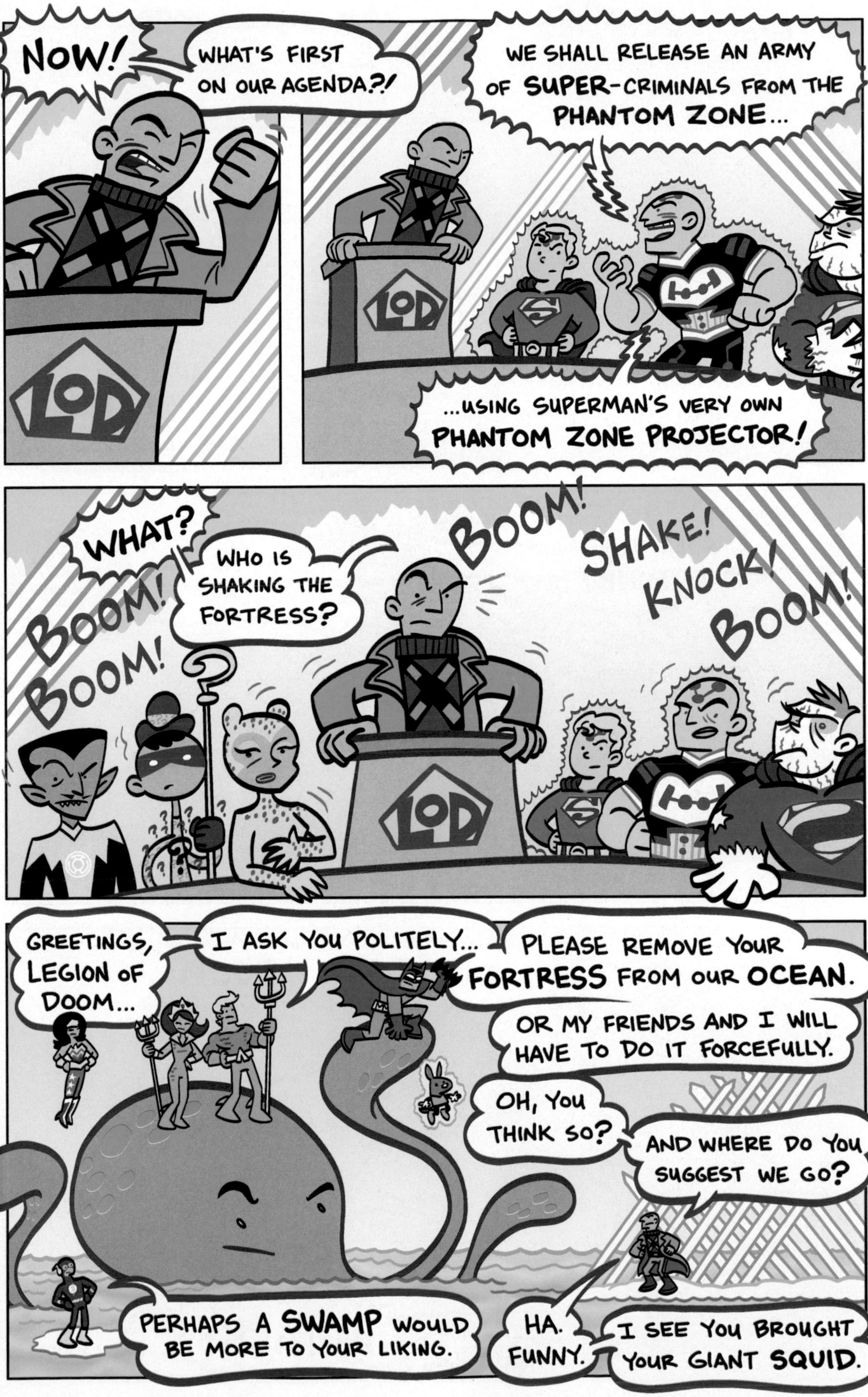
NOW!
WHAT'S FIRST ON OUR AGENDA?!
WE SHALL RELEASE AN ARMY OF SUPER-CRIMINALS FROM THE PHANTOM ZONE...
...USING SUPERMAN'S VERY OWN PHANTOM ZONE PROJECTOR!
WHAT?
BOOM!
BOOM!
WHO IS SHAKING THE FORTRESS?
BOOM!
SHAKE!
KNOCK!
BOOM!
GREETINGS, LEGION OF DOOM...
I ASK YOU POLITELY...
PLEASE REMOVE YOUR FORTRESS FROM OUR OCEAN.
OR MY FRIENDS AND I WILL HAVE TO DO IT FORCEFULLY.
OH, YOU THINK SO?
AND WHERE DO YOU SUGGEST WE GO?
PERHAPS A SWAMP WOULD BE MORE TO YOUR LIKING.
HA. FUNNY.
I SEE YOU BROUGHT YOUR GIANT SQUID.

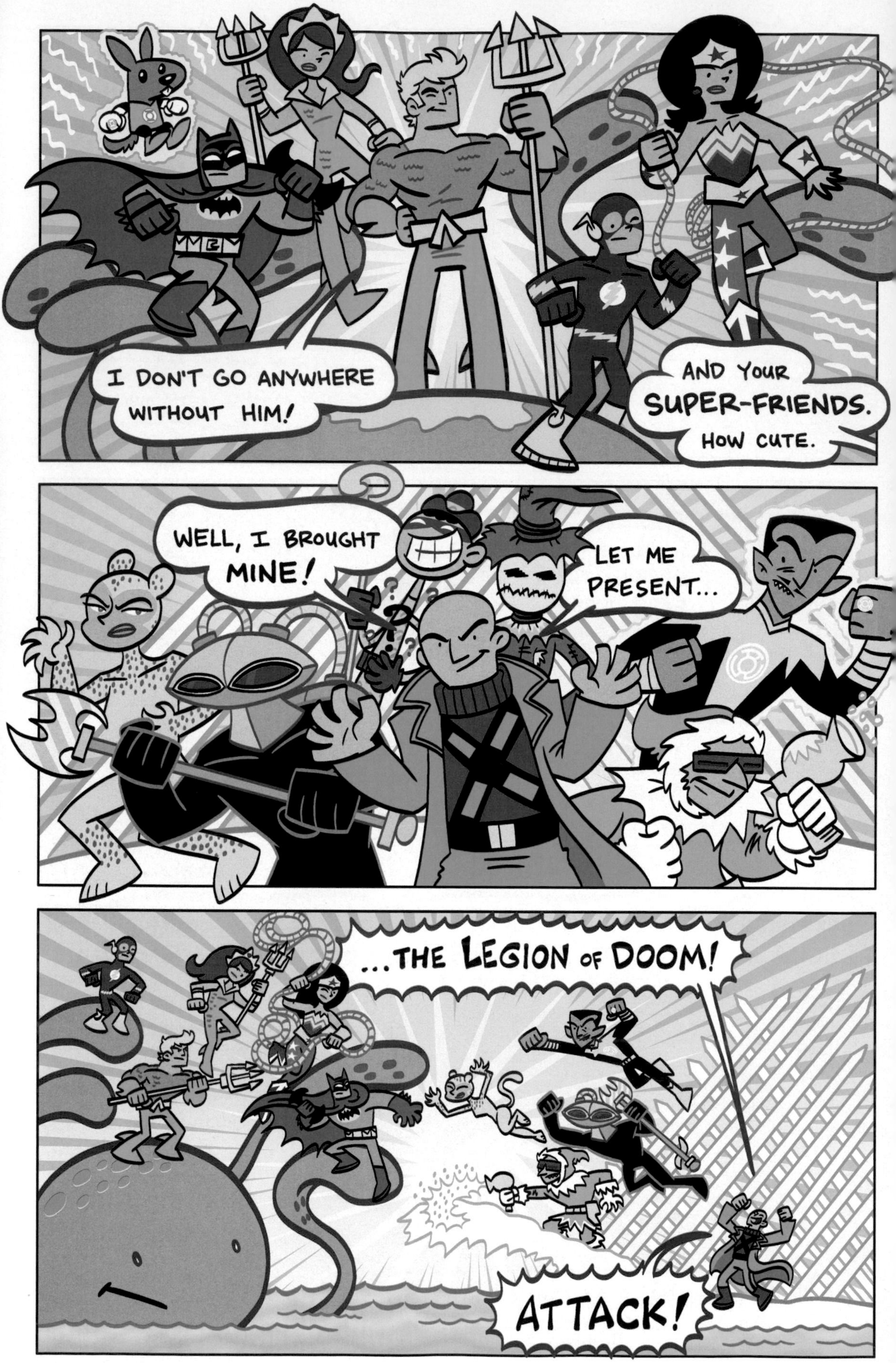
I DON'T GO ANYWHERE WITHOUT HIM!
AND YOUR SUPER-FRIENDS. HOW CUTE.
WELL, I BROUGHT MINE!
LET ME PRESENT...
...THE LEGION OF DOOM!
ATTACK!

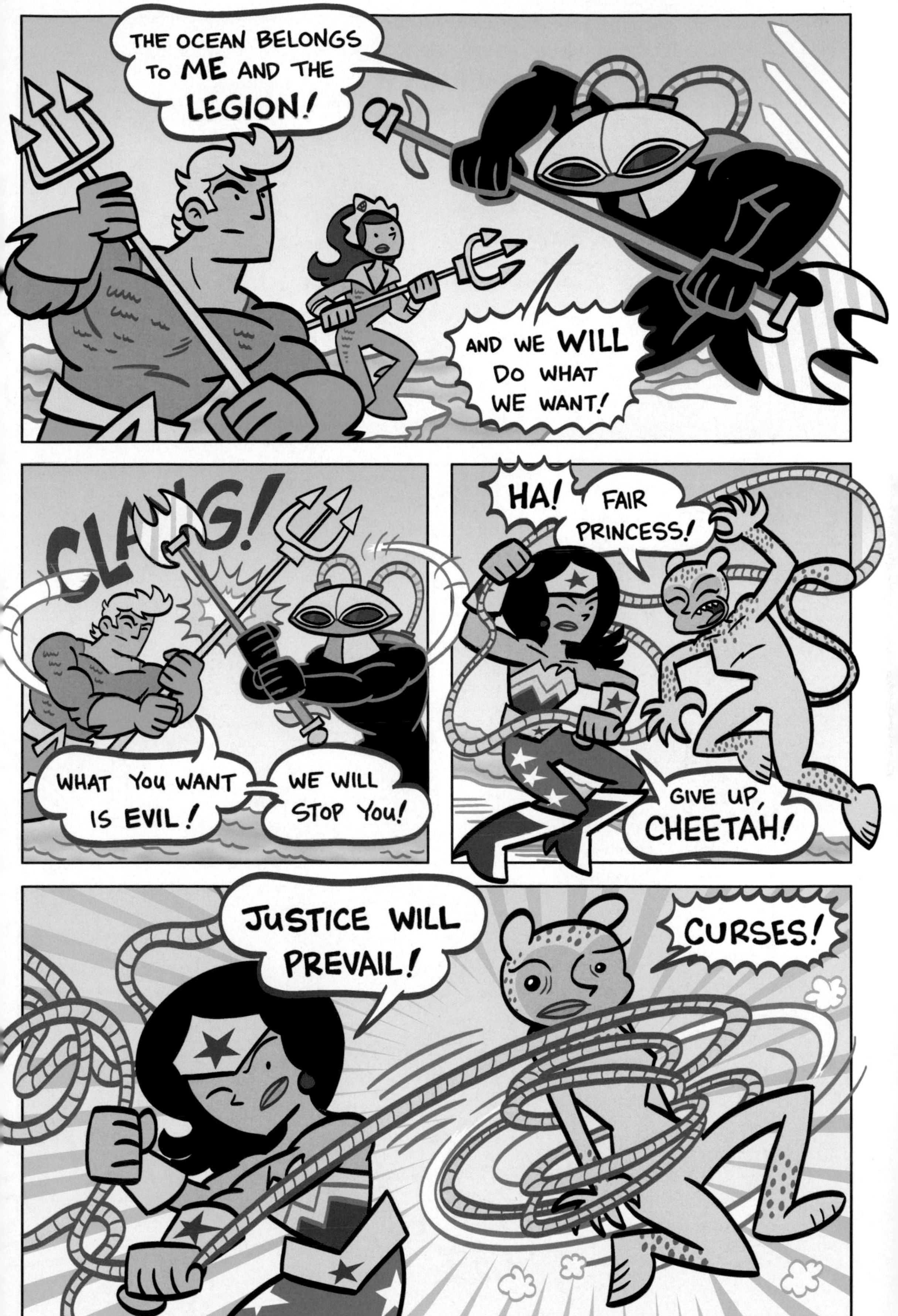
THE OCEAN BELONGS TO ME AND THE LEGION!
AND WE WILL DO WHAT WE WANT!
CLANG!
WHAT YOU WANT IS EVIL!
WE WILL STOP YOU!
HA!
FAIR PRINCESS!
GIVE UP, CHEETAH!
JUSTICE WILL PREVAIL!
CURSES!

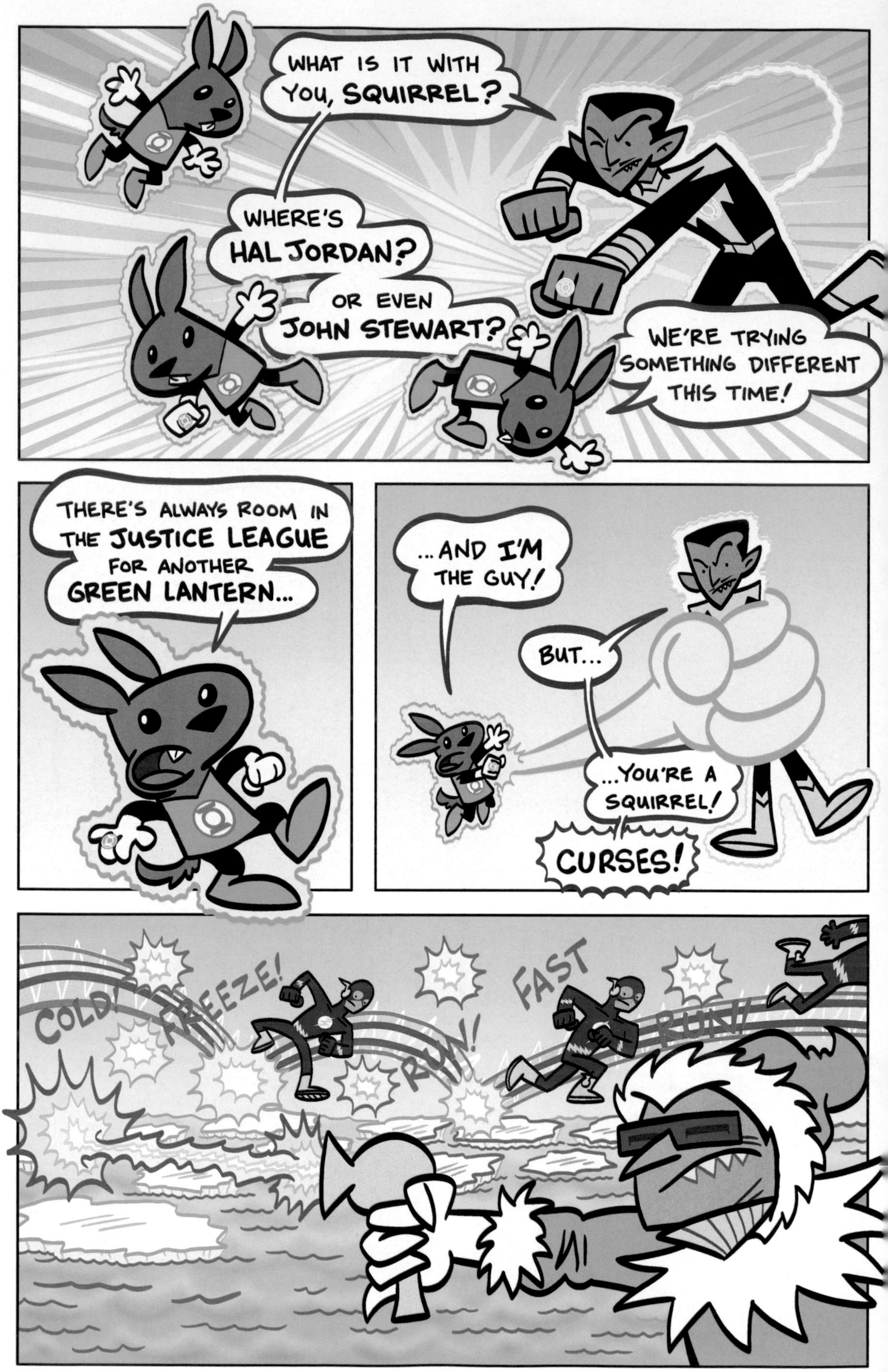

WHAT IS IT WITH YOU, SQUIRREL?
WHERE'S HAL JORDAN?
OR EVEN JOHN STEWART?
WE'RE TRYING SOMETHING DIFFERENT THIS TIME!
THERE'S ALWAYS ROOM IN THE JUSTICE LEAGUE FOR ANOTHER GREEN LANTERN...
...AND I'M THE GUY!
BUT...
...YOU'RE A SQUIRREL!
CURSES!
COLD!
FREEZE!
FAST
RUN!
RUN!

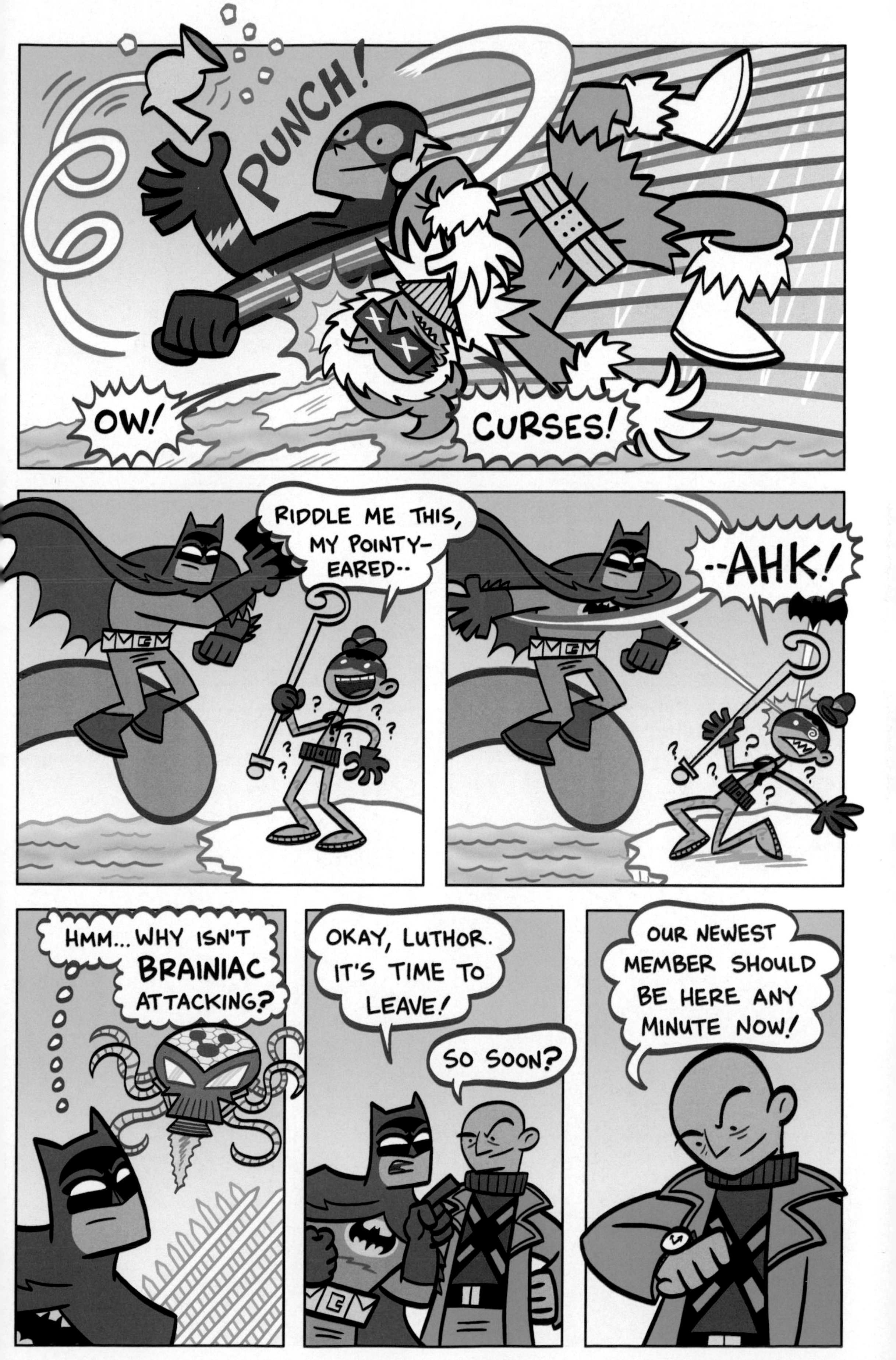
PUNCH!
OW!
CURSES!
RIDDLE ME THIS, MY POINTY-EARED--
--AHK!
HMM... WHY ISN'T BRAINIAC ATTACKING?
OKAY, LUTHOR. IT'S TIME TO LEAVE!
SO SOON?
OUR NEWEST MEMBER SHOULD BE HERE ANY MINUTE NOW!

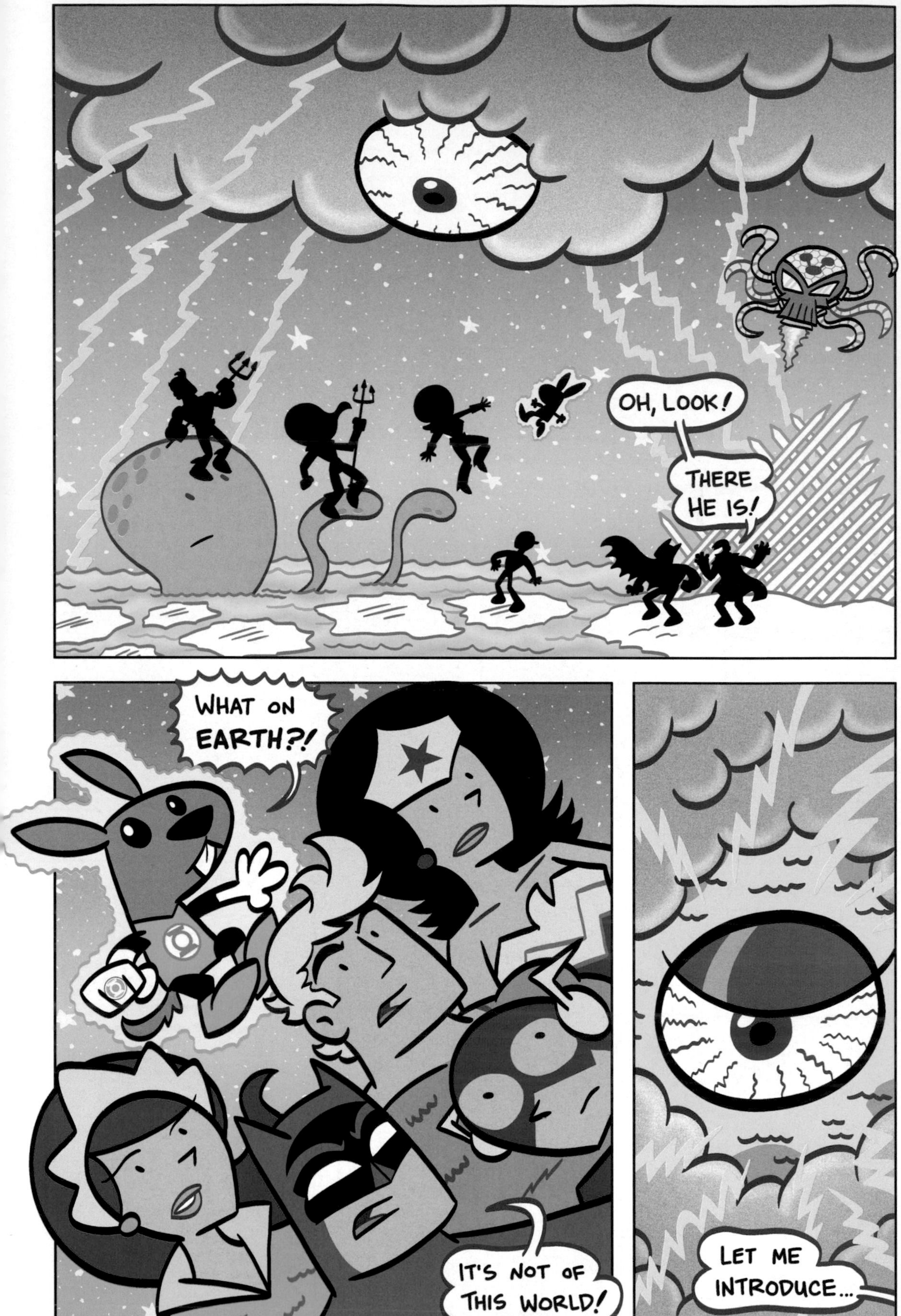
OH, LOOK!
THERE HE IS!
WHAT ON EARTH?!
IT'S NOT OF THIS WORLD!
LET ME INTRODUCE...

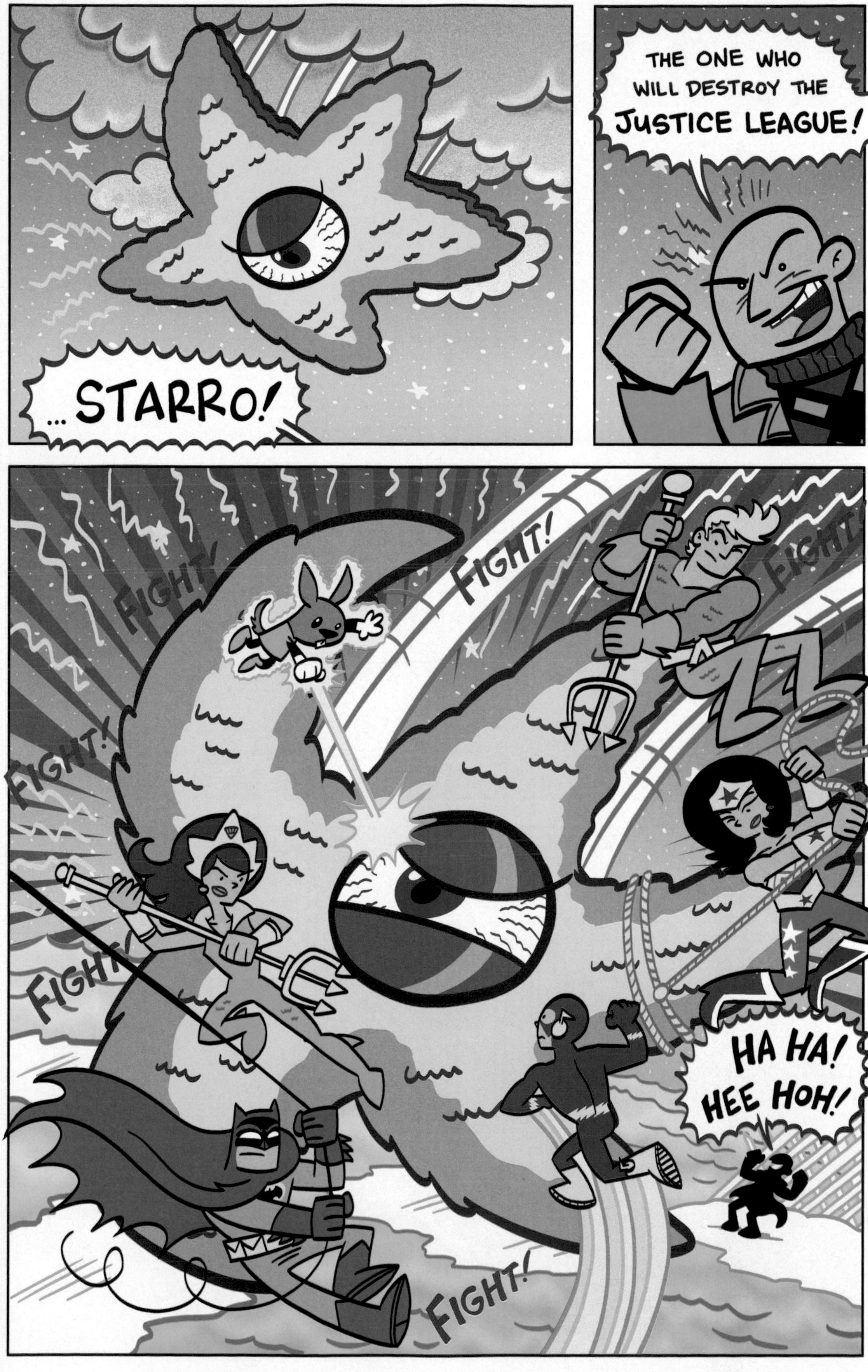
...STARRO!
THE ONE WHO WILL DESTROY THE JUSTICE LEAGUE!
FIGHT!
FIGHT!
FIGHT!
FIGHT!
FIGHT!
FIGHT!
HA HA! HEE HOH!

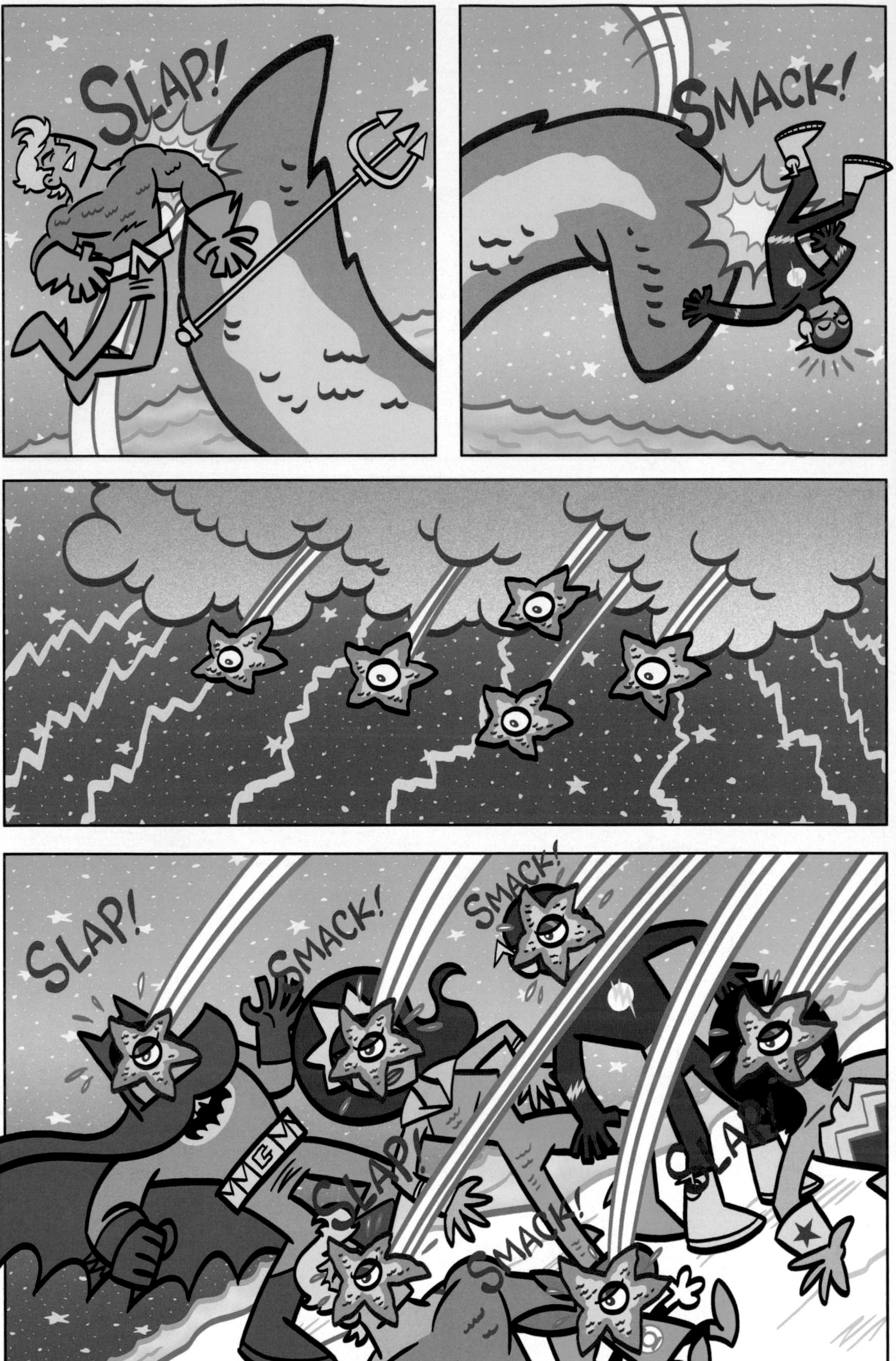
SLAP!
SMACK!
SLAP!
SMACK!
SMACK!
SLAP!
SMACK!

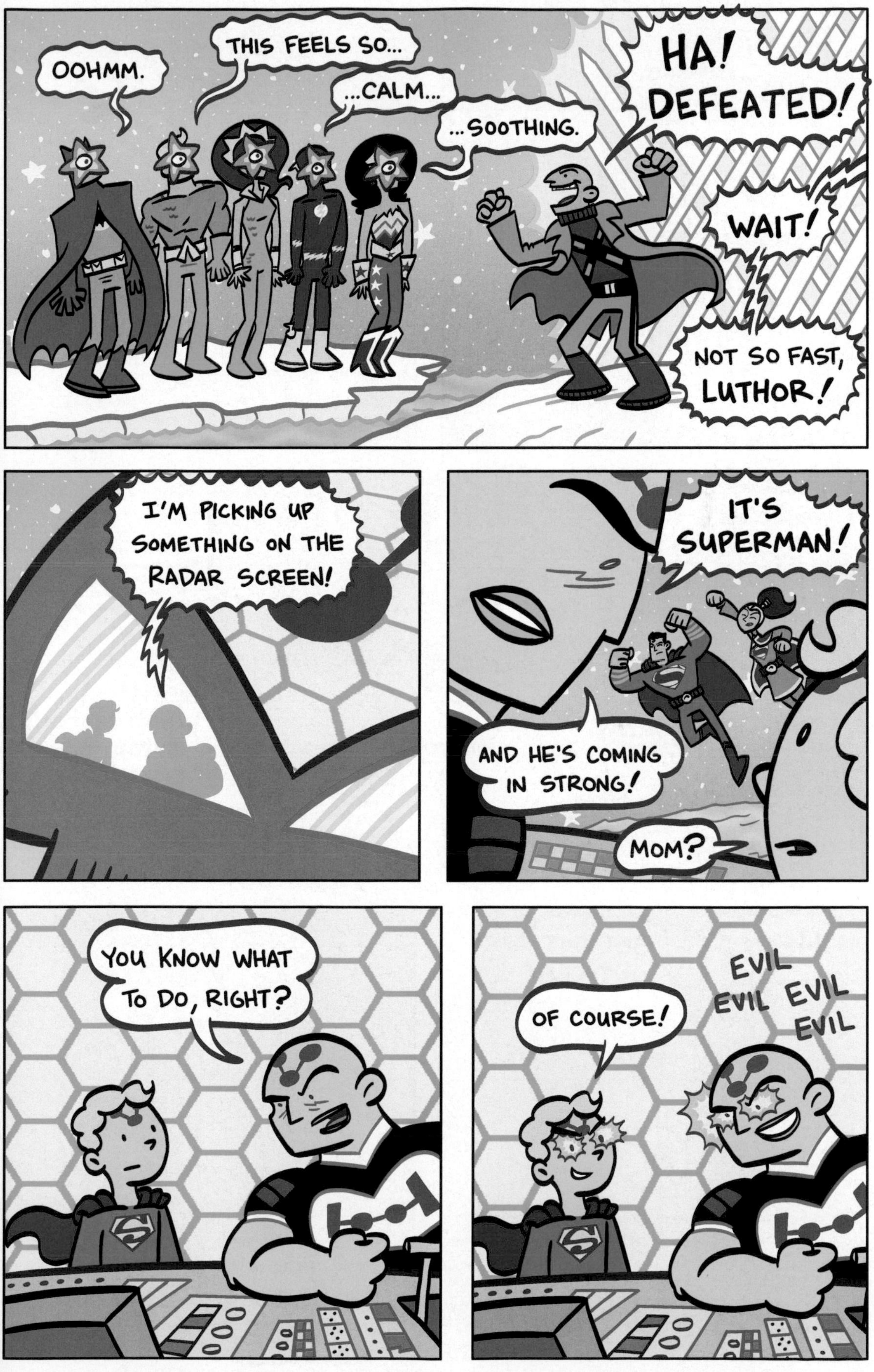
OOHMM.
THIS FEELS SO...
...CALM...
...SOOTHING.
HA! DEFEATED!
WAIT!
NOT SO FAST, LUTHOR!
I'M PICKING UP SOMETHING ON THE RADAR SCREEN!
IT'S SUPERMAN!
AND HE'S COMING IN STRONG!
MOM?
YOU KNOW WHAT TO DO, RIGHT?
OF COURSE!
EVIL EVIL EVIL EVIL

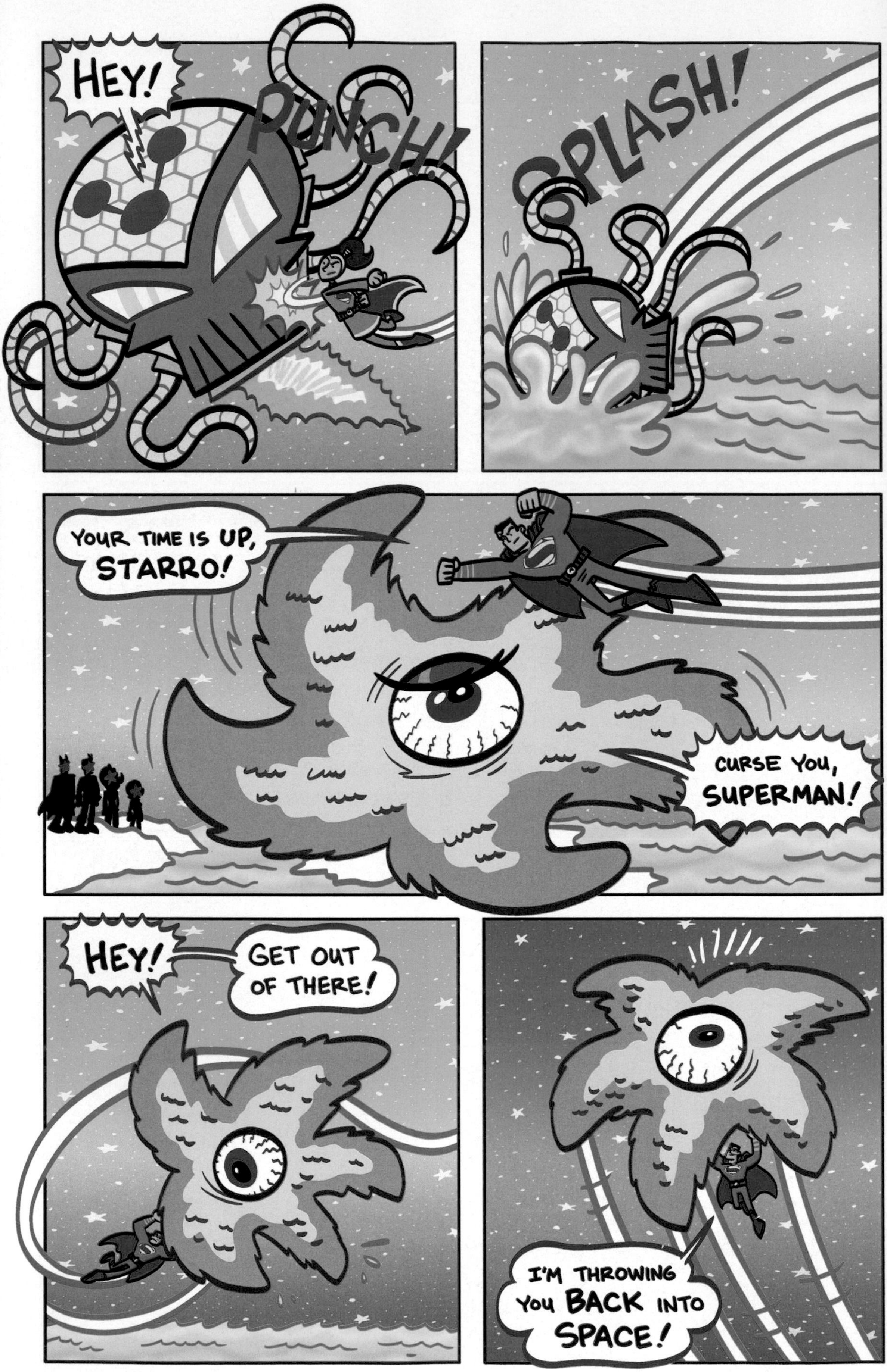
HEY!
PUNCH!
SPLASH!
YOUR TIME IS UP, STARRO!
CURSE YOU, SUPERMAN!
HEY!
GET OUT OF THERE!
I'M THROWING YOU BACK INTO SPACE!

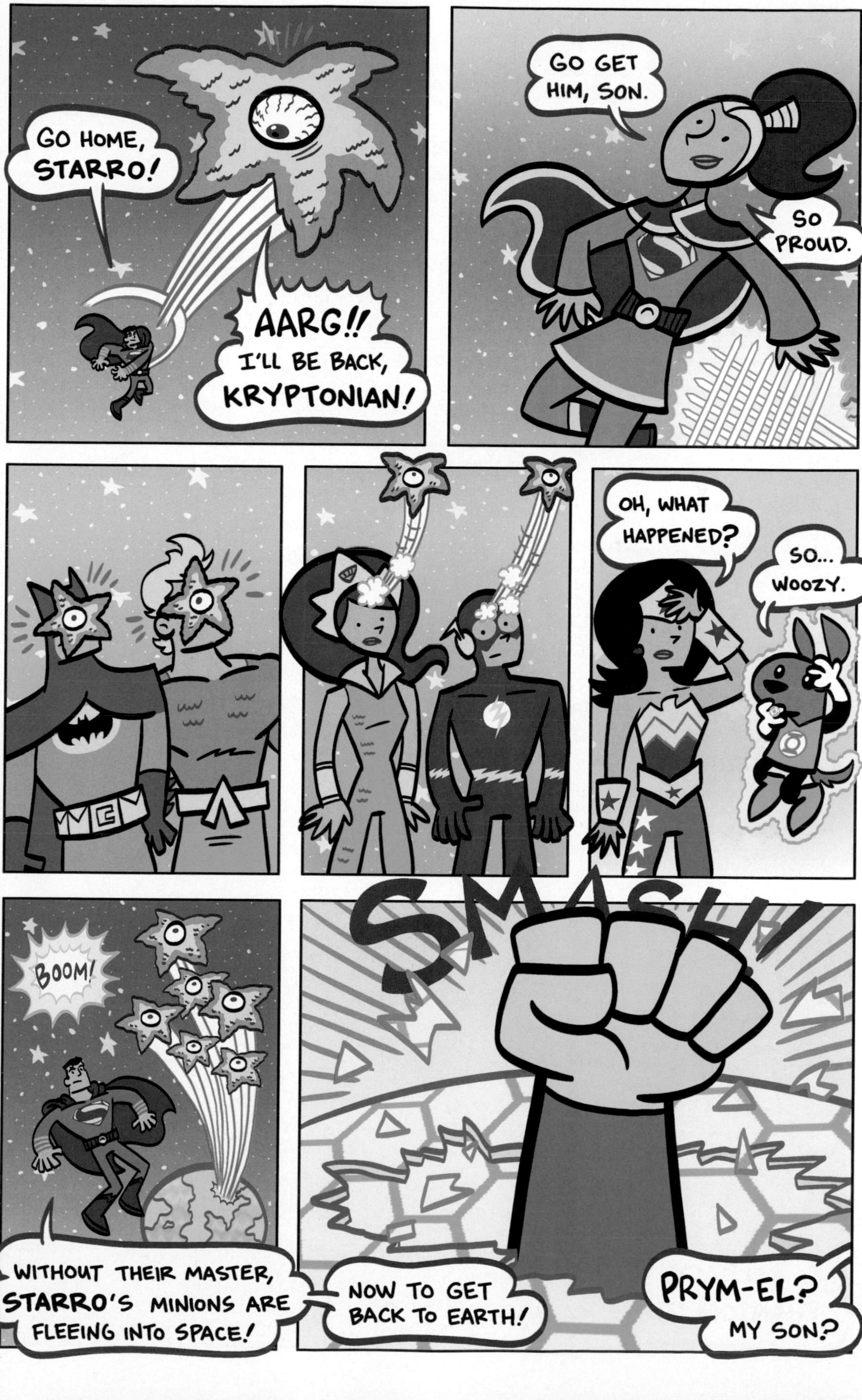
GO HOME, STARRO!
AARG!! I'LL BE BACK, KRYPTONIAN!
GO GET HIM, SON.
SO PROUD.
OH, WHAT HAPPENED?
SO... WOOZY.
BOOM!
WITHOUT THEIR MASTER, STARRO'S MINIONS ARE FLEEING INTO SPACE!
SMASH!
NOW TO GET BACK TO EARTH!
PRYM-EL? MY SON?

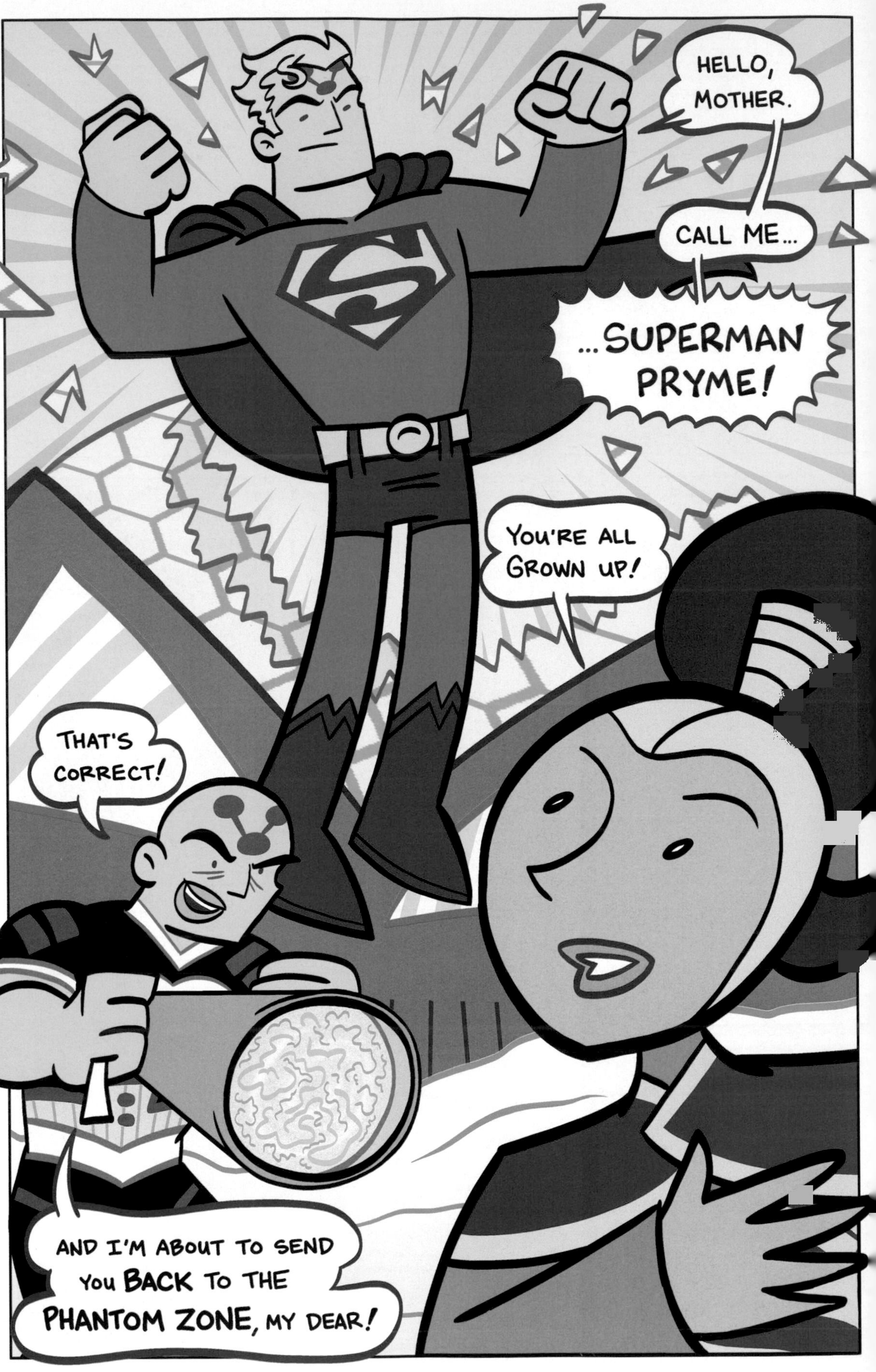
HELLO, MOTHER.
CALL ME...
...SUPERMAN PRYME!
YOU'RE ALL GROWN UP!
THAT'S CORRECT!
AND I'M ABOUT TO SEND YOU BACK TO THE PHANTOM ZONE, MY DEAR!

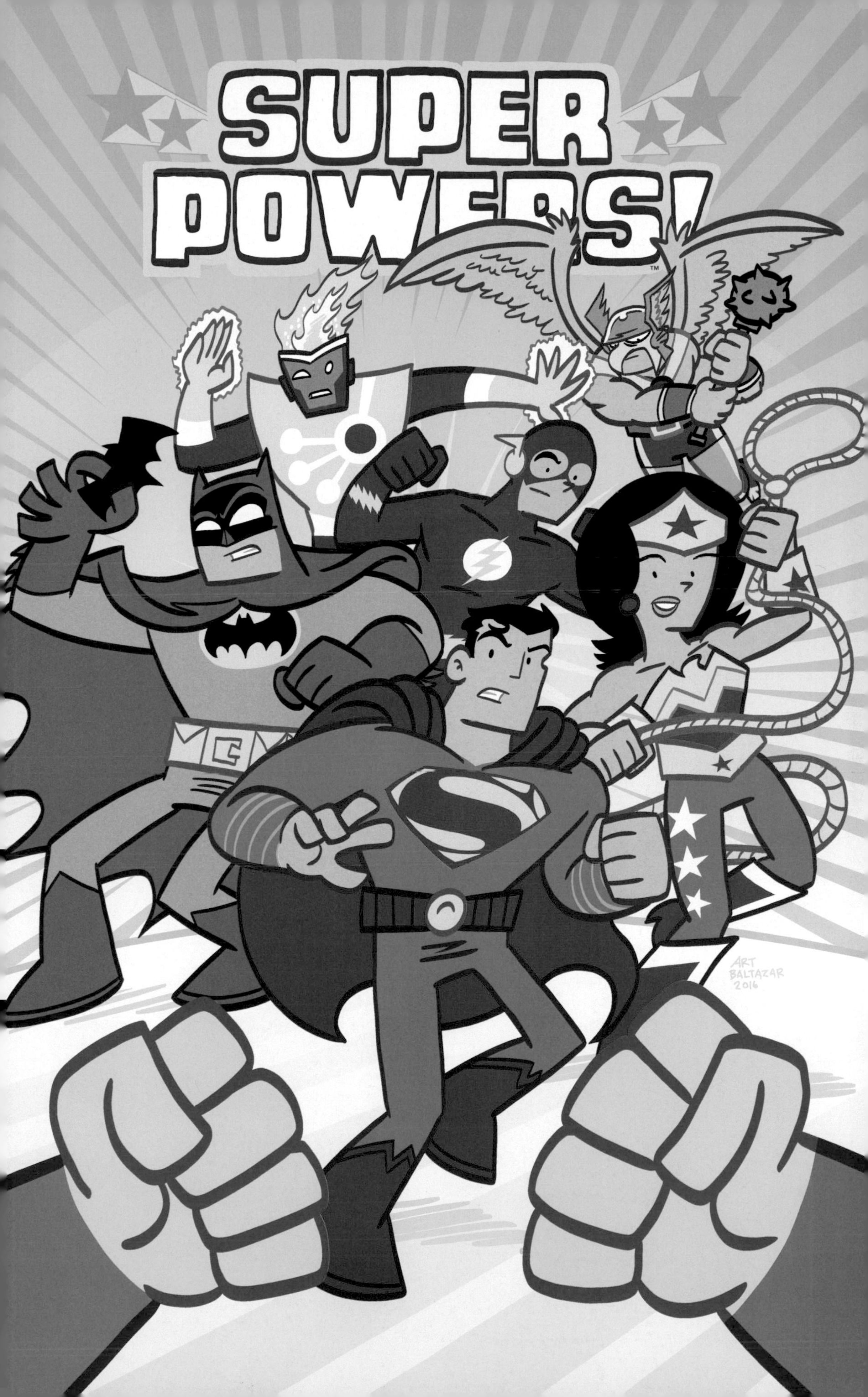
SUPER POWERS!™
ART BALTAZAR 2016

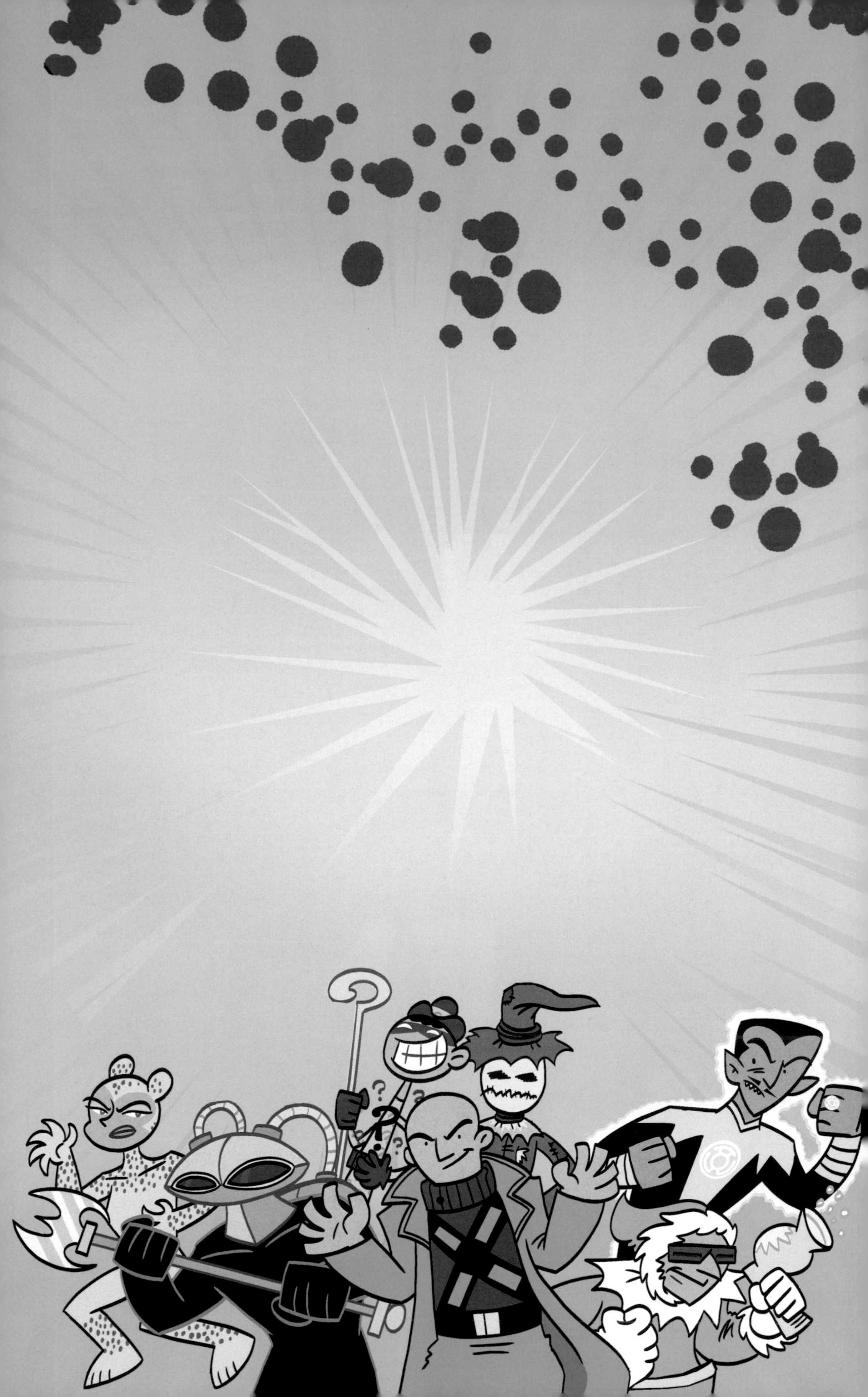

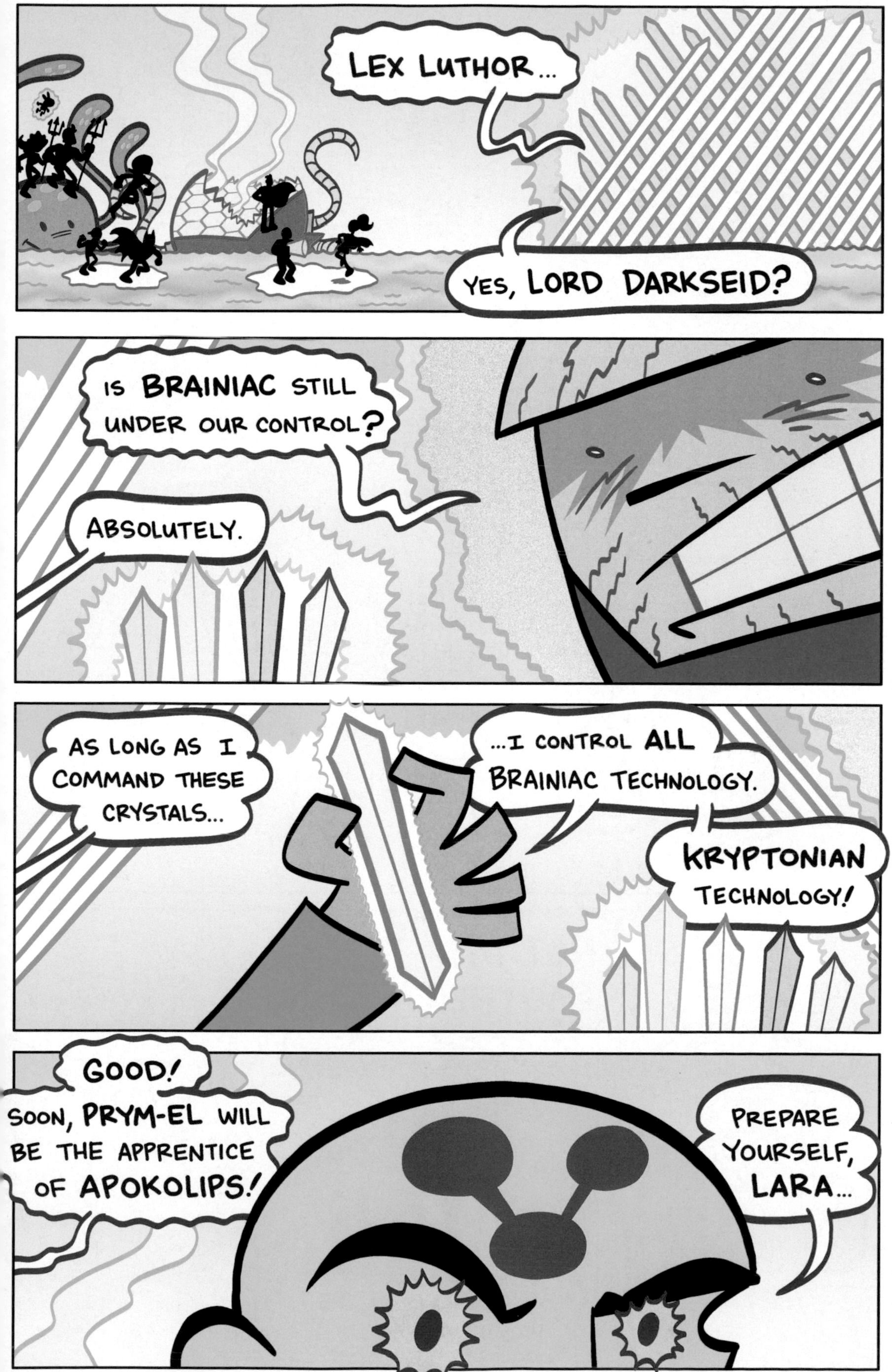
LEX LUTHOR...
YES, LORD DARKSEID?
IS BRAINIAC STILL UNDER OUR CONTROL?
ABSOLUTELY.
AS LONG AS I COMMAND THESE CRYSTALS...
...I CONTROL ALL BRAINIAC TECHNOLOGY.
KRYPTONIAN TECHNOLOGY!
GOOD!
SOON, PRYM-EL WILL BE THE APPRENTICE OF APOKOLIPS!
PREPARE YOURSELF, LARA...

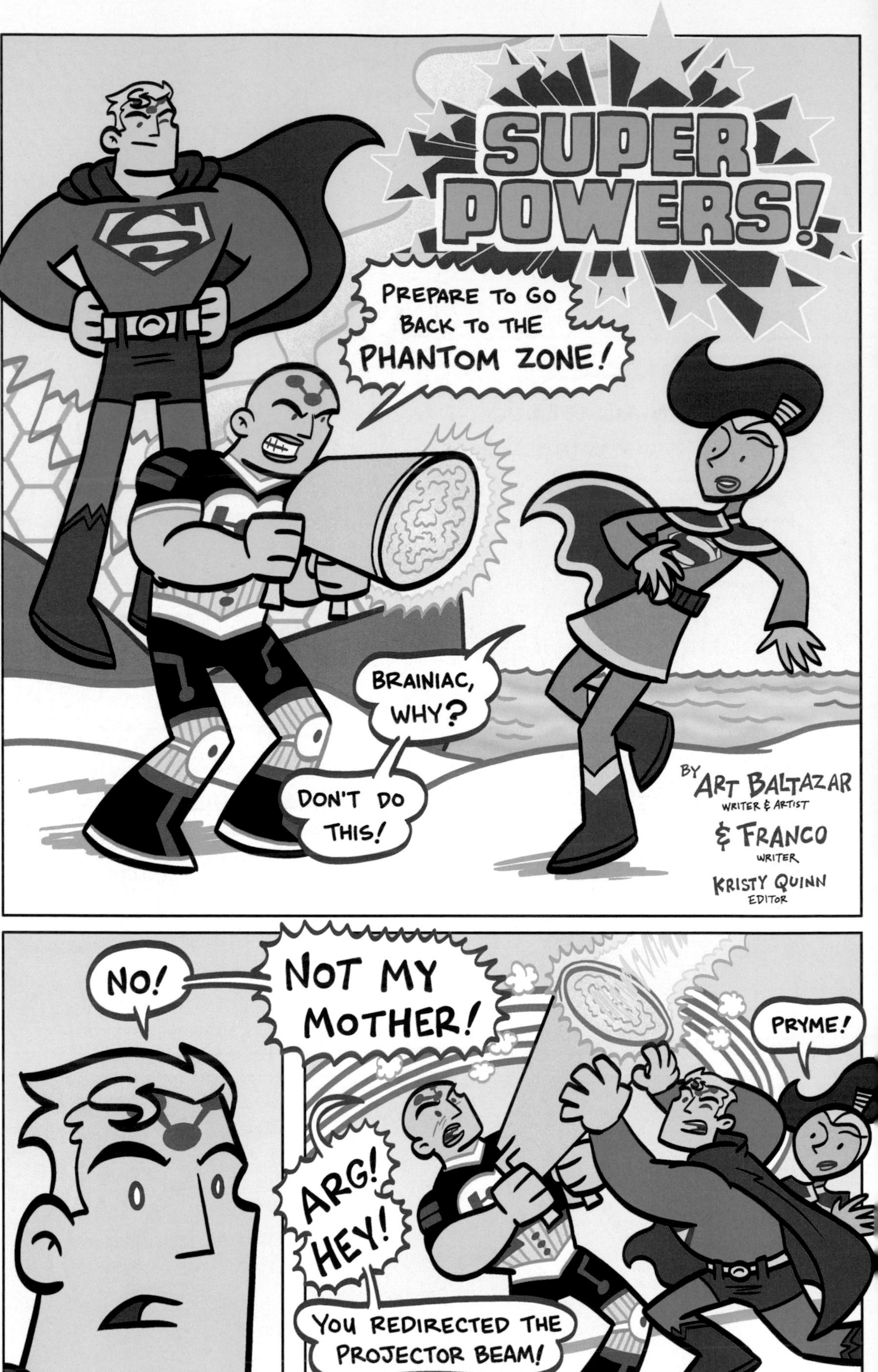
SUPER POWERS!
PREPARE TO GO BACK TO THE PHANTOM ZONE!
BRAINIAC, WHY?
DON'T DO THIS!
BY ART BALTAZAR WRITER & ARTIST
& FRANCO WRITER
KRISTY QUINN EDITOR
NO!
NOT MY MOTHER!
PRYME!
ARG!
HEY!
YOU REDIRECTED THE PROJECTOR BEAM!

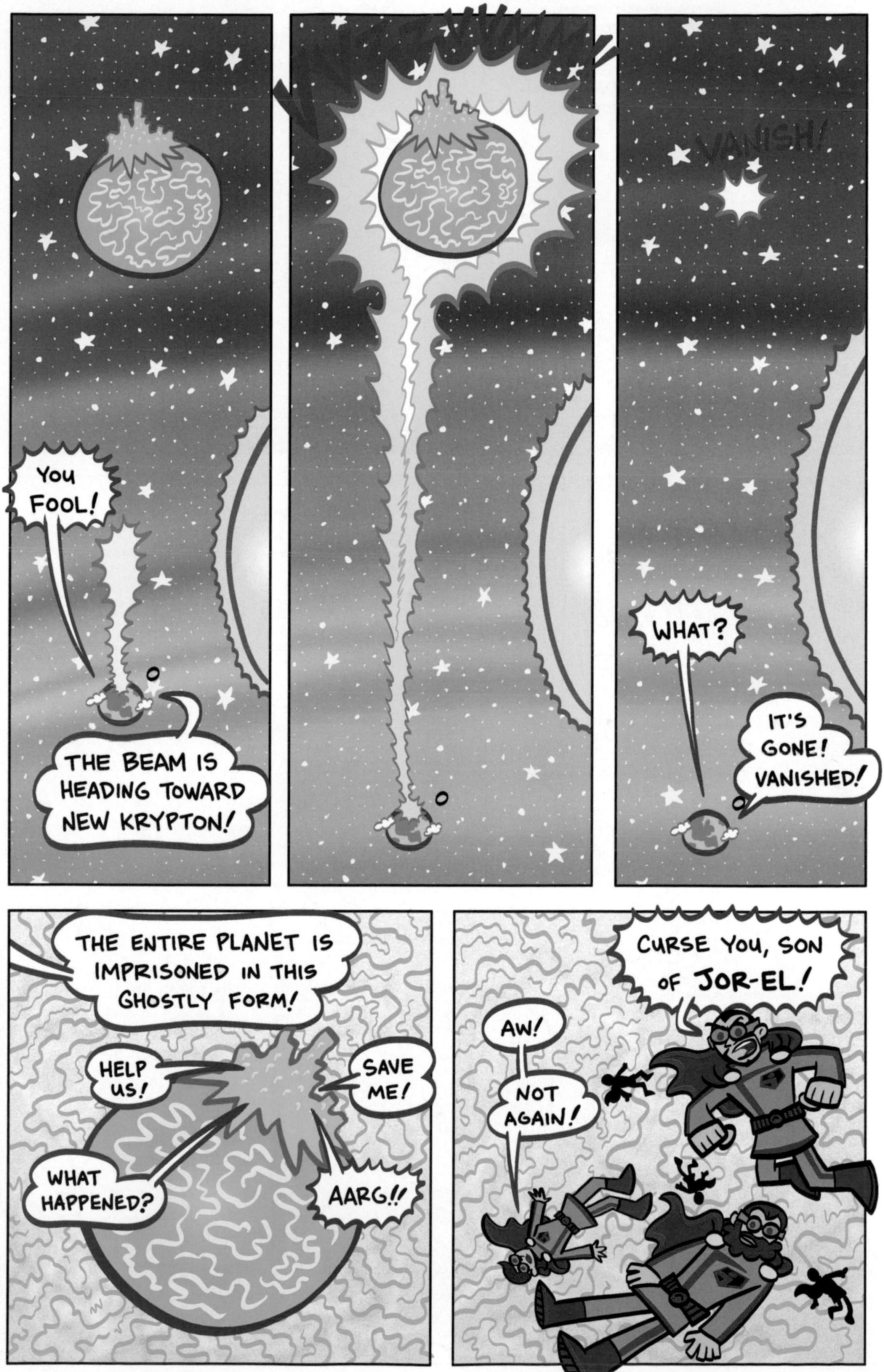
YOU FOOL!
THE BEAM IS HEADING TOWARD NEW KRYPTON!
VANISH!
WHAT?
IT'S GONE! VANISHED!
THE ENTIRE PLANET IS IMPRISONED IN THIS GHOSTLY FORM!
HELP US!
SAVE ME!
WHAT HAPPENED?
AARG!!
CURSE YOU, SON OF JOR-EL!
AW!
NOT AGAIN!

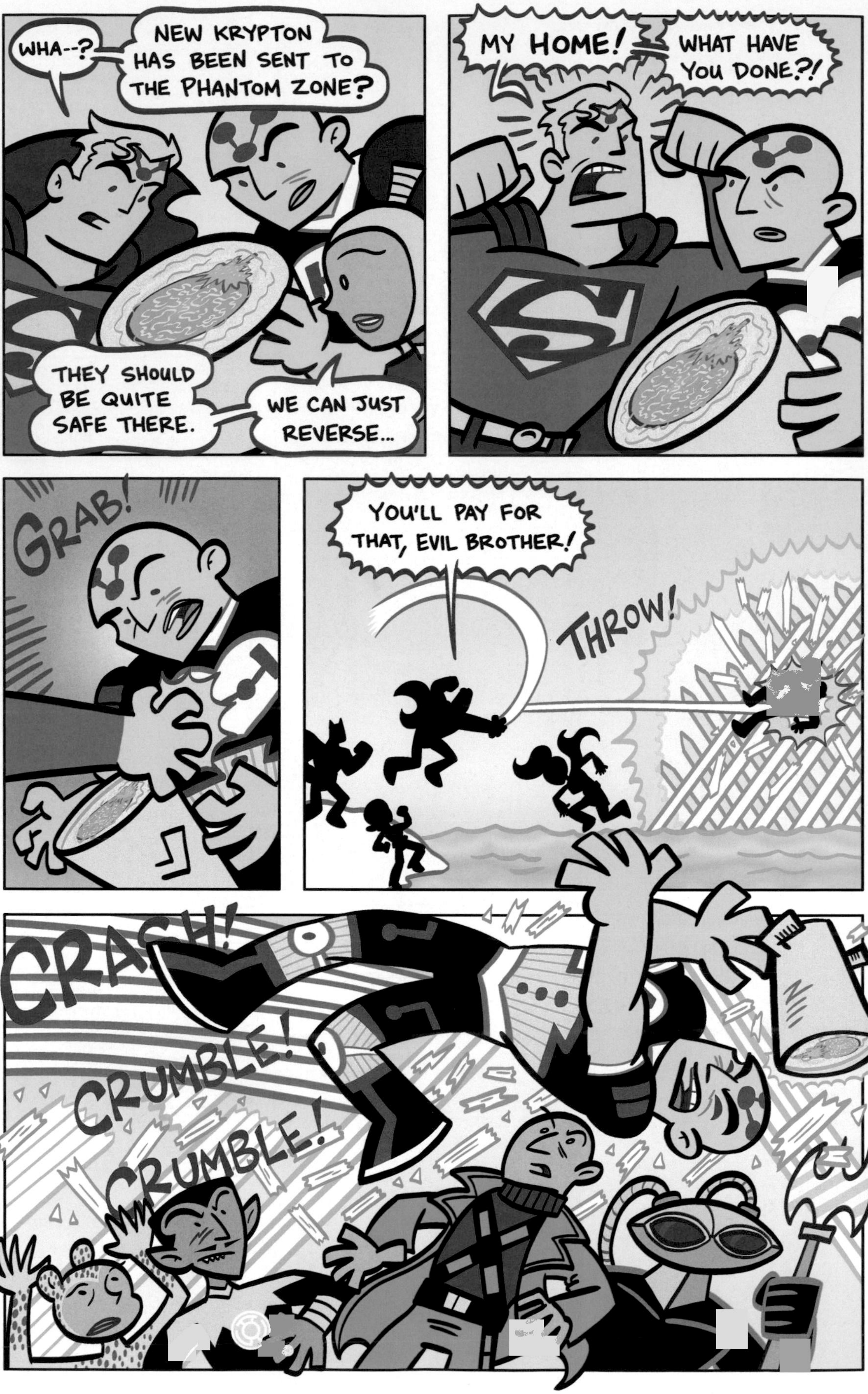
WHA--?
NEW KRYPTON HAS BEEN SENT TO THE PHANTOM ZONE?
THEY SHOULD BE QUITE SAFE THERE.
WE CAN JUST REVERSE...
MY HOME!
WHAT HAVE YOU DONE?!
GRAB!
YOU'LL PAY FOR THAT, EVIL BROTHER!
THROW!
CRASH!
CRUMBLE!
CRUMBLE!

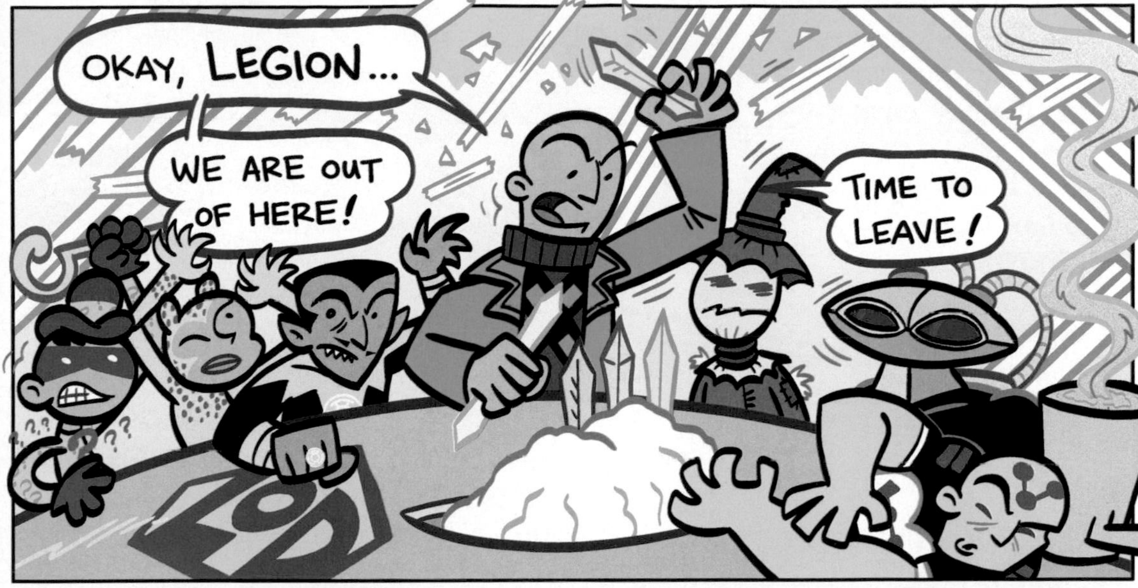
OKAY, LEGION...
WE ARE OUT OF HERE!
TIME TO LEAVE!

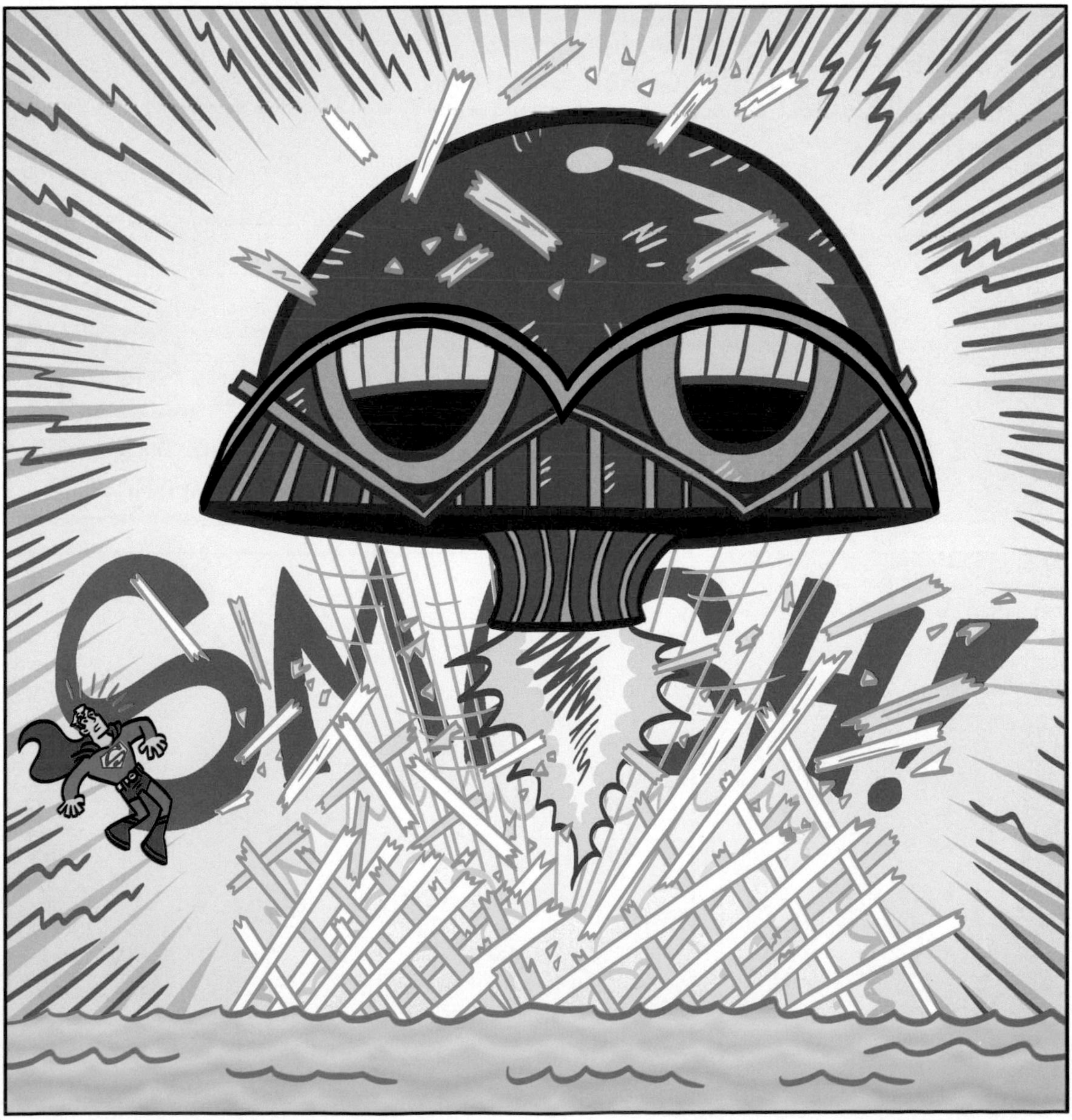
SMASH!

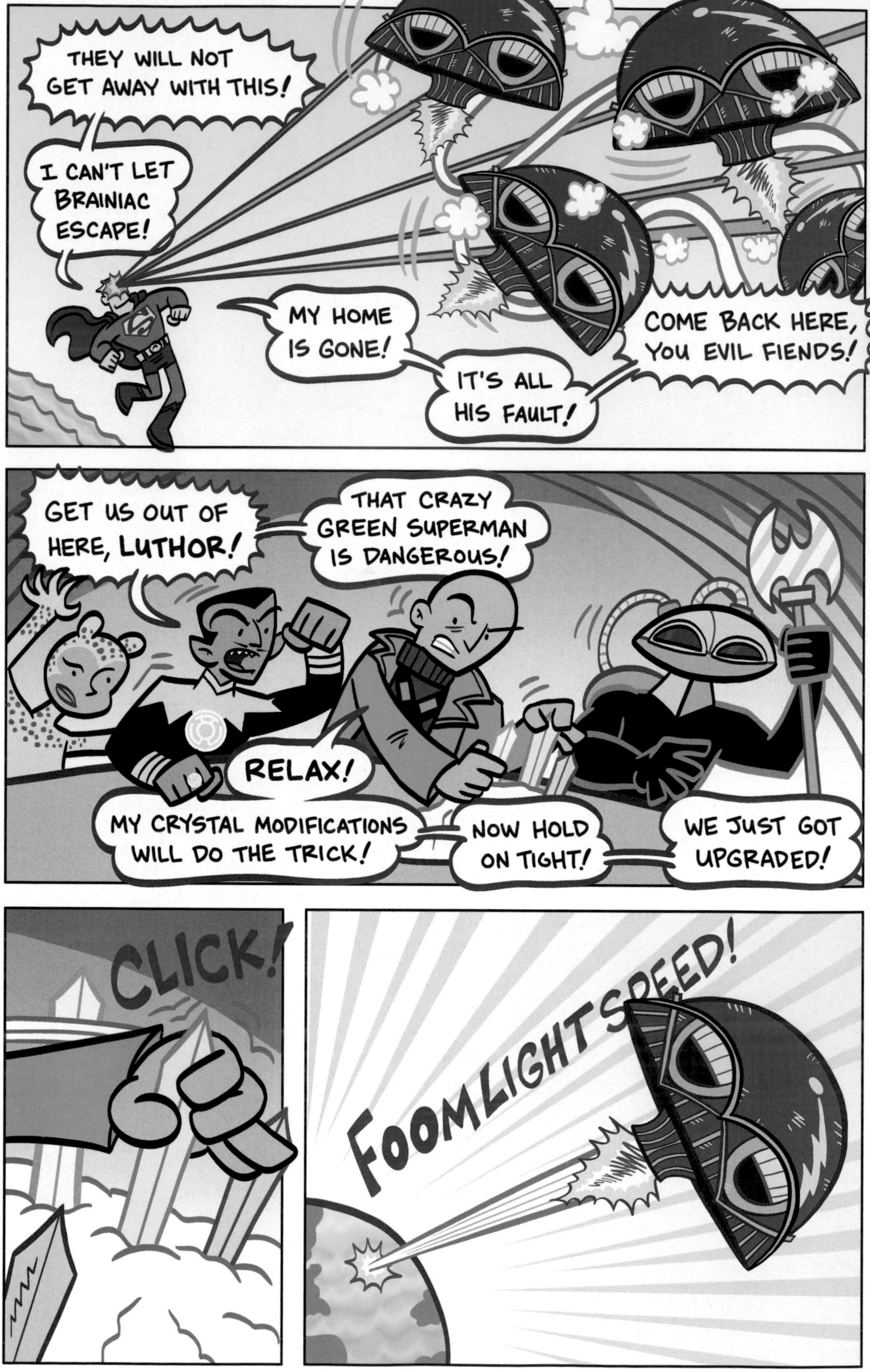
THEY WILL NOT GET AWAY WITH THIS!
I CAN'T LET BRAINIAC ESCAPE!
MY HOME IS GONE!
IT'S ALL HIS FAULT!
COME BACK HERE, YOU EVIL FIENDS!
GET US OUT OF HERE, LUTHOR!
THAT CRAZY GREEN SUPERMAN IS DANGEROUS!
RELAX!
MY CRYSTAL MODIFICATIONS WILL DO THE TRICK!
NOW HOLD ON TIGHT!
WE JUST GOT UPGRADED!
CLICK!
FOOM
LIGHTSPEED!

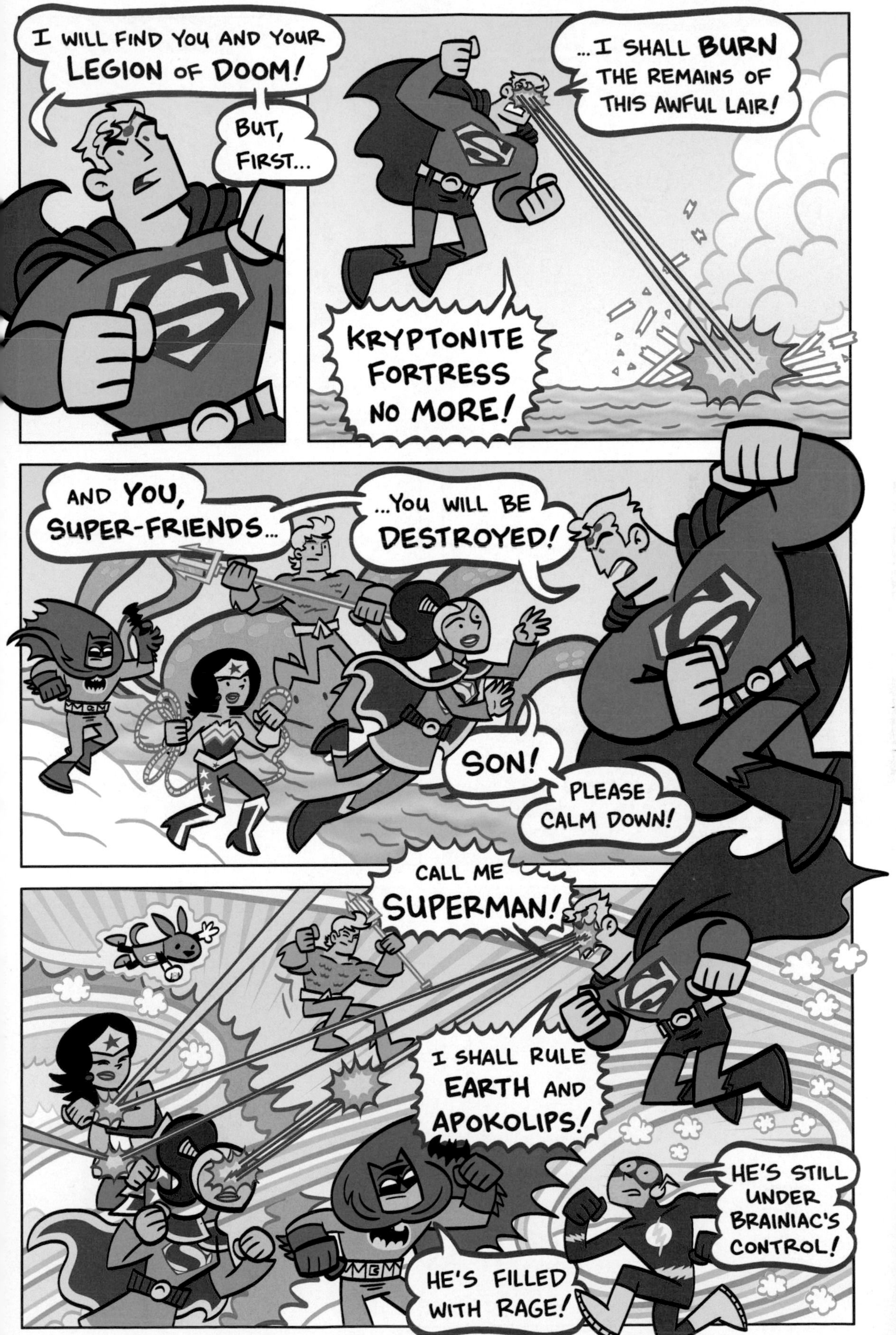
I WILL FIND YOU AND YOUR LEGION OF DOOM!
BUT, FIRST...
...I SHALL BURN THE REMAINS OF THIS AWFUL LAIR!
KRYPTONITE FORTRESS NO MORE!
AND YOU, SUPER-FRIENDS...
...YOU WILL BE DESTROYED!
SON!
PLEASE CALM DOWN!
CALL ME SUPERMAN!
I SHALL RULE EARTH AND APOKOLIPS!
HE'S STILL UNDER BRAINIAC'S CONTROL!
HE'S FILLED WITH RAGE!

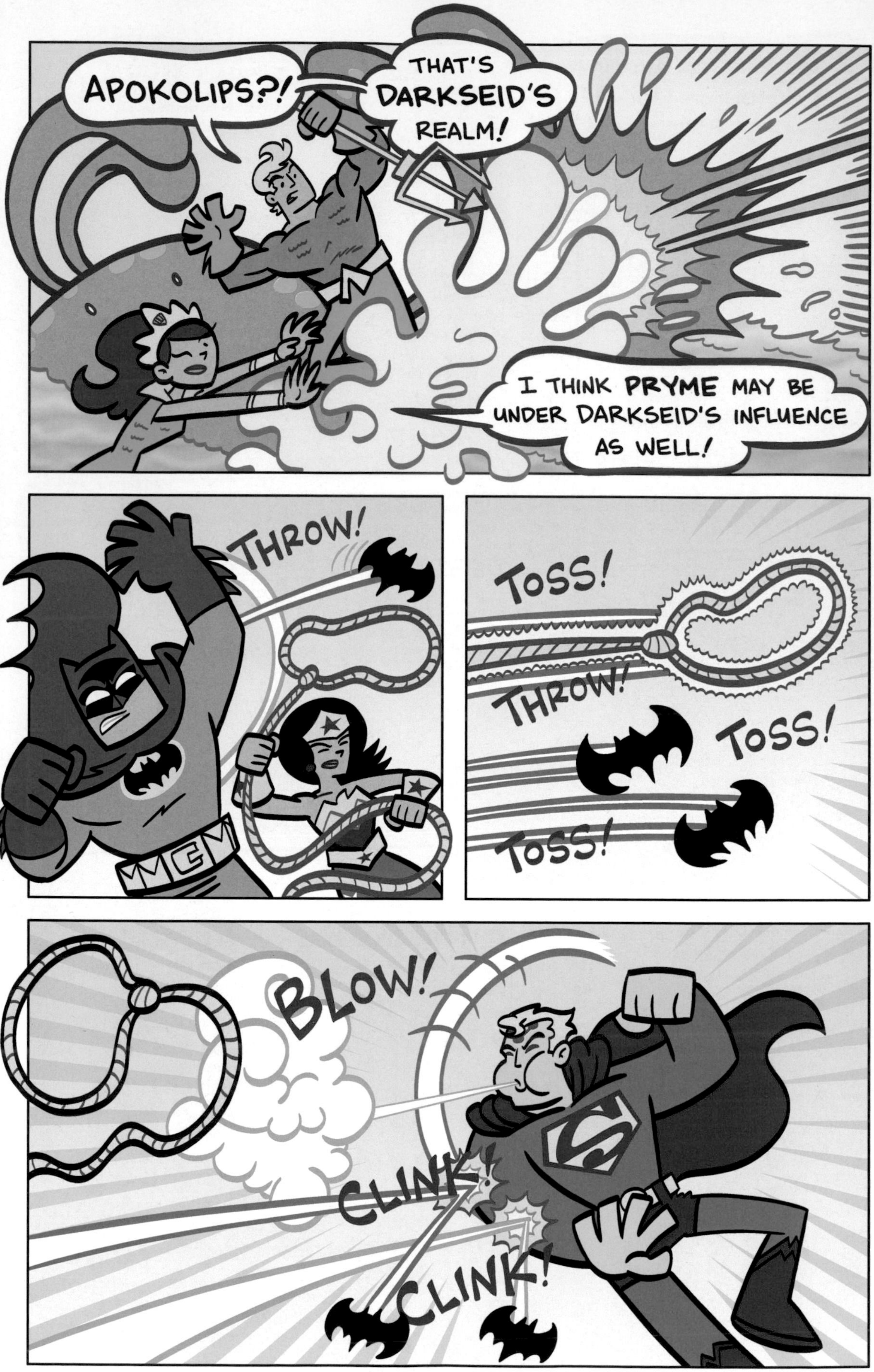
APOKOLIPS?!
THAT'S DARKSEID'S REALM!
I THINK PRYME MAY BE UNDER DARKSEID'S INFLUENCE AS WELL!
THROW!
TOSS!
THROW!
TOSS!
TOSS!
BLOW!
CLINK!
CLINK!

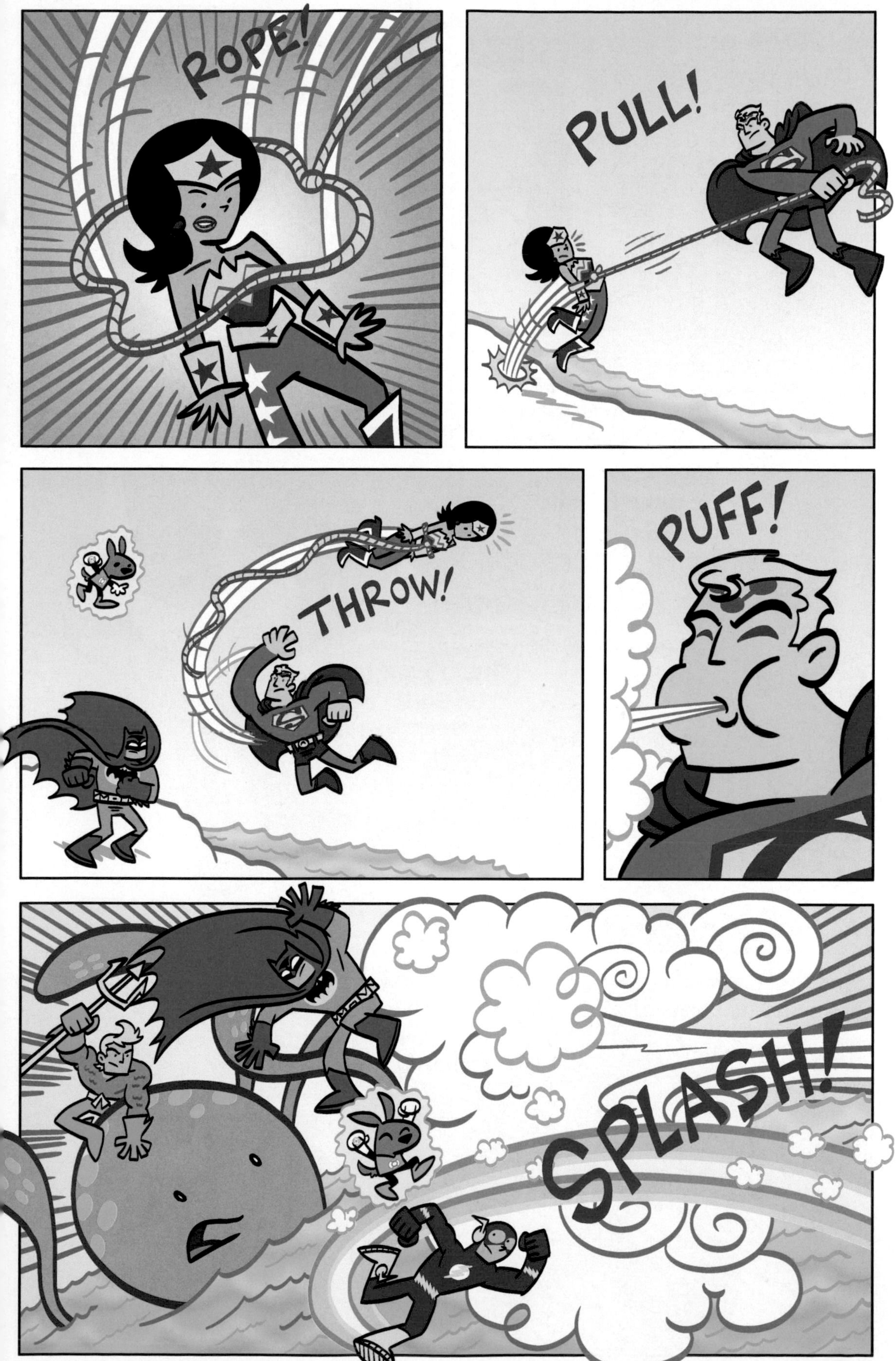

ROPE!
PULL!
THROW!
PUFF!
SPLASH!

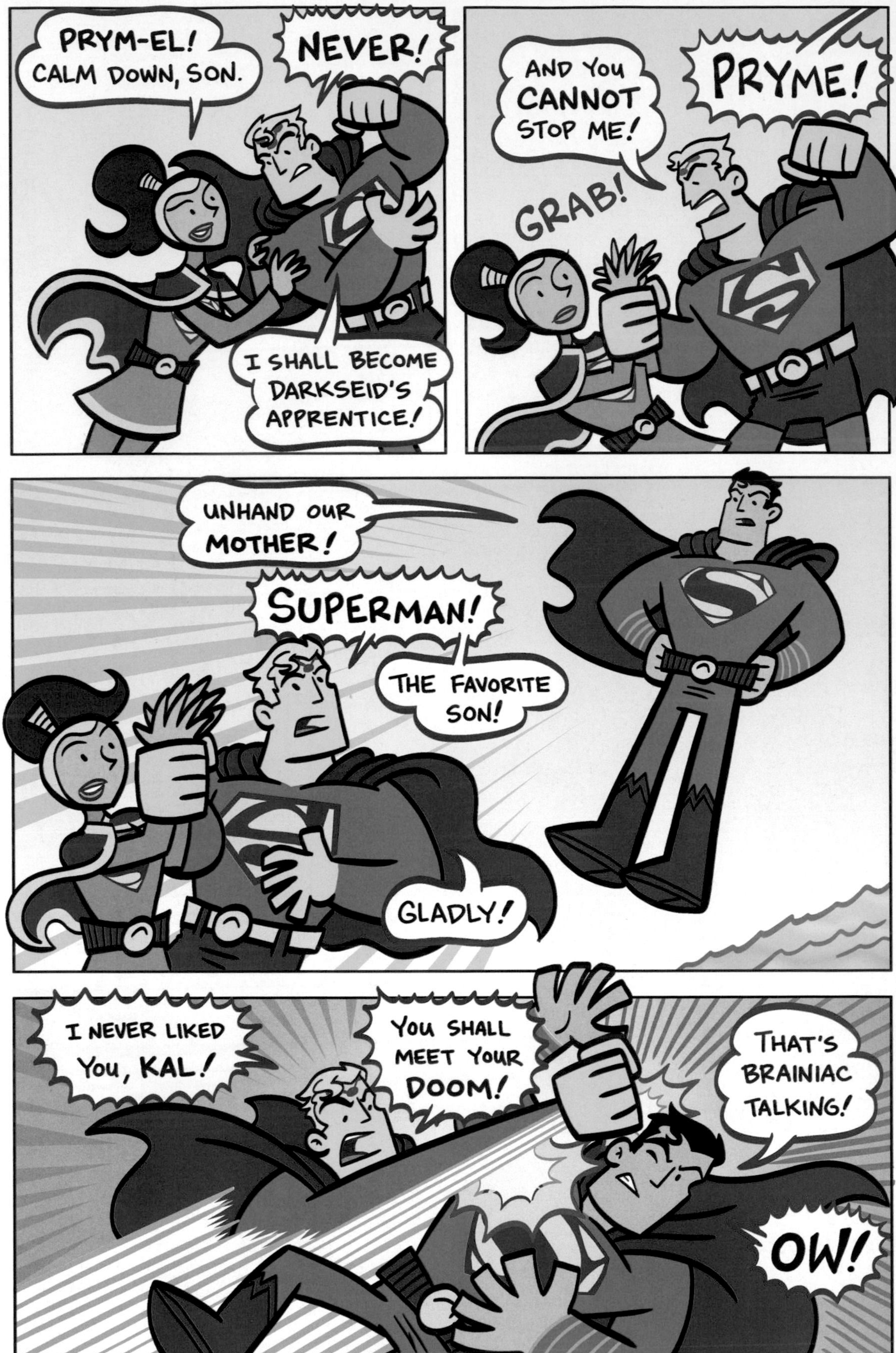
PRYM-EL! CALM DOWN, SON.
NEVER!
I SHALL BECOME DARKSEID'S APPRENTICE!
AND YOU CANNOT STOP ME!
PRYME!
GRAB!
UNHAND OUR MOTHER!
SUPERMAN!
THE FAVORITE SON!
GLADLY!
I NEVER LIKED YOU, KAL!
YOU SHALL MEET YOUR DOOM!
THAT'S BRAINIAC TALKING!
OW!

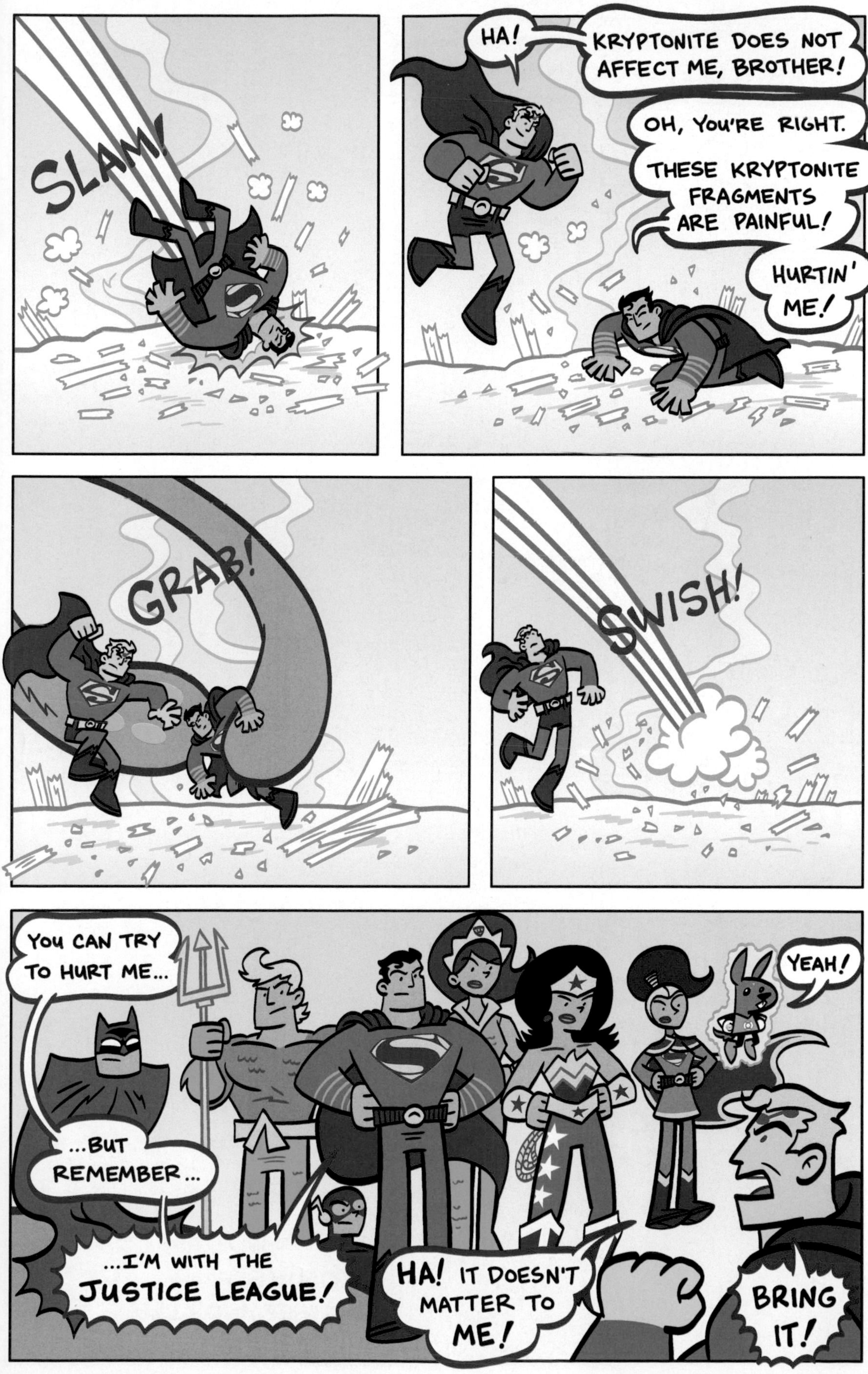
SLAM!
HA!
KRYPTONITE DOES NOT AFFECT ME, BROTHER!
OH, YOU'RE RIGHT.
THESE KRYPTONITE FRAGMENTS ARE PAINFUL!
HURTIN' ME!
GRAB!
SWISH!
YOU CAN TRY TO HURT ME...
...BUT REMEMBER...
...I'M WITH THE JUSTICE LEAGUE!
YEAH!
HA! IT DOESN'T MATTER TO ME!
BRING IT!

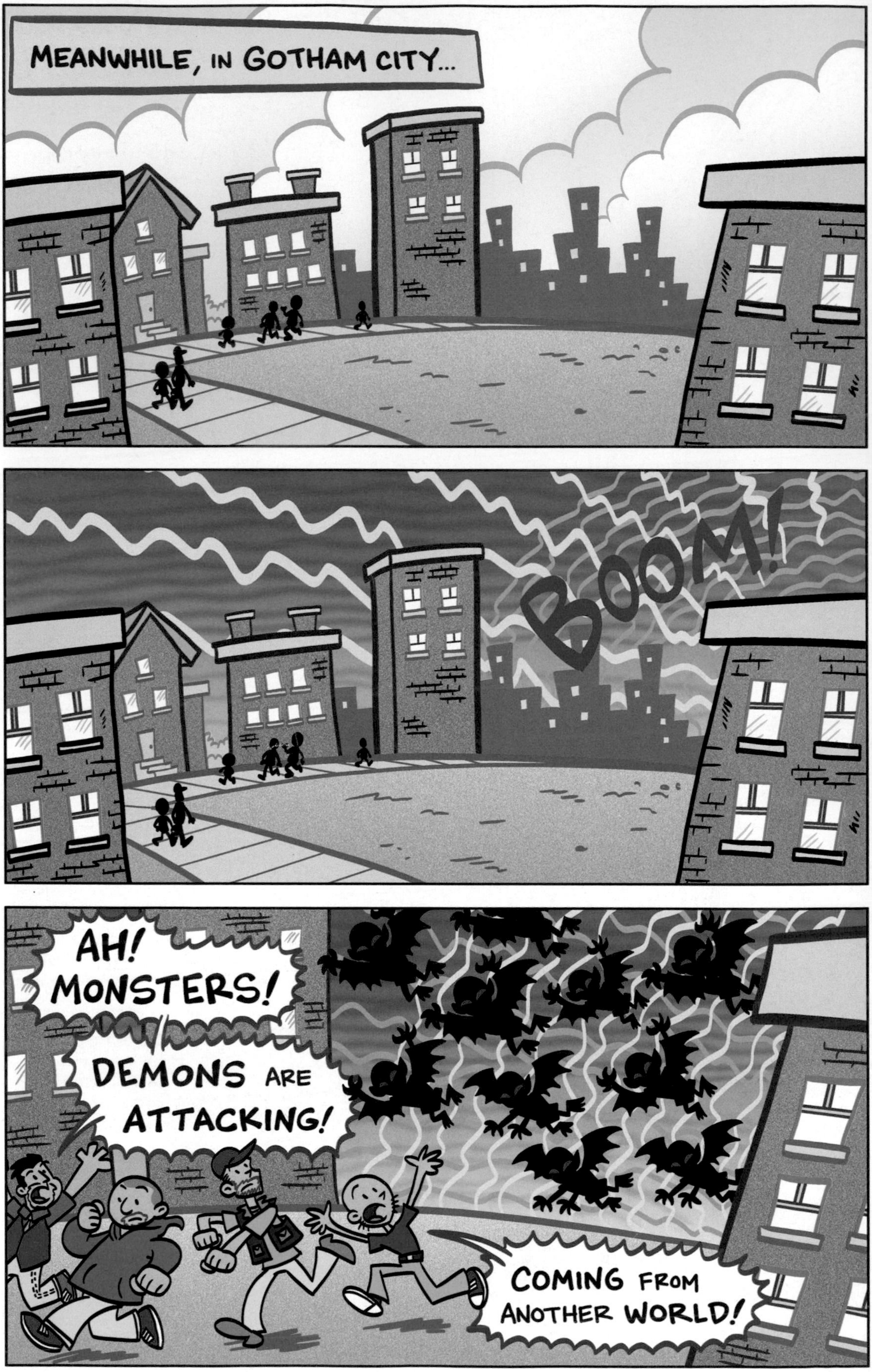
MEANWHILE, IN GOTHAM CITY...
BOOM!
AH! MONSTERS!
DEMONS ARE ATTACKING!
COMING FROM ANOTHER WORLD!

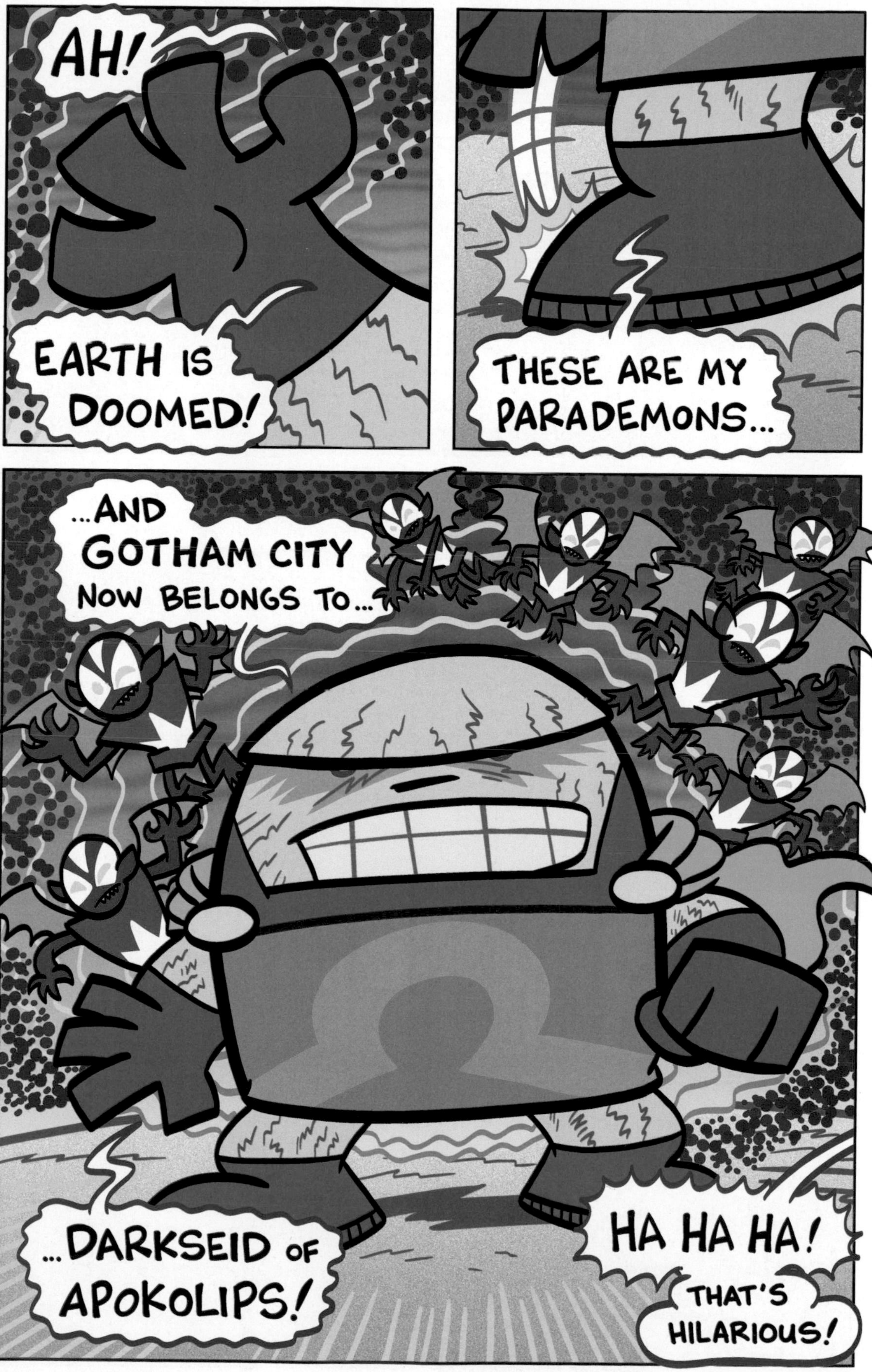
AH!
EARTH IS DOOMED!
THESE ARE MY PARADEMONS...
...AND GOTHAM CITY NOW BELONGS TO...
...DARKSEID OF APOKOLIPS!
HA HA HA!
THAT'S HILARIOUS!

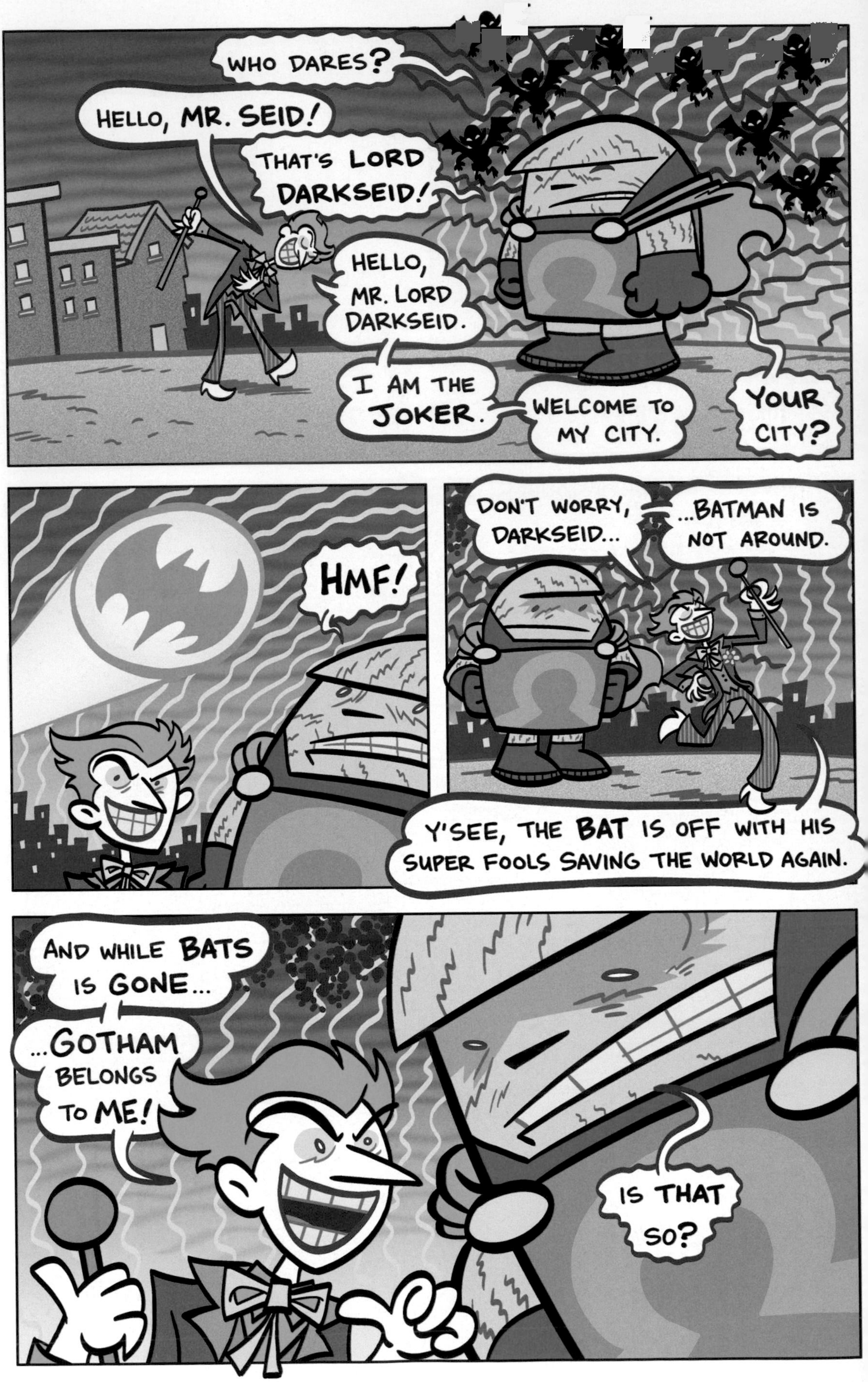
WHO DARES?
HELLO, MR. SEID!
THAT'S LORD DARKSEID!
HELLO, MR. LORD DARKSEID.
I AM THE JOKER.
WELCOME TO MY CITY.
YOUR CITY?
HMF!
DON'T WORRY, DARKSEID...
...BATMAN IS NOT AROUND.
Y'SEE, THE BAT IS OFF WITH HIS SUPER FOOLS SAVING THE WORLD AGAIN.
AND WHILE BATS IS GONE...
...GOTHAM BELONGS TO ME!
IS THAT SO?

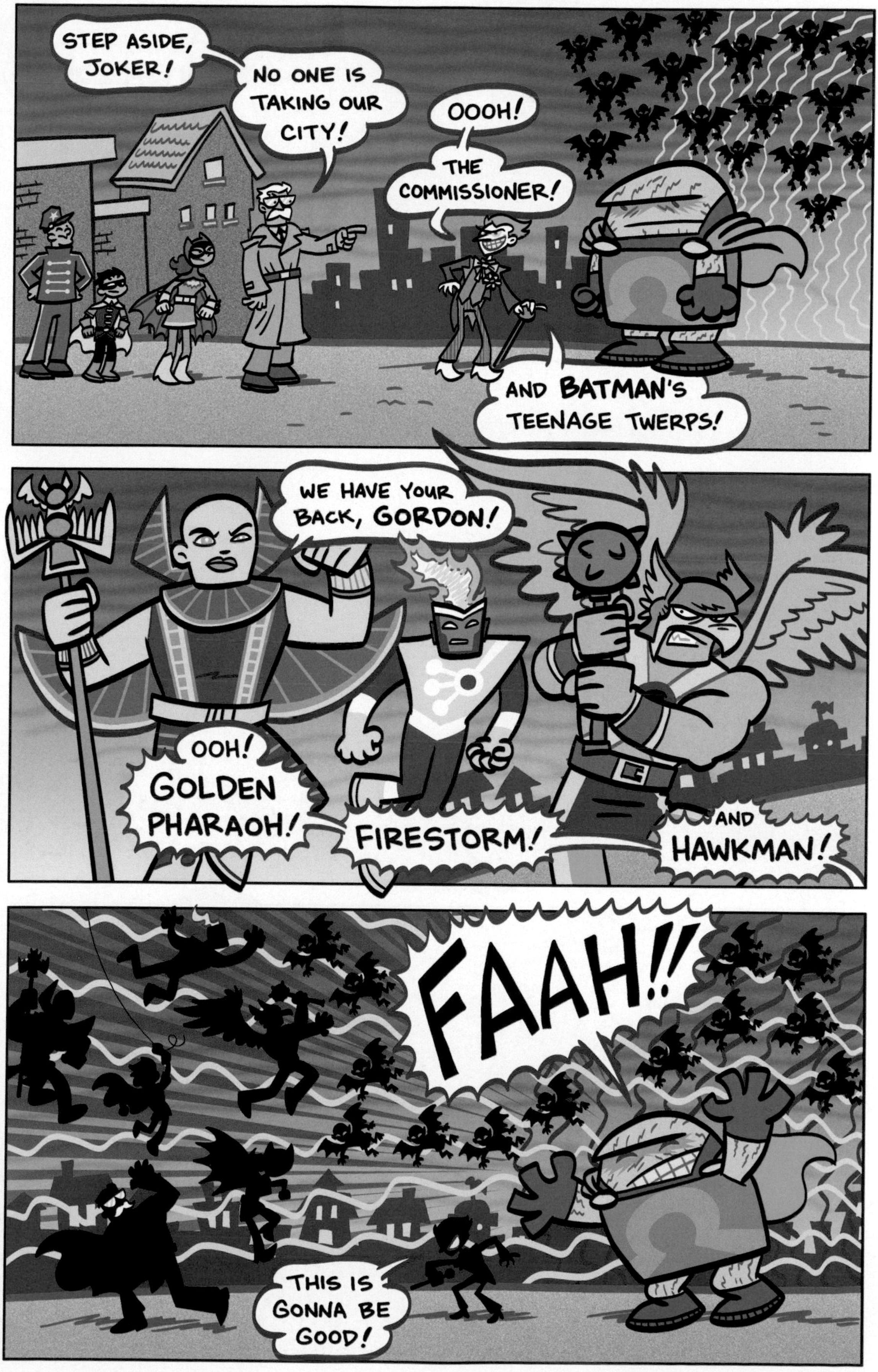
STEP ASIDE, JOKER!
NO ONE IS TAKING OUR CITY!
OOOH!
THE COMMISSIONER!
AND BATMAN'S TEENAGE TWERPS!
WE HAVE YOUR BACK, GORDON!
OOH! GOLDEN PHARAOH!
FIRESTORM!
AND HAWKMAN!
FAAH!!
THIS IS GONNA BE GOOD!

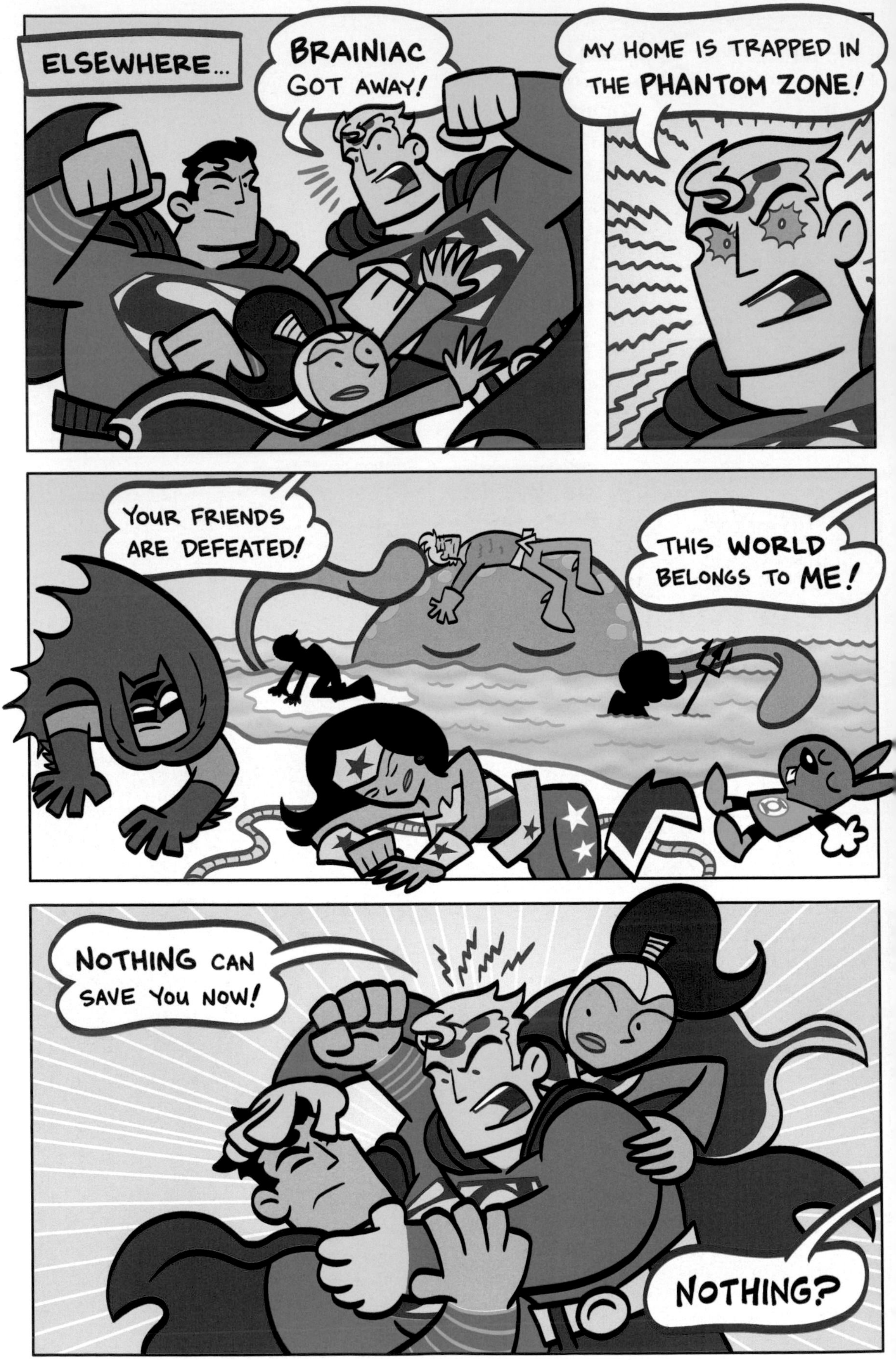
ELSEWHERE...
BRAINIAC GOT AWAY!
MY HOME IS TRAPPED IN THE PHANTOM ZONE!
YOUR FRIENDS ARE DEFEATED!
THIS WORLD BELONGS TO ME!
NOTHING CAN SAVE YOU NOW!
NOTHING?

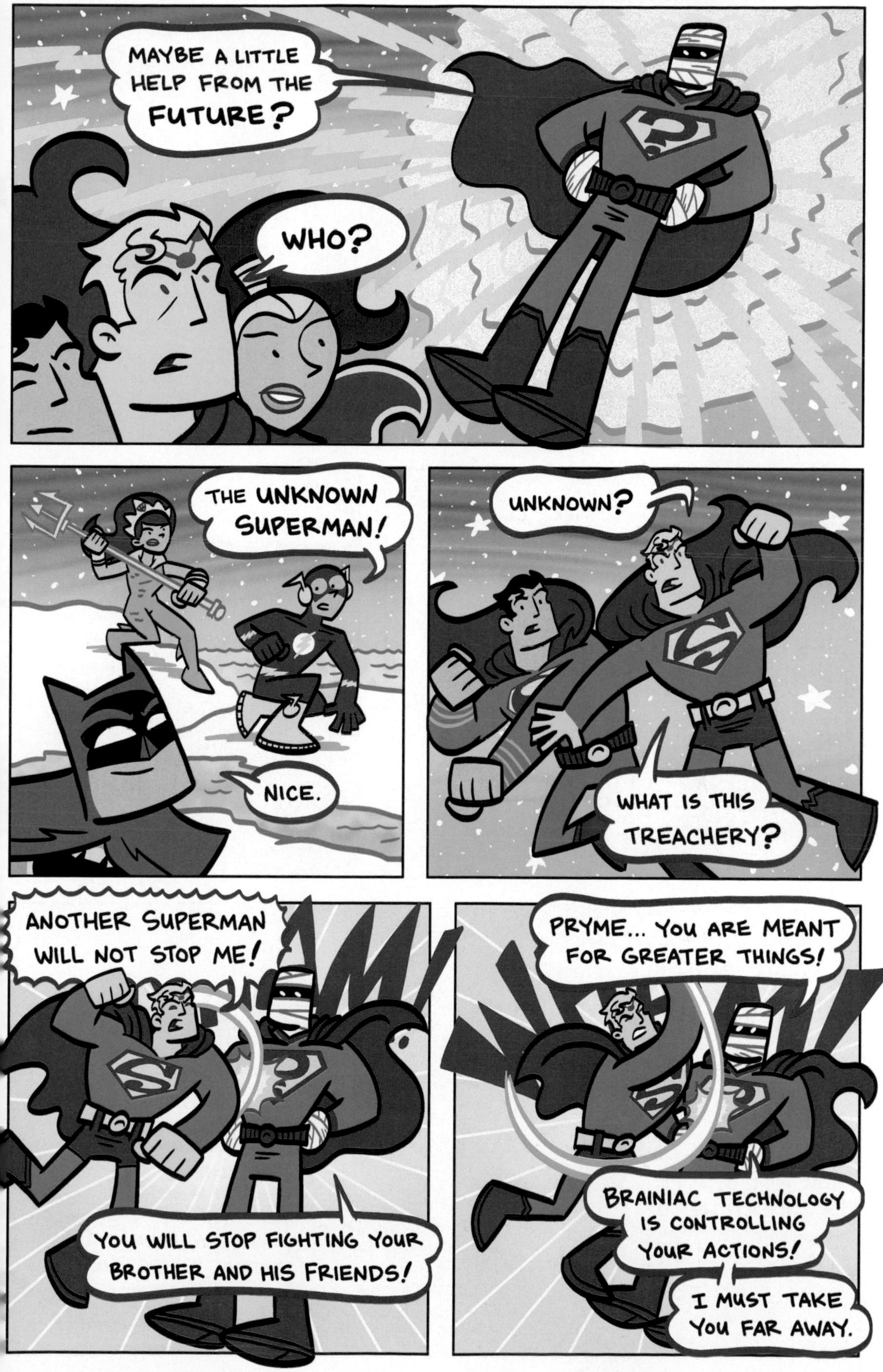
MAYBE A LITTLE HELP FROM THE FUTURE?
WHO?
THE UNKNOWN SUPERMAN!
NICE.
UNKNOWN?
WHAT IS THIS TREACHERY?
ANOTHER SUPERMAN WILL NOT STOP ME!
YOU WILL STOP FIGHTING YOUR BROTHER AND HIS FRIENDS!
PRYME... YOU ARE MEANT FOR GREATER THINGS!
BRAINIAC TECHNOLOGY IS CONTROLLING YOUR ACTIONS!
I MUST TAKE YOU FAR AWAY.

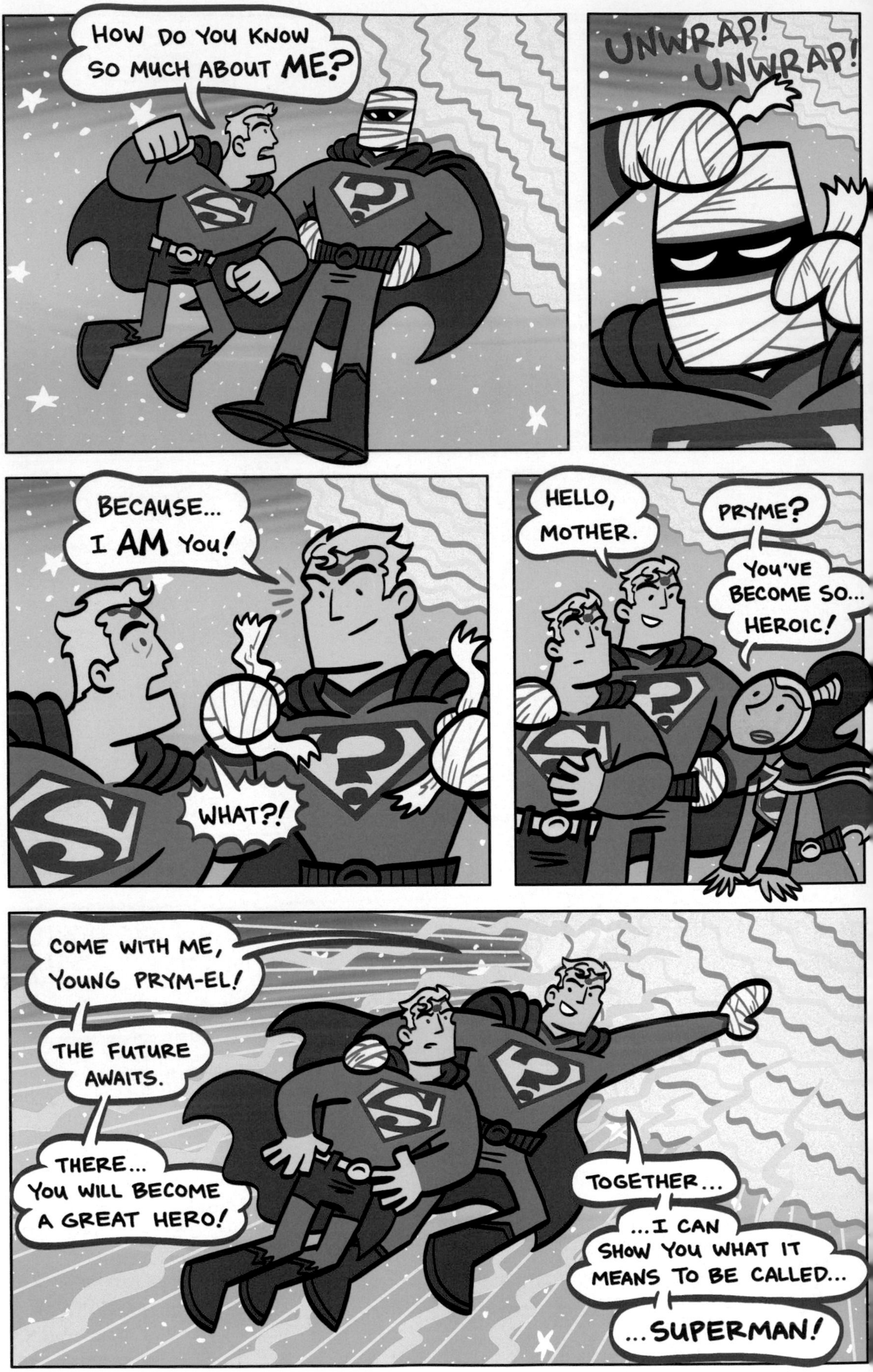
HOW DO YOU KNOW SO MUCH ABOUT ME?
UNWRAP! UNWRAP!
BECAUSE... I AM YOU!
WHAT?!
HELLO, MOTHER.
PRYME?
YOU'VE BECOME SO... HEROIC!
COME WITH ME, YOUNG PRYM-EL!
THE FUTURE AWAITS.
THERE... YOU WILL BECOME A GREAT HERO!
TOGETHER...
...I CAN SHOW YOU WHAT IT MEANS TO BE CALLED...
...SUPERMAN!

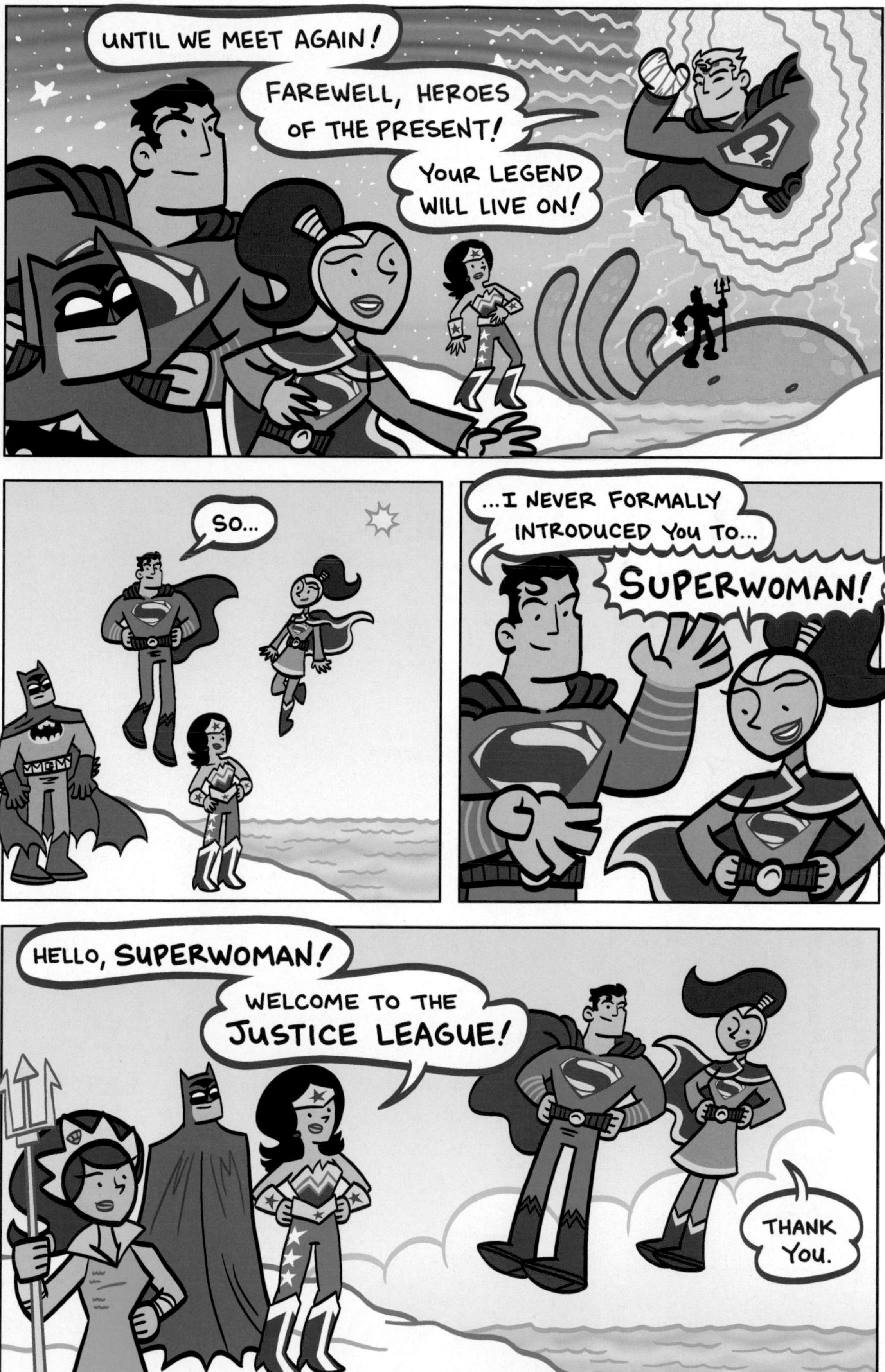
UNTIL WE MEET AGAIN!
FAREWELL, HEROES OF THE PRESENT!
YOUR LEGEND WILL LIVE ON!
SO...
...I NEVER FORMALLY INTRODUCED YOU TO...
SUPERWOMAN!
HELLO, SUPERWOMAN!
WELCOME TO THE JUSTICE LEAGUE!
THANK YOU.

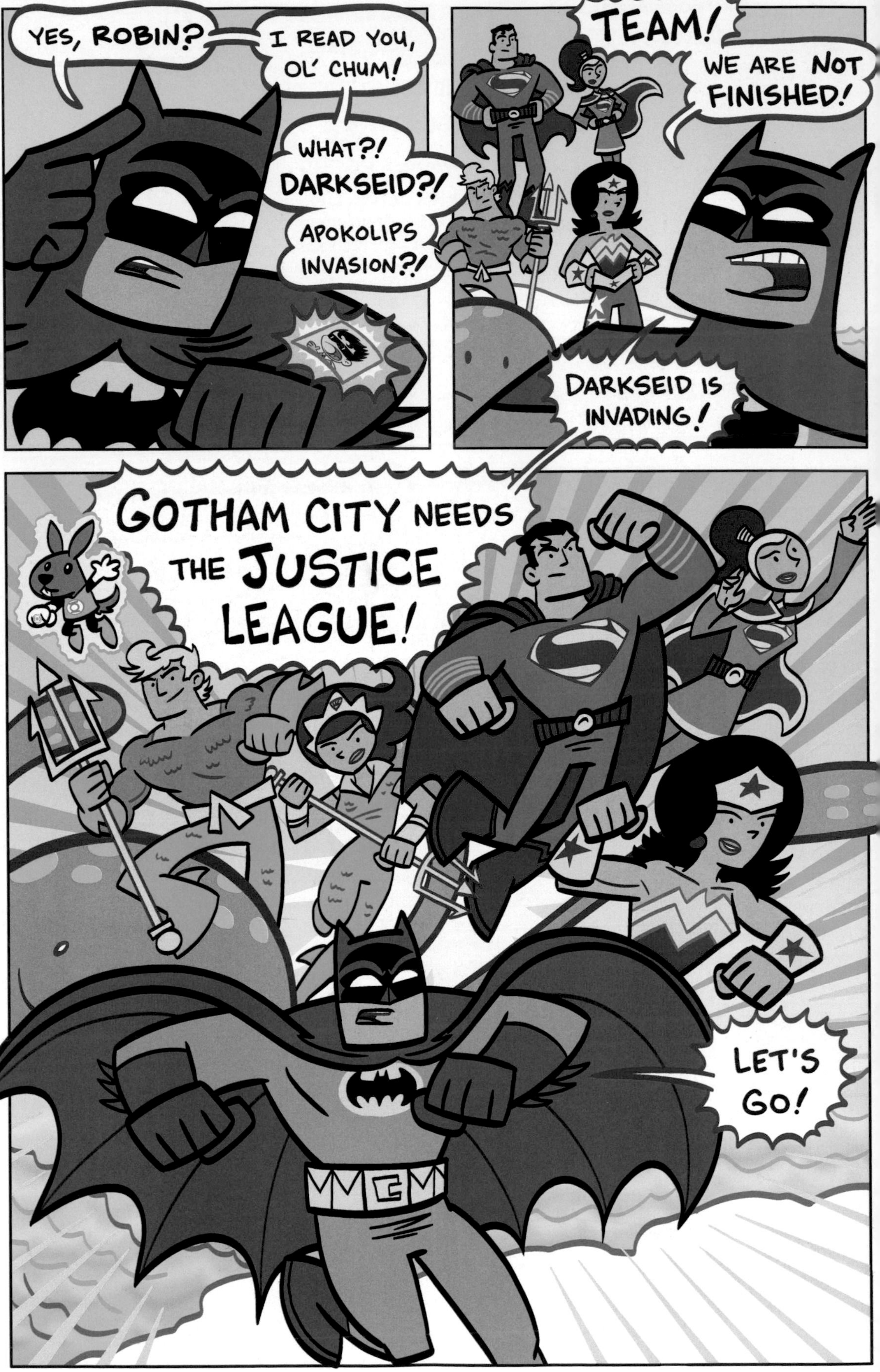
YES, ROBIN?
I READ YOU, OL' CHUM!
WHAT?! DARKSEID?!
APOKOLIPS INVASION?!
TEAM!
WE ARE NOT FINISHED!
DARKSEID IS INVADING!
GOTHAM CITY NEEDS THE JUSTICE LEAGUE!
LET'S GO!

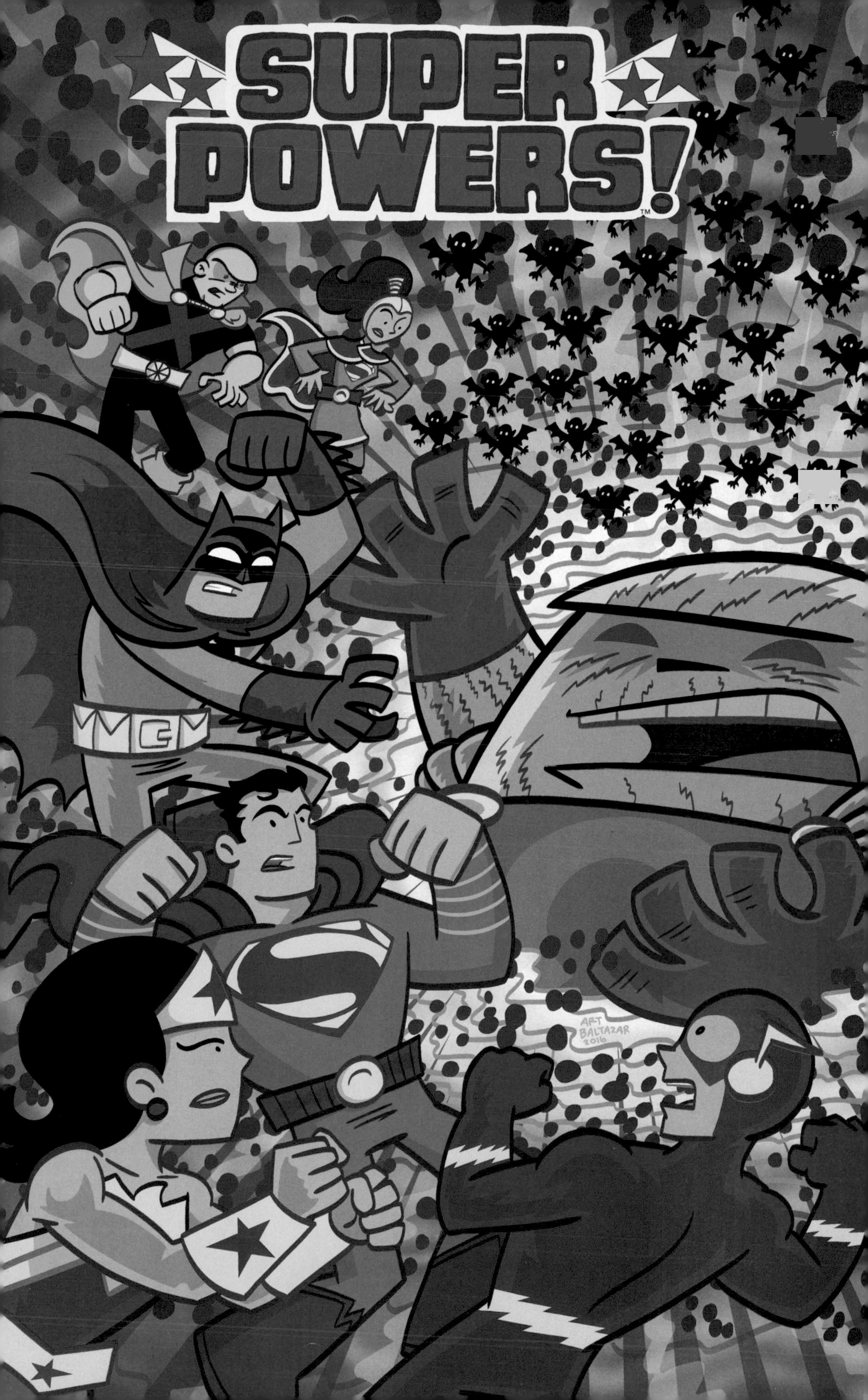
SUPER POWERS!™
ART BALTAZAR 2016

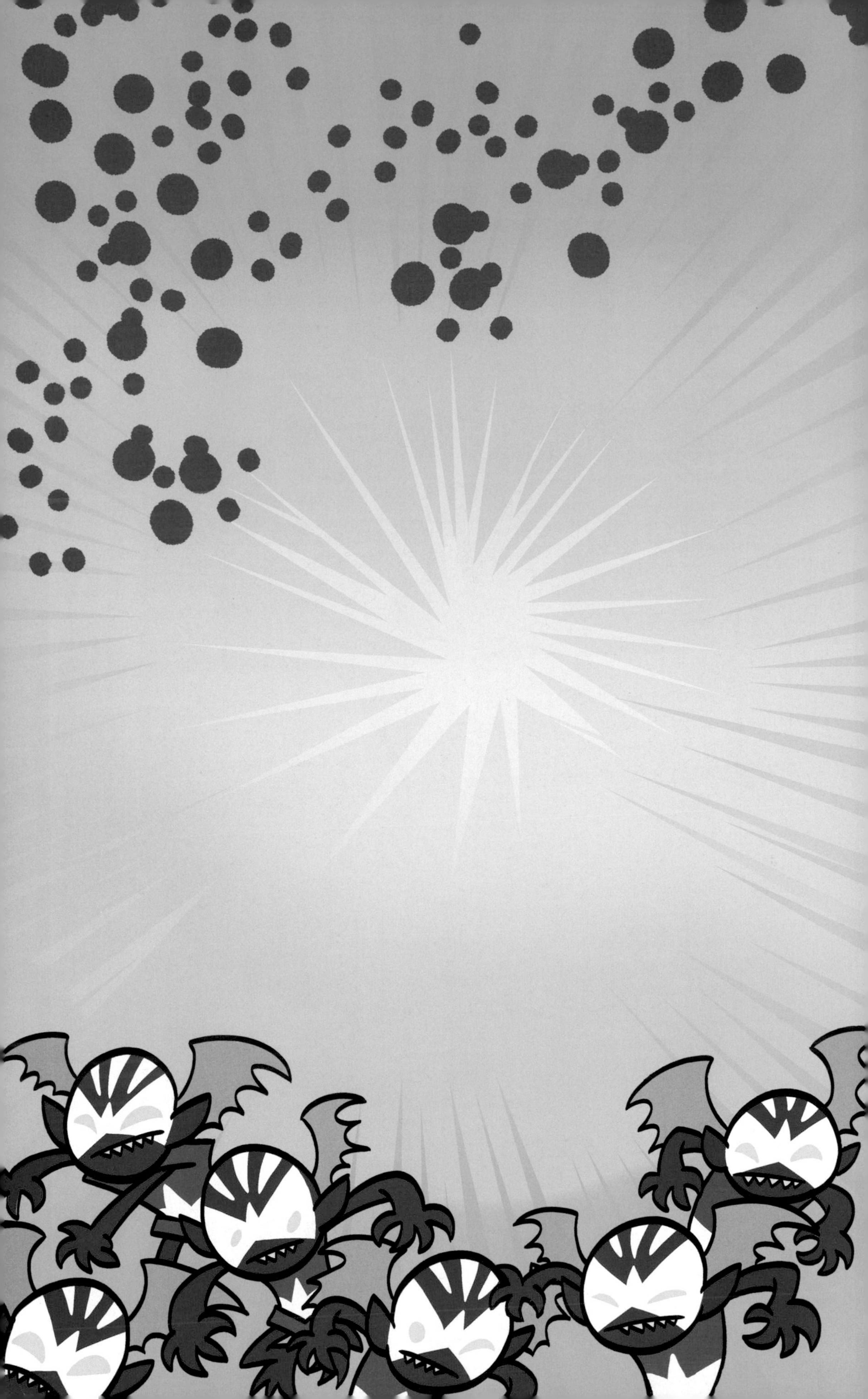

DC COMICS PROUDLY PRESENTS...

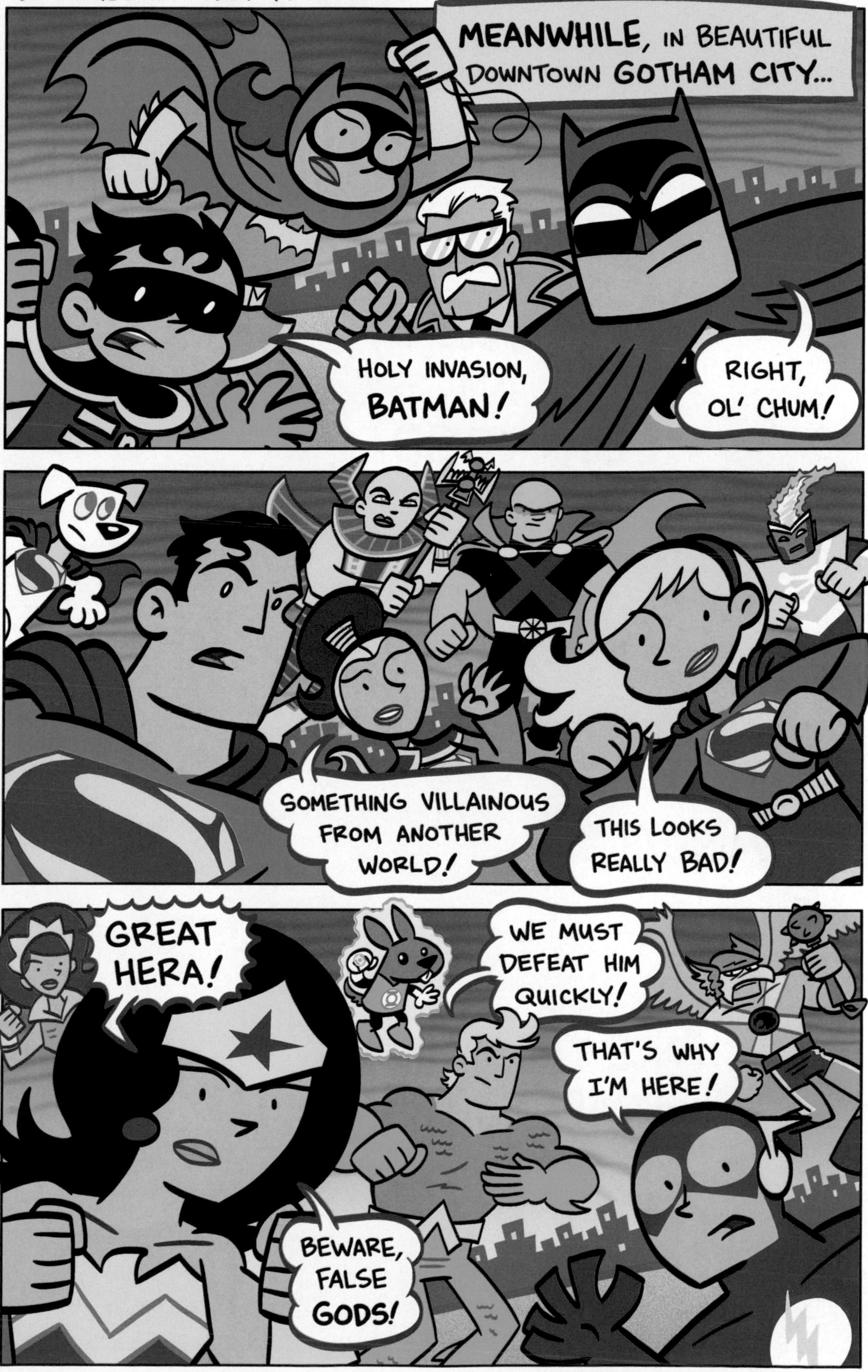

MEANWHILE, IN BEAUTIFUL DOWNTOWN GOTHAM CITY...
HOLY INVASION, BATMAN!
RIGHT, OL' CHUM!
SOMETHING VILLAINOUS FROM ANOTHER WORLD!
THIS LOOKS REALLY BAD!
GREAT HERA!
WE MUST DEFEAT HIM QUICKLY!
THAT'S WHY I'M HERE!
BEWARE, FALSE GODS!

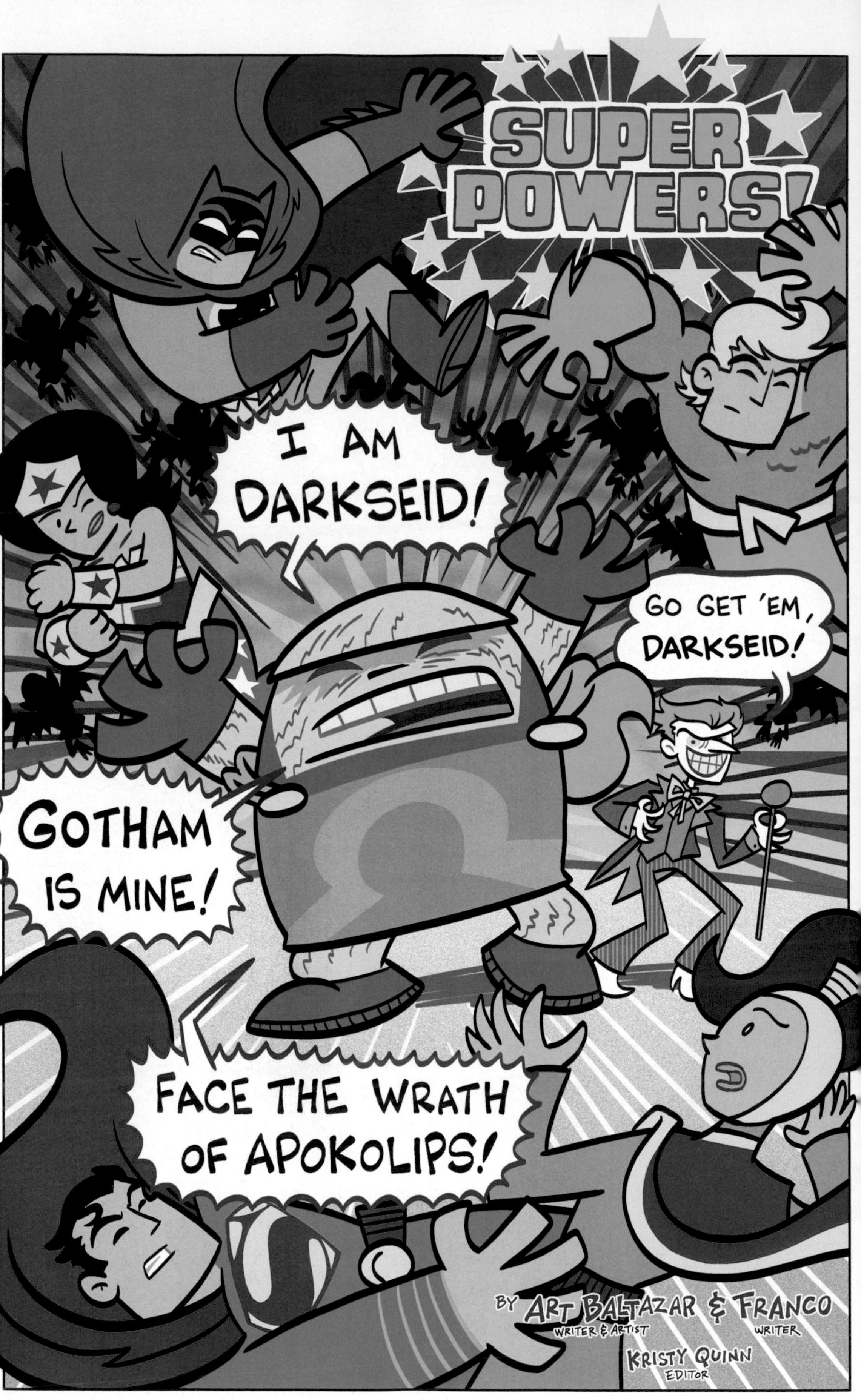
SUPER POWERS!
I AM DARKSEID!
GO GET 'EM, DARKSEID!
GOTHAM IS MINE!
FACE THE WRATH OF APOKOLIPS!
BY ART BALTAZAR WRITER & ARTIST & FRANCO WRITER
KRISTY QUINN EDITOR

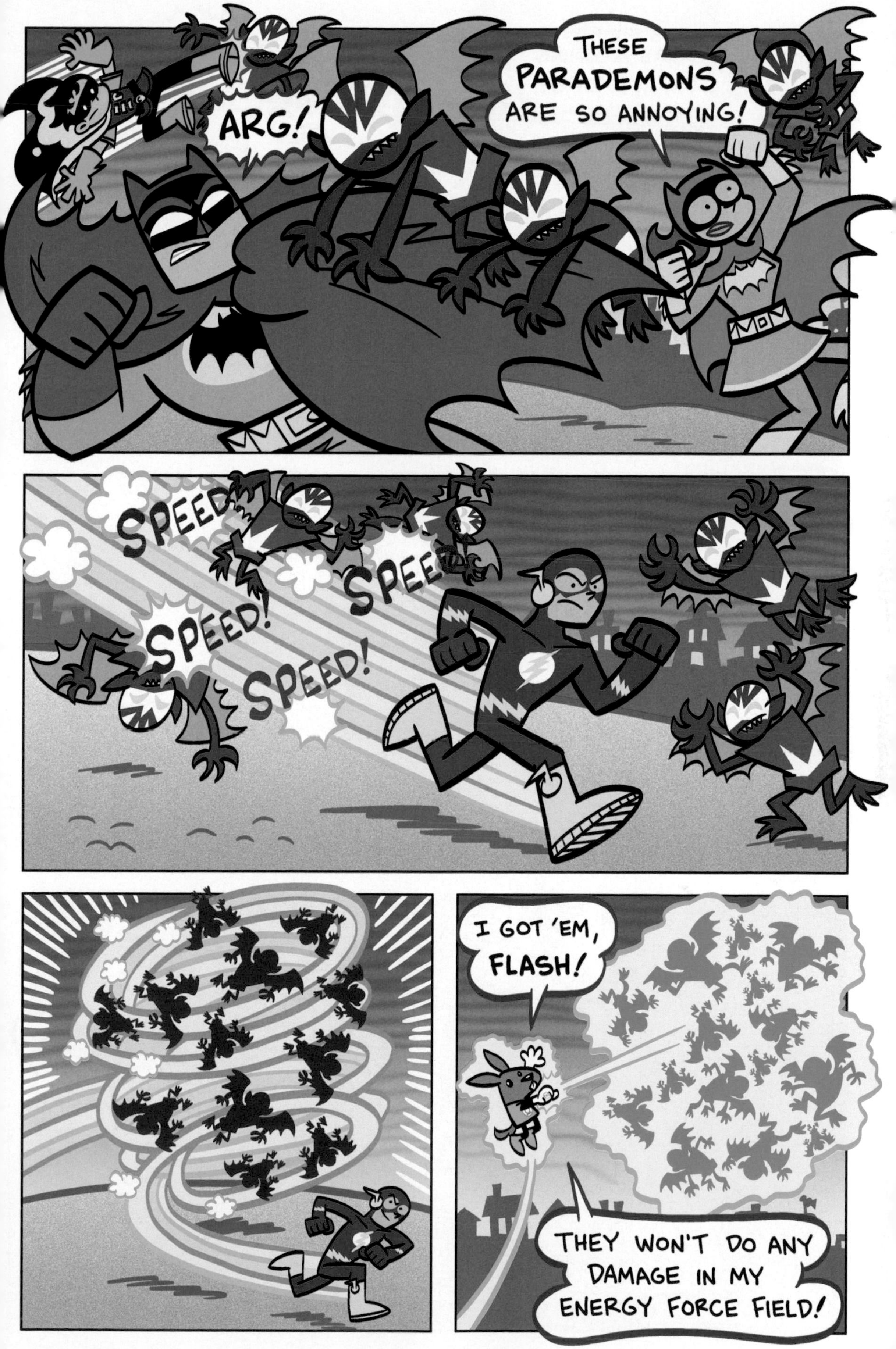
ARG!
THESE PARADEMONS ARE SO ANNOYING!
SPEED!
SPEED!
SPEED!
SPEED!
I GOT 'EM, FLASH!
THEY WON'T DO ANY DAMAGE IN MY ENERGY FORCE FIELD!

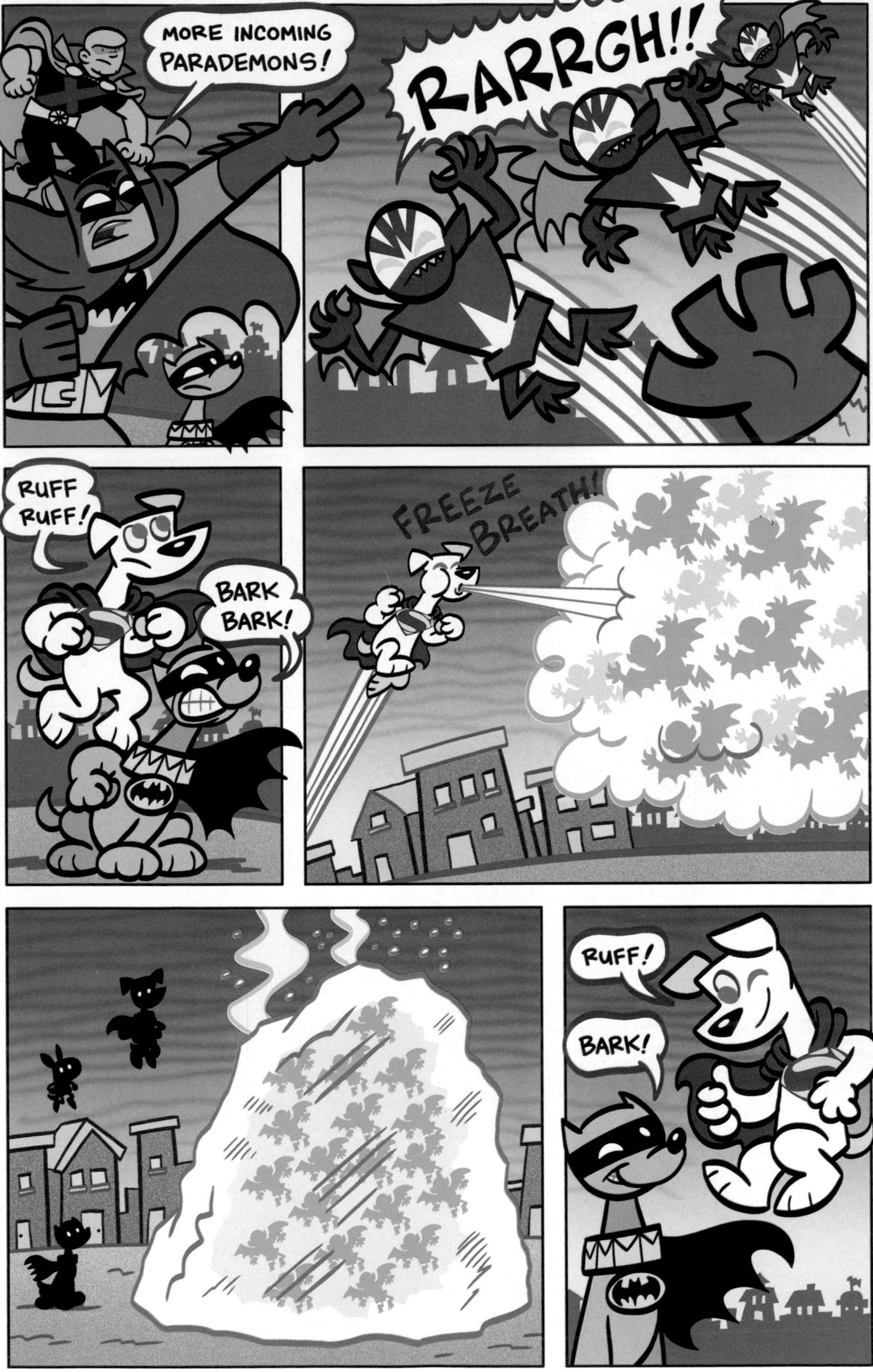
MORE INCOMING PARADEMONS!
RARRGH!!
RUFF RUFF!
BARK BARK!
FREEZE BREATH!
RUFF!
BARK!

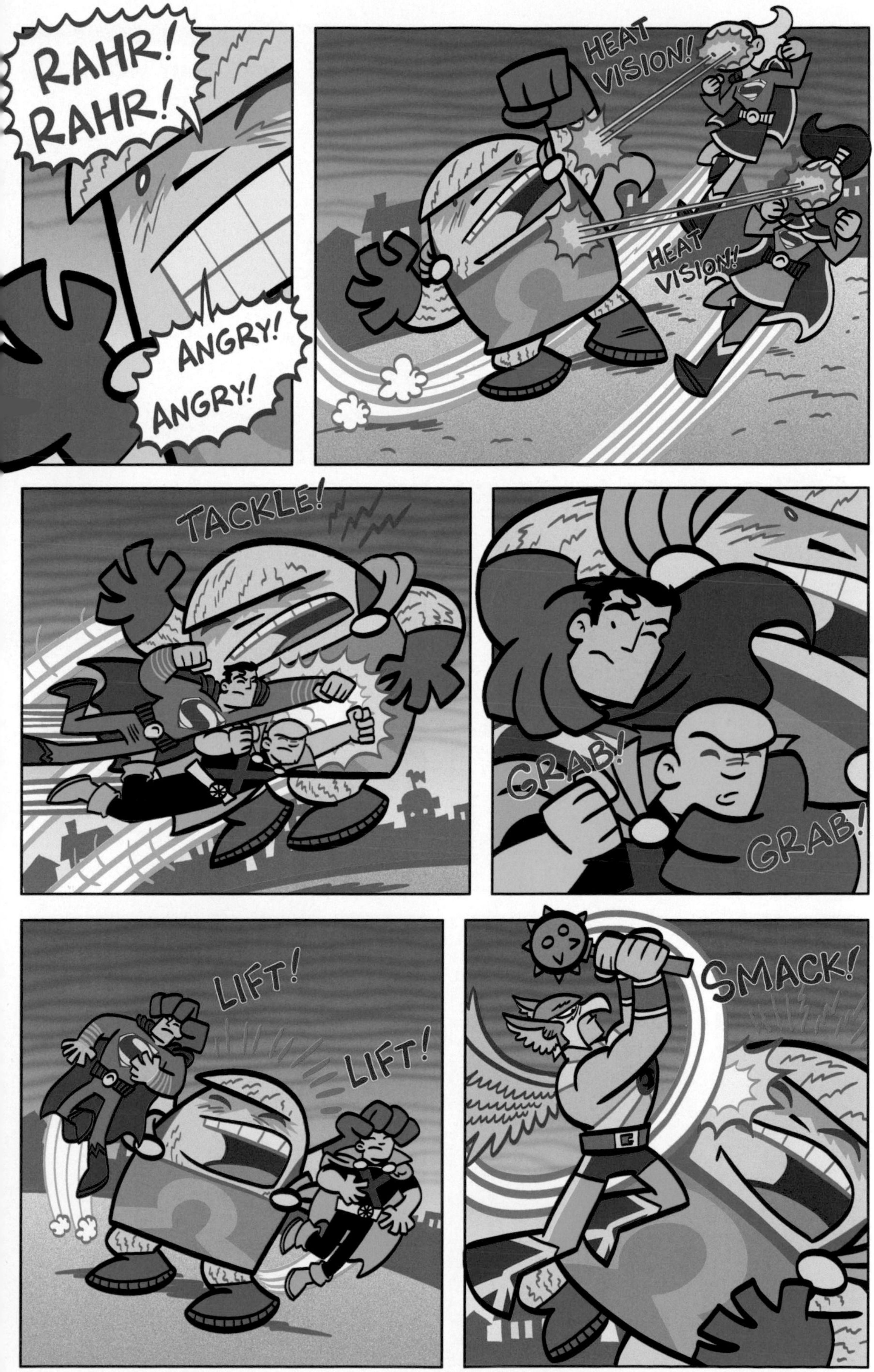
RAHR! RAHR!
ANGRY! ANGRY!
HEAT VISION!
HEAT VISION!
TACKLE!
GRAB!
GRAB!
LIFT!
LIFT!
SMACK!

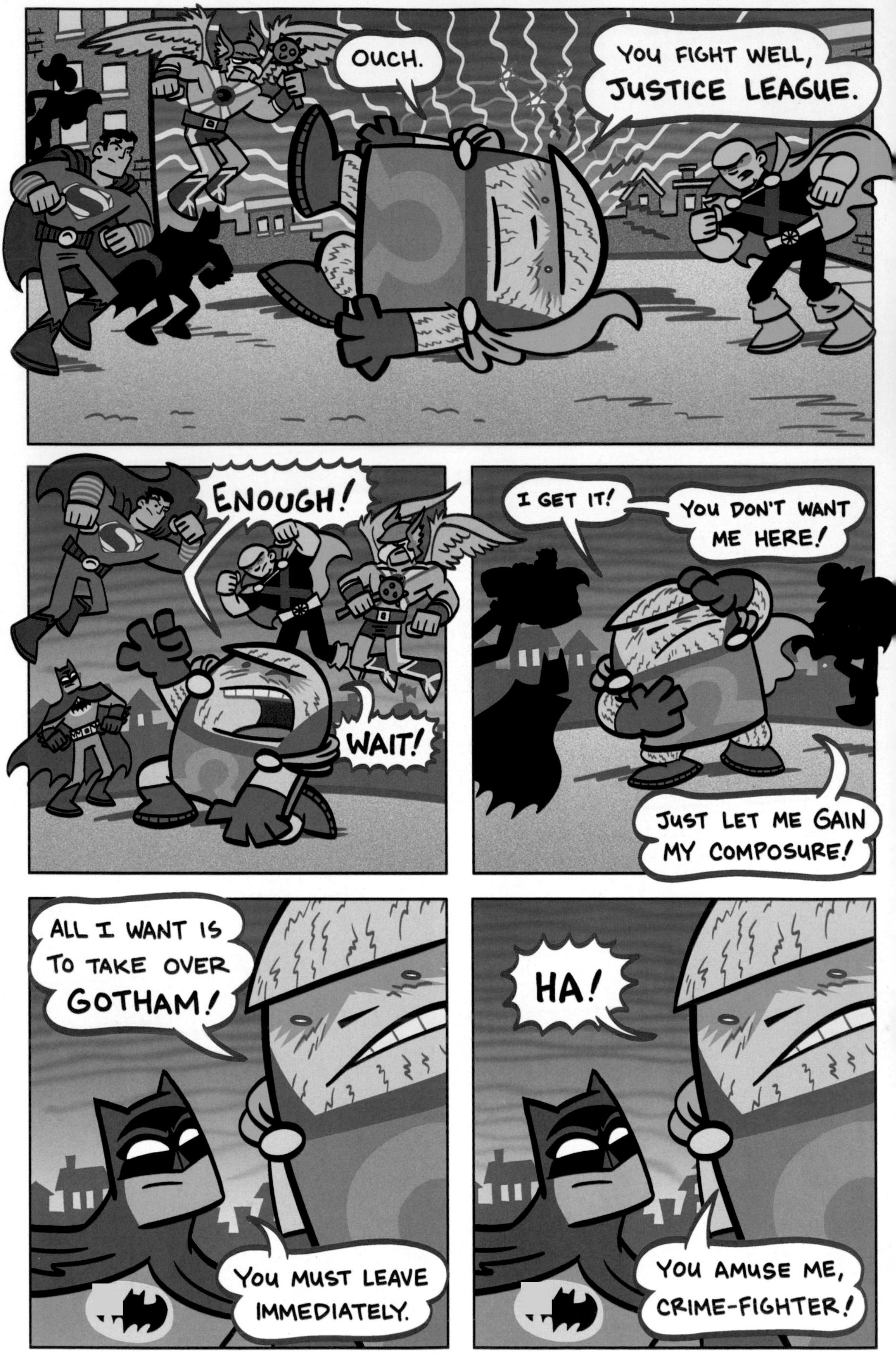
OUCH.
YOU FIGHT WELL, JUSTICE LEAGUE.
ENOUGH!
WAIT!
I GET IT!
YOU DON'T WANT ME HERE!
JUST LET ME GAIN MY COMPOSURE!
ALL I WANT IS TO TAKE OVER GOTHAM!
YOU MUST LEAVE IMMEDIATELY.
HA!
YOU AMUSE ME, CRIME-FIGHTER!

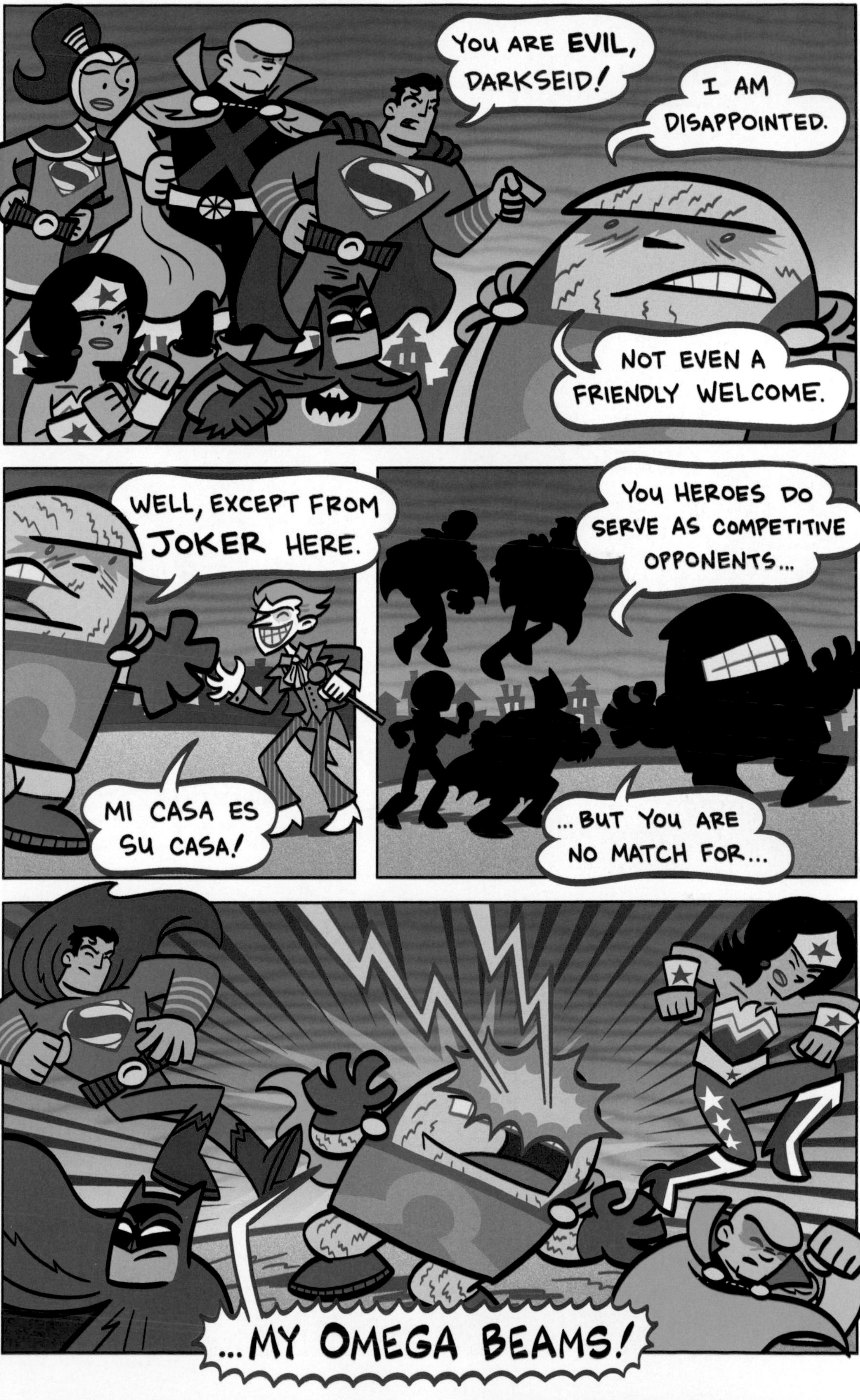
YOU ARE EVIL, DARKSEID!
I AM DISAPPOINTED.
NOT EVEN A FRIENDLY WELCOME.
WELL, EXCEPT FROM JOKER HERE.
MI CASA ES SU CASA!
YOU HEROES DO SERVE AS COMPETITIVE OPPONENTS...
...BUT YOU ARE NO MATCH FOR...
...MY OMEGA BEAMS!

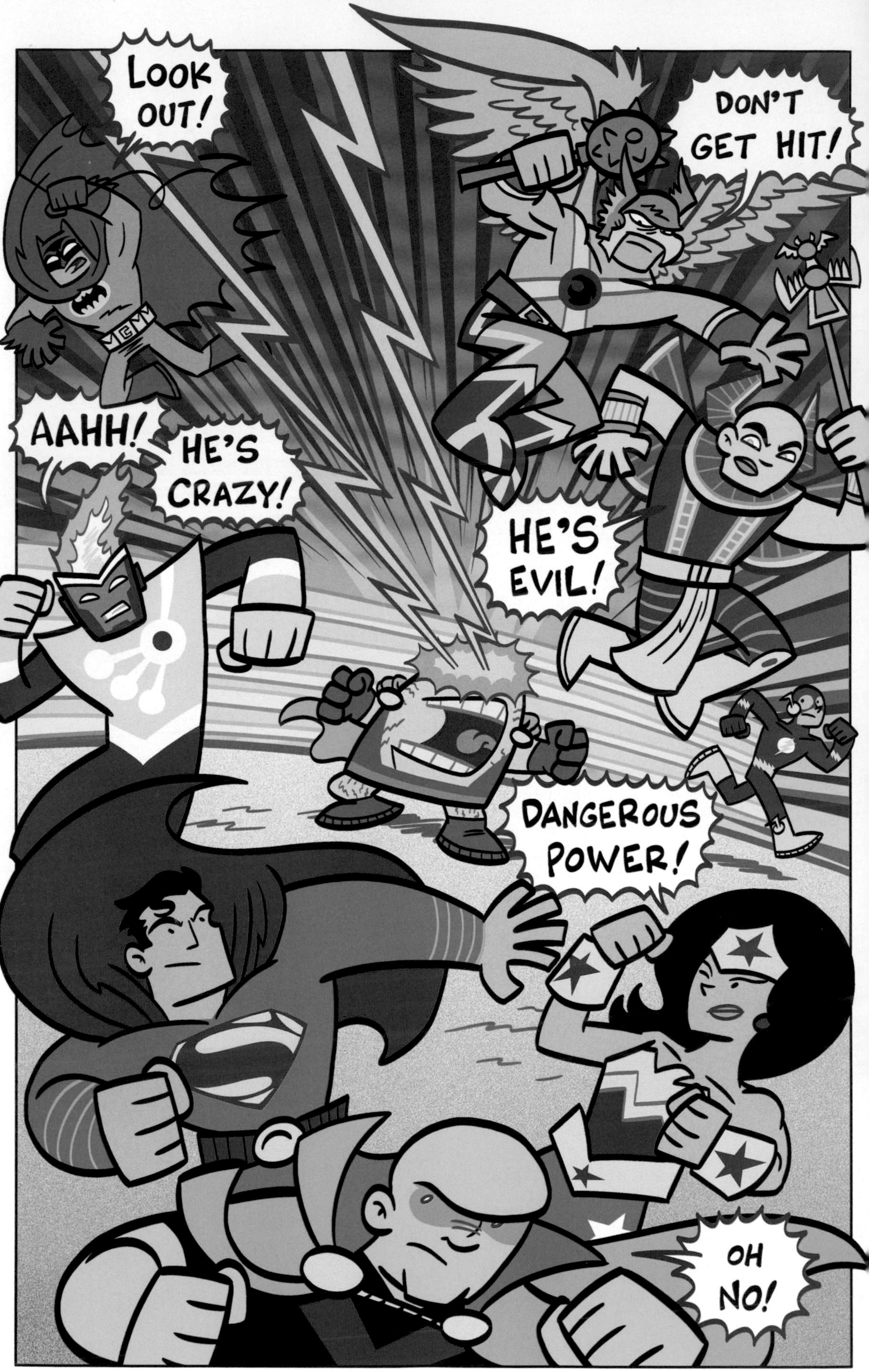
LOOK OUT!
DON'T GET HIT!
AAHH!
HE'S CRAZY!
HE'S EVIL!
DANGEROUS POWER!
OH NO!

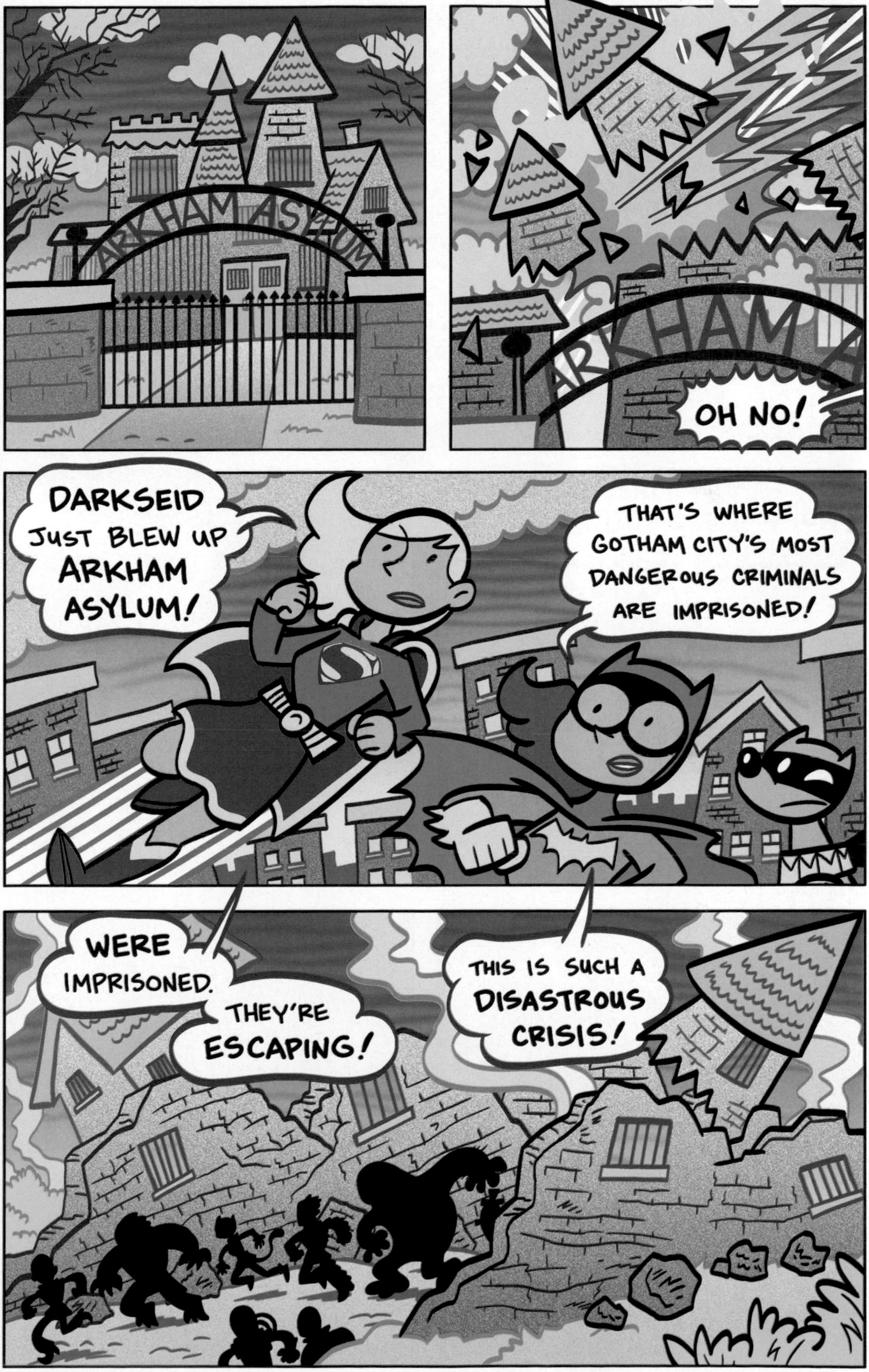
ARKHAM ASYLUM
ARKHAM
OH NO!
DARKSEID JUST BLEW UP ARKHAM ASYLUM!
THAT'S WHERE GOTHAM CITY'S MOST DANGEROUS CRIMINALS ARE IMPRISONED!
WERE IMPRISONED.
THEY'RE ESCAPING!
THIS IS SUCH A DISASTROUS CRISIS!

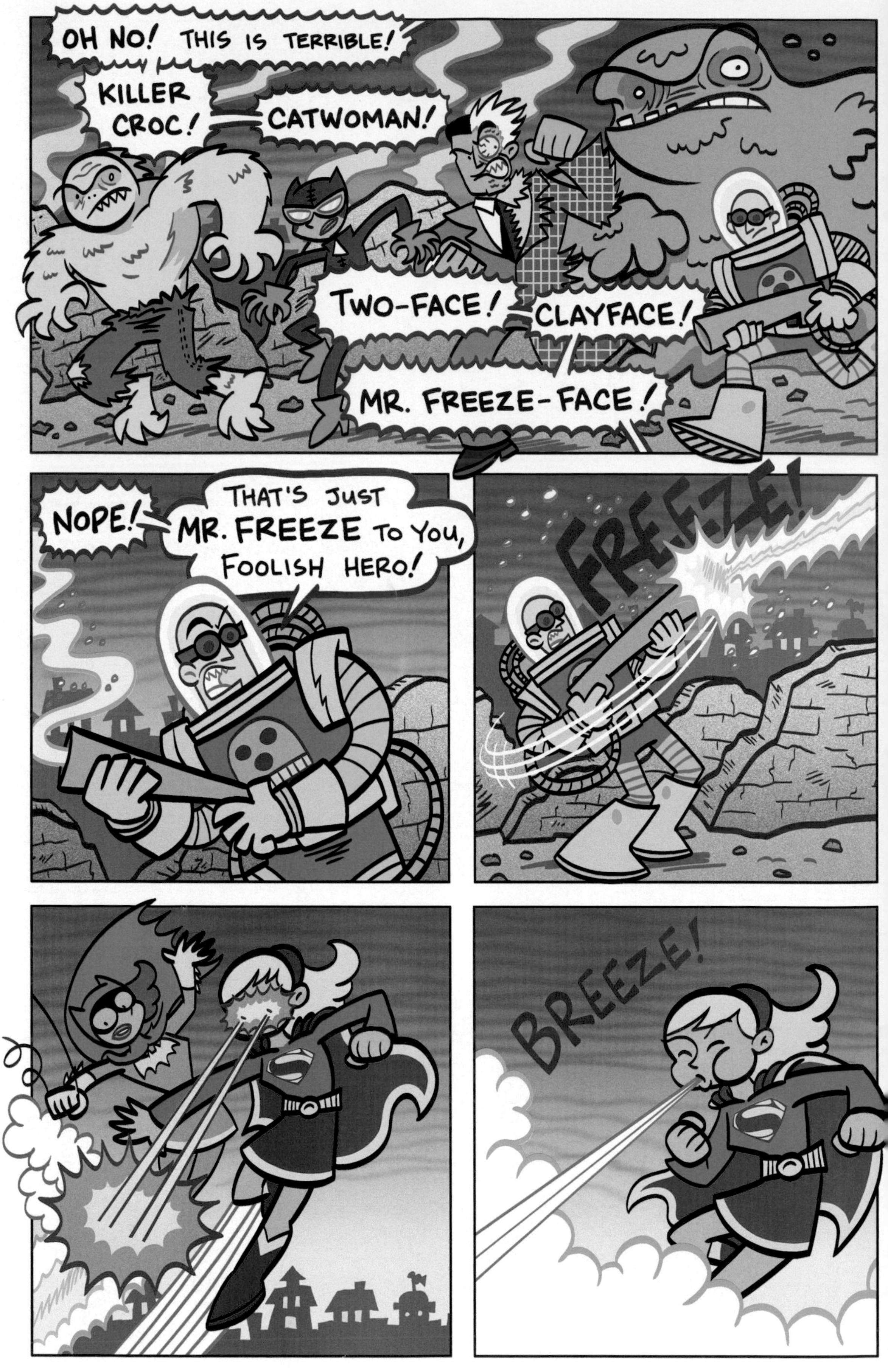
OH NO! THIS IS TERRIBLE!
KILLER CROC!
CATWOMAN!
TWO-FACE!
CLAYFACE!
MR. FREEZE-FACE!
NOPE!
THAT'S JUST MR. FREEZE TO YOU, FOOLISH HERO!
FREEZE!
BREEZE!

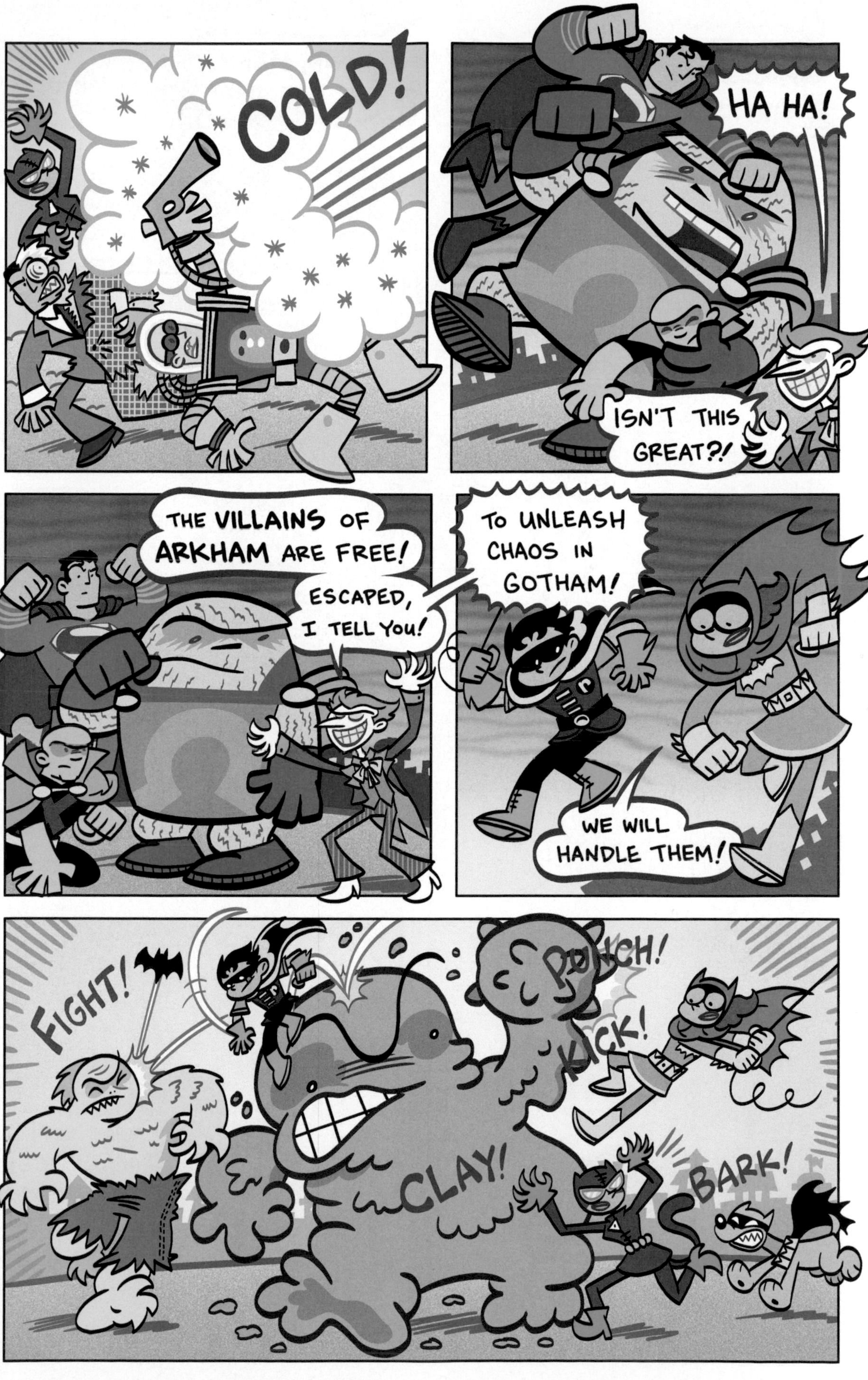

COLD!
HA HA!
ISN'T THIS GREAT?!
THE VILLAINS OF ARKHAM ARE FREE!
ESCAPED, I TELL YOU!
TO UNLEASH CHAOS IN GOTHAM!
WE WILL HANDLE THEM!
FIGHT!
PUNCH!
KICK!
CLAY!
BARK!

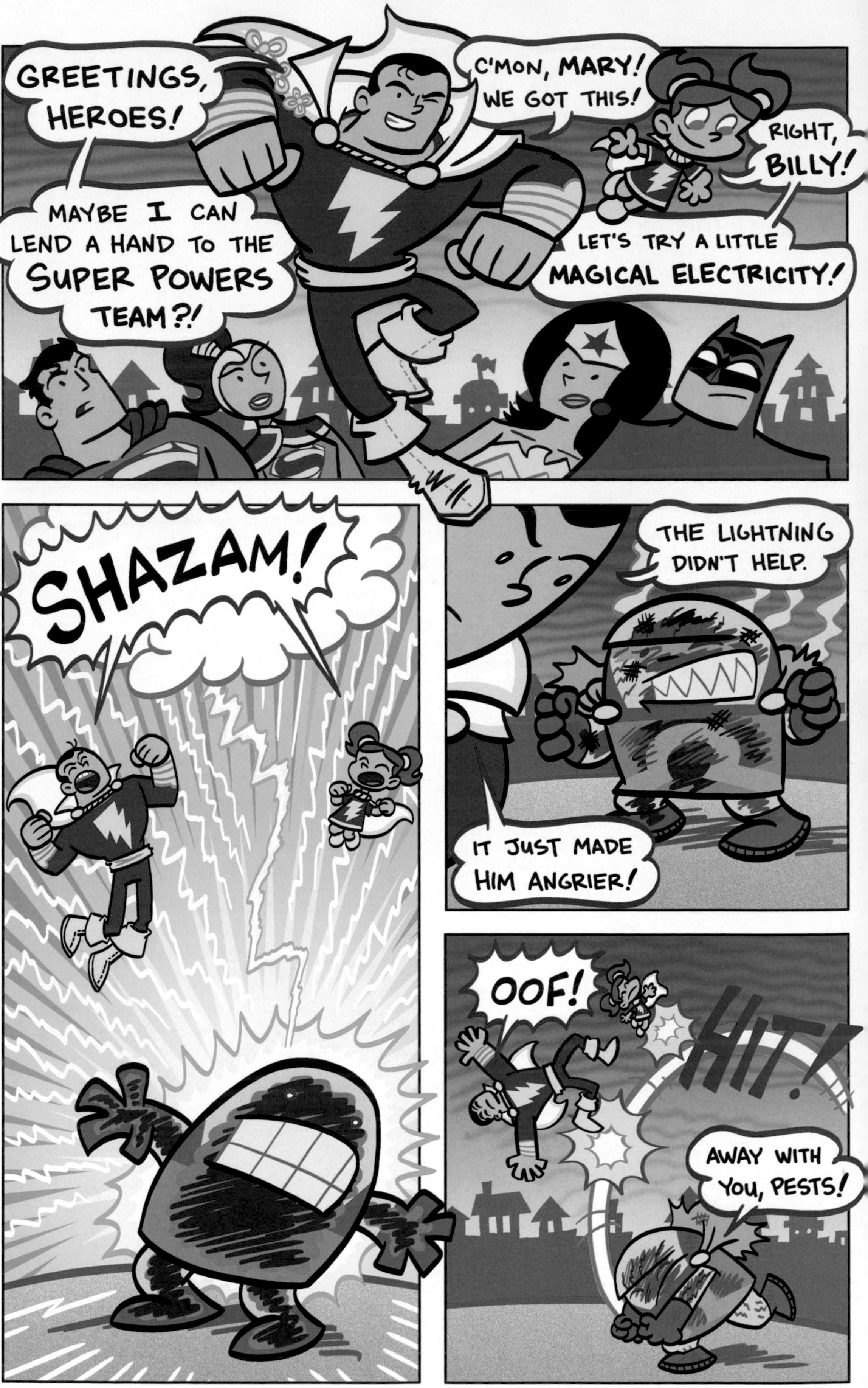
GREETINGS, HEROES!
MAYBE I CAN LEND A HAND TO THE SUPER POWERS TEAM?!
C'MON, MARY! WE GOT THIS!
RIGHT, BILLY!
LET'S TRY A LITTLE MAGICAL ELECTRICITY!
SHAZAM!
THE LIGHTNING DIDN'T HELP.
IT JUST MADE HIM ANGRIER!
OOF!
HIT!
AWAY WITH YOU, PESTS!

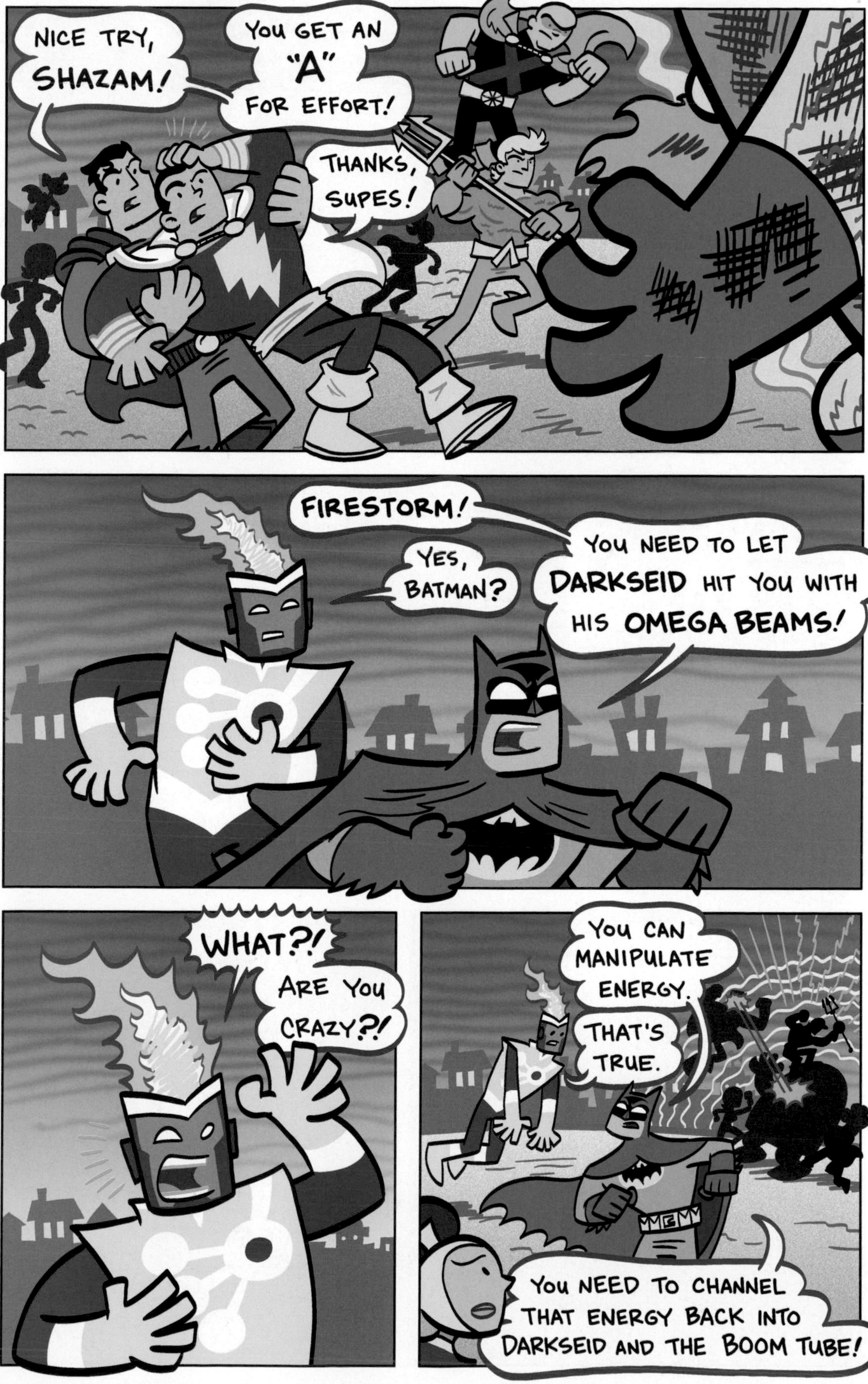
NICE TRY, SHAZAM!
YOU GET AN "A" FOR EFFORT!
THANKS, SUPES!
FIRESTORM!
YES, BATMAN?
YOU NEED TO LET DARKSEID HIT YOU WITH HIS OMEGA BEAMS!
WHAT?!
ARE YOU CRAZY?!
YOU CAN MANIPULATE ENERGY.
THAT'S TRUE.
YOU NEED TO CHANNEL THAT ENERGY BACK INTO DARKSEID AND THE BOOM TUBE!

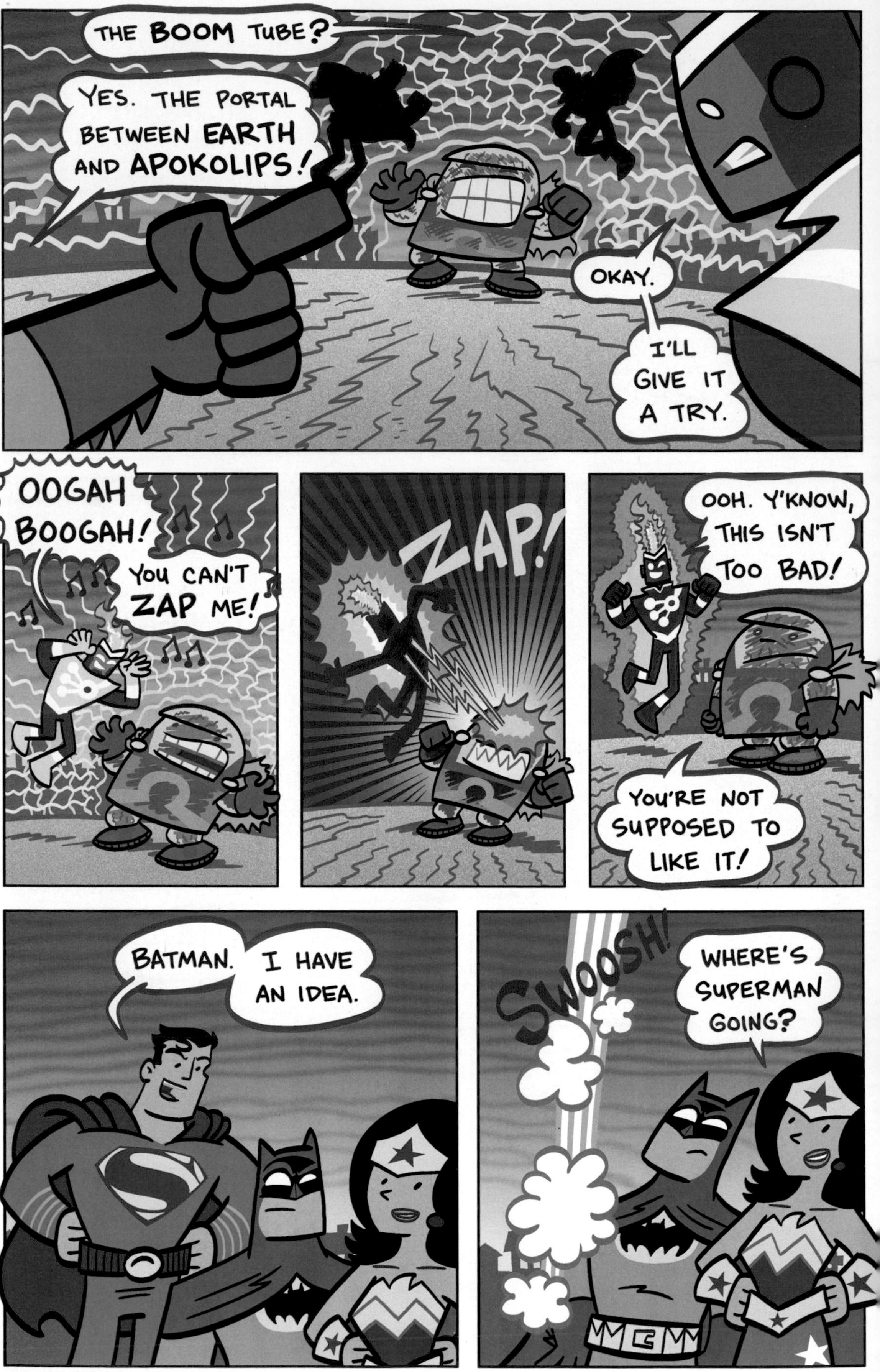
THE BOOM TUBE?
YES. THE PORTAL BETWEEN EARTH AND APOKOLIPS!
OKAY.
I'LL GIVE IT A TRY.
OOGAH BOOGAH!
YOU CAN'T ZAP ME!
ZAP!
OOH. Y'KNOW, THIS ISN'T TOO BAD!
YOU'RE NOT SUPPOSED TO LIKE IT!
BATMAN.
I HAVE AN IDEA.
SWOOSH!
WHERE'S SUPERMAN GOING?

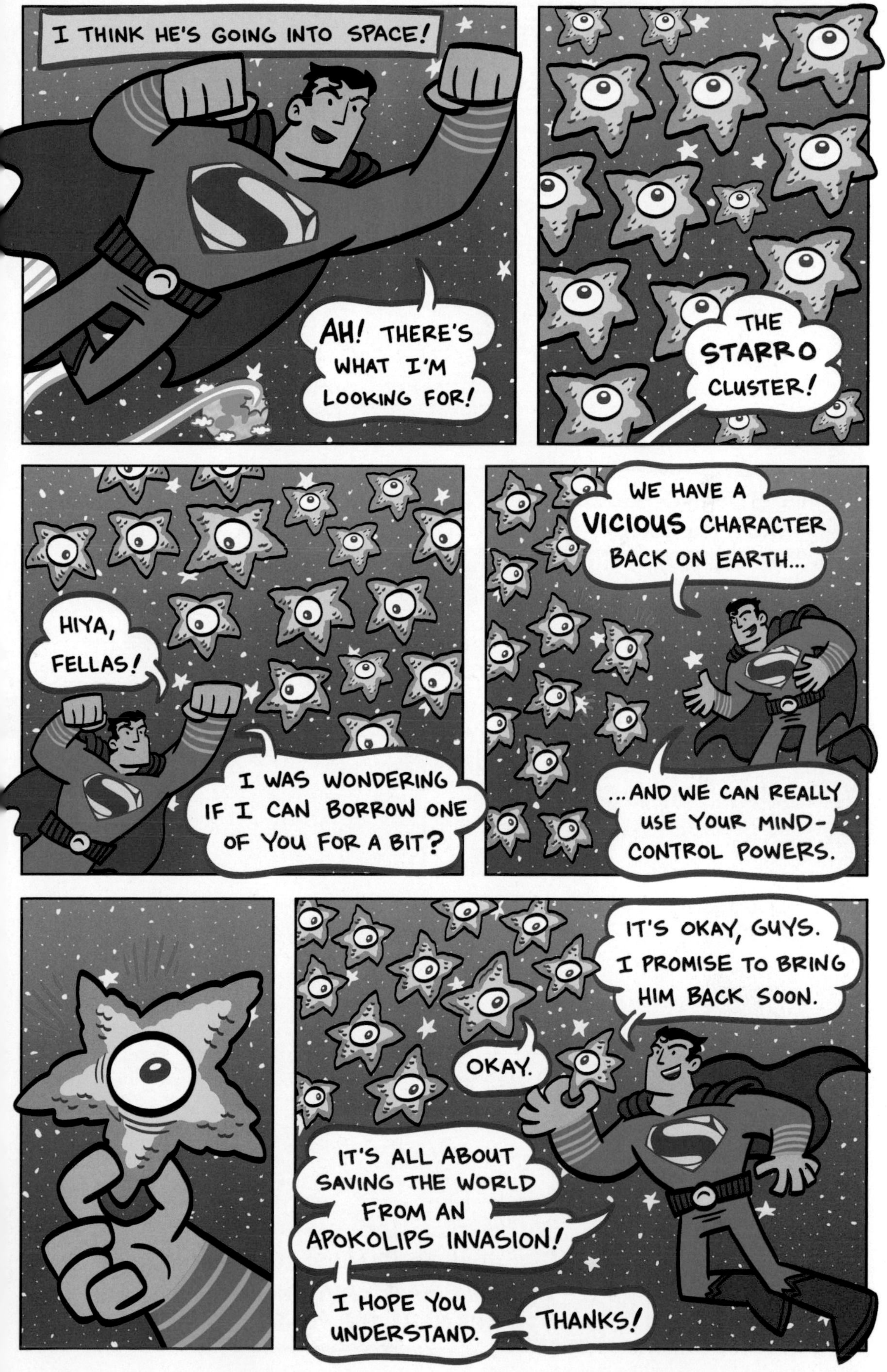
I THINK HE'S GOING INTO SPACE!
AH! THERE'S WHAT I'M LOOKING FOR!
THE STARRO CLUSTER!
HIYA, FELLAS!
I WAS WONDERING IF I CAN BORROW ONE OF YOU FOR A BIT?
WE HAVE A VICIOUS CHARACTER BACK ON EARTH...
...AND WE CAN REALLY USE YOUR MIND-CONTROL POWERS.
IT'S OKAY, GUYS. I PROMISE TO BRING HIM BACK SOON.
OKAY.
IT'S ALL ABOUT SAVING THE WORLD FROM AN APOKOLIPS INVASION!
I HOPE YOU UNDERSTAND.
THANKS!

OKAY!
DARKSEID'S DISTRACTED!
YOU'RE THE DISTRACTION, SPEEDSTER!
WHAT ARE YOU UP TO?
HEY, DARKSEID!
DID YOU MISS ME?
WHAT?!
I HAVE SOMETHING FOR YOU!
THIS STARRO SHOULD CALM YOU DOWN!
SLAP!
OH...SOO... SOOTHING...
IT WORKED!
YEAH!
THAT'S NOT GONNA HOLD HIM FOR LONG!
NOW, TO CHANNEL THAT OMEGA BEAM ENERGY THROUGH THE PORTAL!

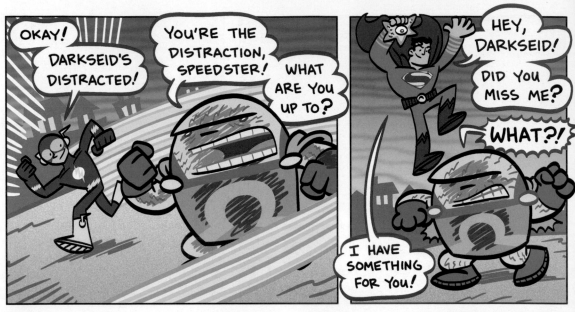

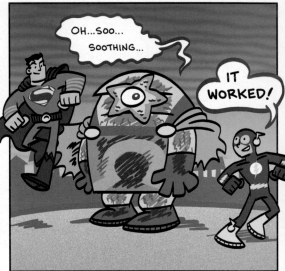

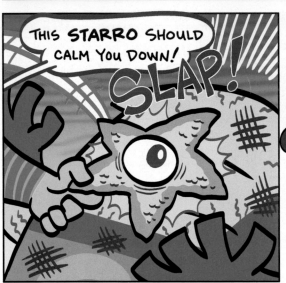

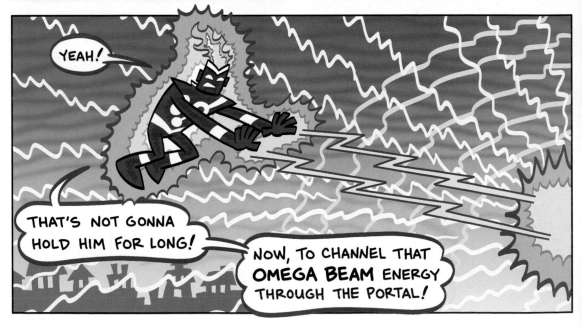

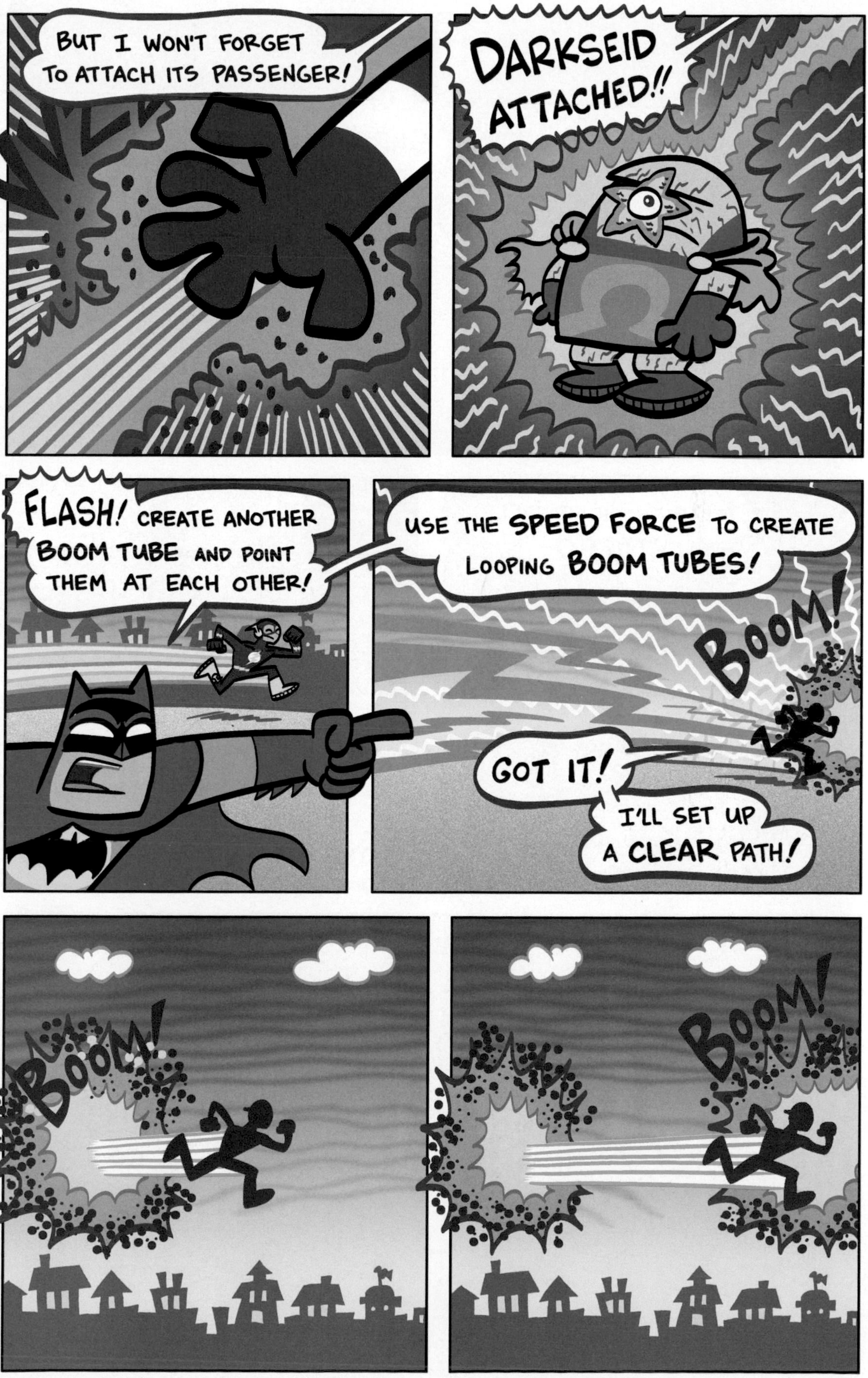
BUT I WON'T FORGET TO ATTACH ITS PASSENGER!
DARKSEID ATTACHED!!
FLASH! CREATE ANOTHER BOOM TUBE AND POINT THEM AT EACH OTHER!
USE THE SPEED FORCE TO CREATE LOOPING BOOM TUBES!
BOOM!
GOT IT!
I'LL SET UP A CLEAR PATH!
BOOM!
BOOM!

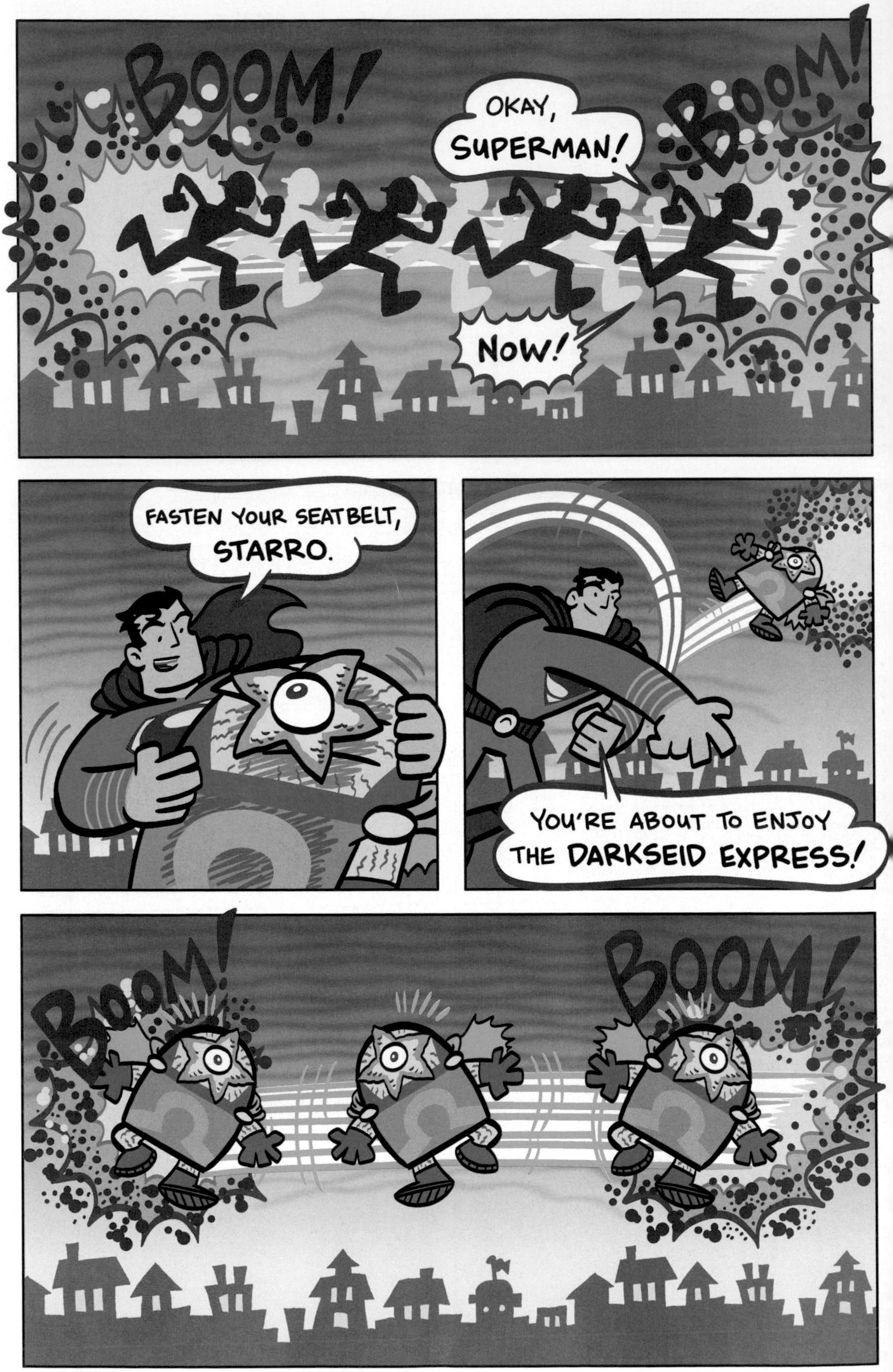
BOOM!
OKAY, SUPERMAN!
BOOM!
NOW!
FASTEN YOUR SEATBELT, STARRO.
YOU'RE ABOUT TO ENJOY THE DARKSEID EXPRESS!
BOOM!
BOOM!

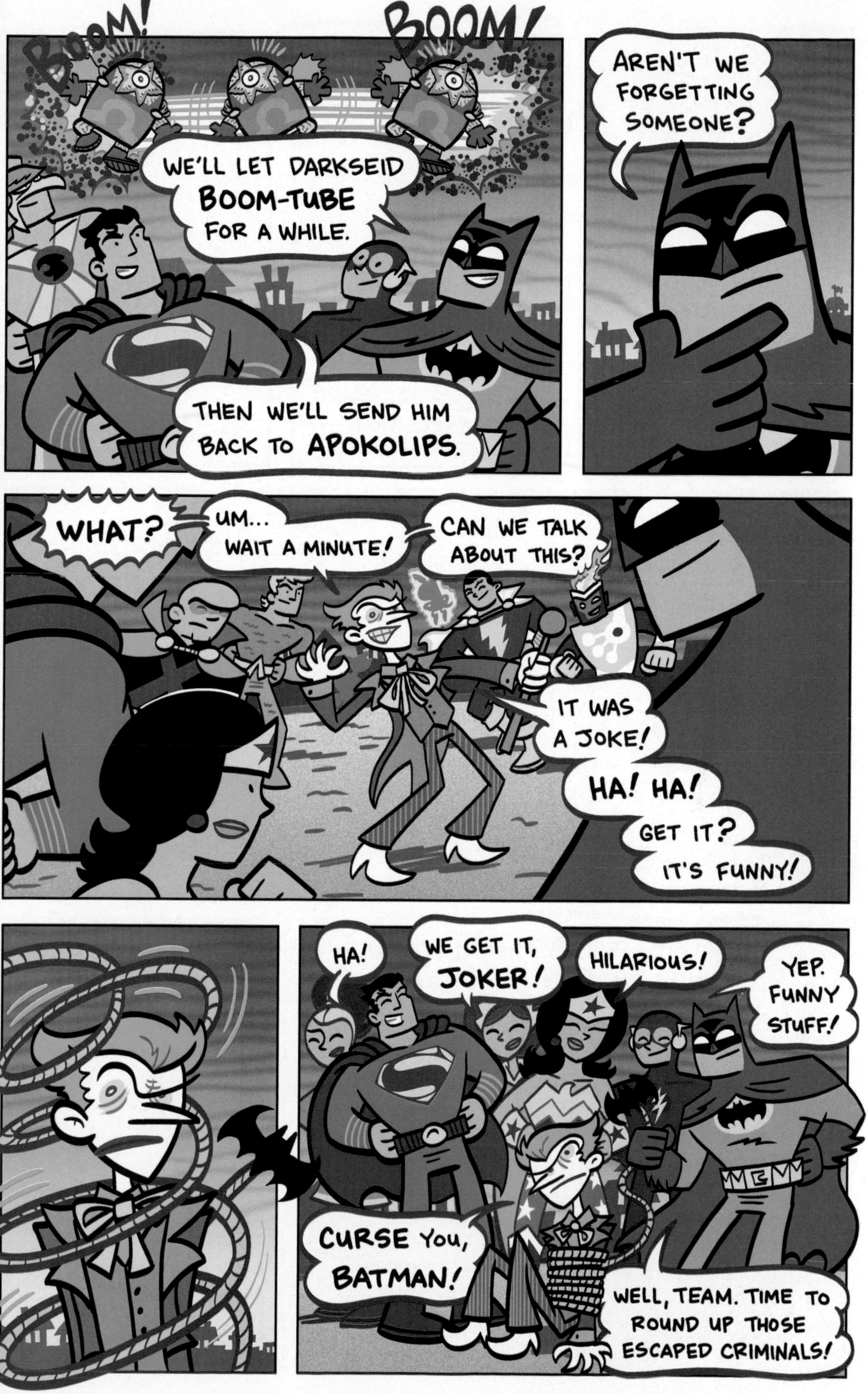
BOOM!
BOOM!
WE'LL LET DARKSEID BOOM-TUBE FOR A WHILE.
THEN WE'LL SEND HIM BACK TO APOKOLIPS.
AREN'T WE FORGETTING SOMEONE?
WHAT?
UM... WAIT A MINUTE!
CAN WE TALK ABOUT THIS?
IT WAS A JOKE!
HA! HA!
GET IT?
IT'S FUNNY!
HA!
WE GET IT, JOKER!
HILARIOUS!
YEP. FUNNY STUFF!
CURSE YOU, BATMAN!
WELL, TEAM. TIME TO ROUND UP THOSE ESCAPED CRIMINALS!

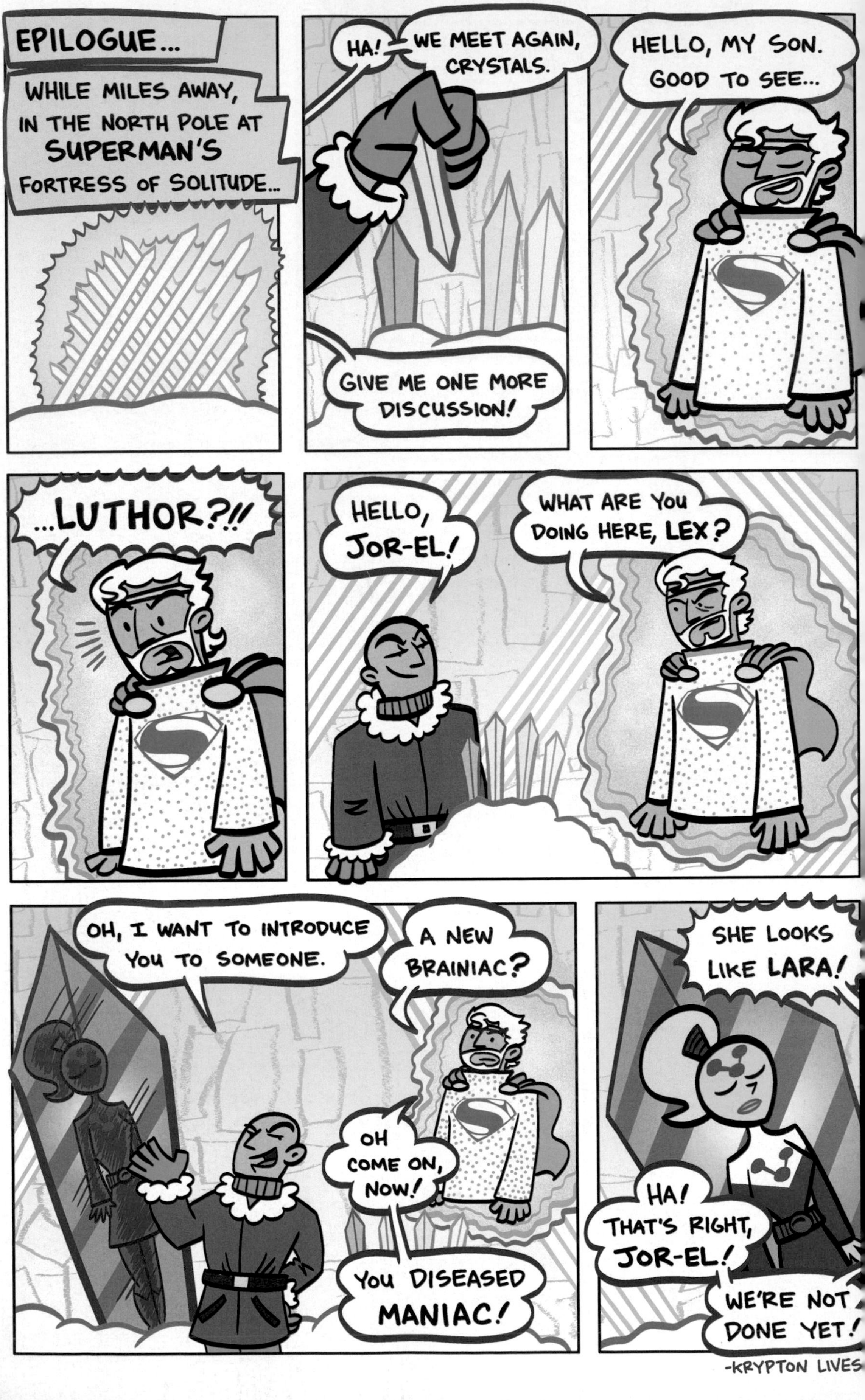
EPILOGUE...
WHILE MILES AWAY, IN THE NORTH POLE AT SUPERMAN'S FORTRESS OF SOLITUDE...
HA!
WE MEET AGAIN, CRYSTALS.
GIVE ME ONE MORE DISCUSSION!
HELLO, MY SON. GOOD TO SEE...
...LUTHOR?!!
HELLO, JOR-EL!
WHAT ARE YOU DOING HERE, LEX?
OH, I WANT TO INTRODUCE YOU TO SOMEONE.
A NEW BRAINIAC?
OH COME ON, NOW!
YOU DISEASED MANIAC!
SHE LOOKS LIKE LARA!
HA! THAT'S RIGHT, JOR-EL!
WE'RE NOT DONE YET!
-KRYPTON LIVES

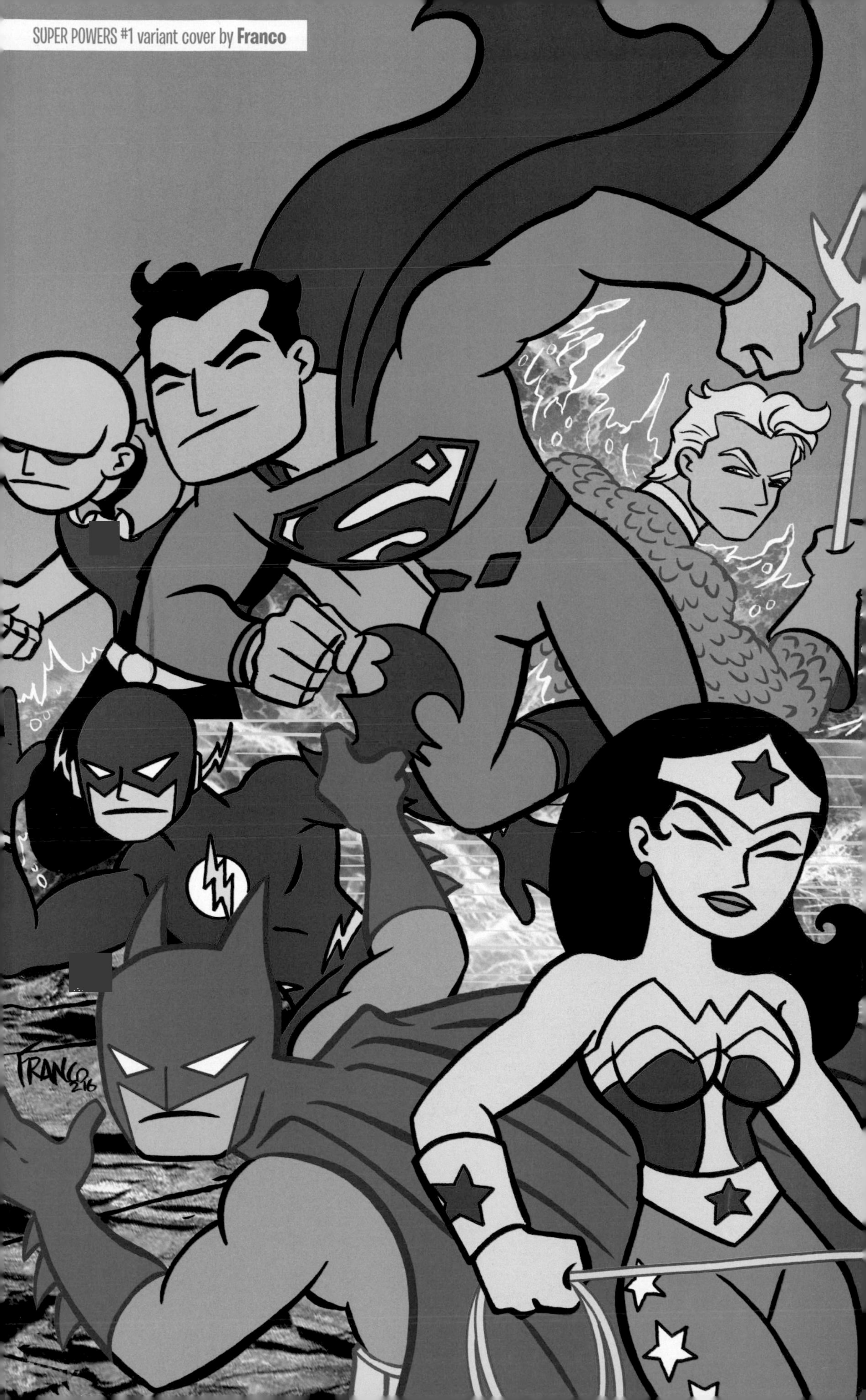
FRANCO

SUPER POWERS #1 variant cover by **Franco**

"Some really thrilling artwork that establishes incredible scope and danger."

–IGN

DC UNIVERSE REBIRTH

JUSTICE LEAGUE

VOL. 1: The Extinction Machines

BRYAN HITCH
with TONY S. DANIEL

DC UNIVERSE REBIRTH

JUSTICE LEAGUE

VOL.1 THE EXTINCTION MACHINES

BRYAN HITCH • TONY S. DANIEL • SANDU FLOREA • TOMEU MOREY

CYBORG VOL. 1:
THE IMITATION OF LIFE

GREEN LANTERNS VOL. 1:
RAGE PLANET

AQUAMAN VOL. 1:
THE DROWNING

Get more DC graphic novels wherever comics and books are sold!